NED KELLY:
A Lawless Life

Ned Kelly in chains, 10 November 1880

DOUG MORRISSEY

Introduction by John Hirst

TED KELLY

A LAWLESS LIFE

connorcourt
PUBLISHING

Connor Court Publishing Pty Ltd

Copyright © Doug Morrissey 2015 (including maps)

ALL RIGHTS RESERVED. This book contains material protected under International and Federal Copyright Laws and Treaties. Any unauthorised reprint or use of this material is prohibited. No part of this book may be reproduced or transmitted in any form or by any means, electronic or mechanical, including photocopying, recording, or by any information storage and retrieval system without express written permission from the publisher.

PO Box 224W
Ballarat VIC 3350
sales@connorcourt.com
www.connorcourt.com

ISBN: 9781925138481 (pbk.)

Cover design by Ian James

Cover illustration: Sidney Nolan's 'Stringybark Creek' (1947), enamel paint on composition board 90.7 x 121.5 cm, National Gallery of Australia, Canberra. Gift of Sunday Reed, 1977.

Printed in Australia

The criminal mind has a peculiar cast; it has great powers of dissimulation. Nearly every ruffian it may be said has something of the histrionic art about him and the constant effort of these men is to posture when under the public eye as generous, large-hearted beings, persecuted by a wicked police but really entitled to the sympathy of their fellows. The practice is an instinct with them. They pose as injured innocents, as naturally as a girl attitudinises before a mirror. The account these scoundrels give of themselves affords a further proof of the truth of the elementary lesson that thieving and lying go hand in hand and this does not cease when the thief becomes a murderer. The 'Kelly lot' or 'Greta gang' have lived from their infancy the common life of low thieves, pilfering by night and trusting to get off if detected by false swearing at the police court by day. Men of this sort are never at a loss for a plausible lie to put themselves in a good position. They have lived in an atmosphere of deceit and consequently every statement in which they figure to advantage should be scrutinised to see who it emanates from and if it comes from them or their sympathisers the gloss should be taken off. The ruffians stand in a very different light to that in which they desire to be represented.

The Argus, 16 December 1878.

CONTENTS

Introduction	ix
Preface	xi
Acknowledgements	xiv
Part I: Larrikin Thief	
1 Horse Stealing	3
2 Mrs Kelly's Selection	13
3 Whitty and Byrne	21
4 Constable Hall's Farewell	29
Part II: Bushranger and Outlaw	
5 That Bloody Fitzpatrick	43
6 Murdering Police	69
7 Going Public	99
8 Operation Massacre	117
9 A Bank Robbers' Republic	145
Conclusion A Lawless Life	159
Appendices	
I The James Murdock Connection	167
II The Diseased Stock Agent	173
III Superintendent Hare's wound at Glenrowan	178
IV The Makers of the Modern Kelly Myth	181
V The Jerilderie Letter Annotated	191
Index	238

Introduction

The books on Ned Kelly multiply without adding to our understanding. Instead the mythologising becomes more intense and uncritical. Doug Morrissey, by contrast, has something new to say on this well-worn subject. He has a clear-sighted view of Kelly, free from romantic illusions and delusions. It is still possible to produce a new take on Kelly by refusing to believe what he said about himself. Doug has that scepticism in abundance. He also knows more than anyone else about the people of Kelly Country and how they lived. This informs the interpretations he offers here.

I first knew Doug at La Trobe University as the supervisor of his honours history thesis on Ned Kelly's sympathisers. Then I became the supervisor of his PhD thesis on 'Selectors, Squatters and Stock Thieves: A Social History of Kelly Country' (1987). Recently he contacted me again because he had finished a major work on Ned Kelly himself. I offered to edit the work and see that it became published. This is the result.

All the research has been done by Doug; the broad interpretation of Kelly is his. I have shortened and re-ordered a much longer manuscript and ensured that the argument emerges with clarity and force. Over the years I have learnt so much about Ned and his world from Doug that I had no problem presenting his Kelly to the world.

Many significant works of historical re-interpretation have emerged from the History Department at La Trobe University. I believe this is a work worthy to take its place beside them. I am honoured to have helped put it in print.

John Hirst

Preface

Ned's iconic status as Australia's premier bushranger rests on the undoubted success of the Kelly myth in whitewashing the bushranger's criminal action. Ned's heavily mythologised role is that of the underdog defiantly fighting against injustice and oppression; a surrogate rebel leader of the poverty-stricken and downtrodden selector farmer. At the centre of selector grievance and regional strife is a bitter land war between wealthy squatters and struggling selectors. This is a classic morality tale of good and evil, where the dividing line is suffering, poverty and exclusion for selectors and wealth, power and dominance for squatters. Land war, squatter tyranny and police harassment are the trinity of Kelly myth assumptions.

Ned is lionised as a bushranging hero, while his enemies are vilified as tyrants. The poor showing of the police throughout the two year hunt for the Kelly Gang is ridiculed and characterised as corrupt, shifting in a topsy-turvy fashion the moral blame for the gang's outlawry from the pursued to those who pursued them. Alleged police harassment of the Kelly family, rather than the criminal behaviour of the Kelly clan itself, emerges from the myth as the principal cause behind the Kelly outbreak. Ned is seen as essentially a good man, driven to crime and bad behaviour by circumstance and the machinations of others.

The aim of the current work is to test these widely-held assumptions against the reality of Ned's behaviour, looking at what actually happened and what Ned intended should have happened if circumstances had been favourable. The failed intention, of course, is every bit as revealing as the actual course of events.

I have chosen to let the participants speak for themselves using their actual words taken from primary sources. In Ned's case there is a lot of primary material available including his letters, police reports, extensive and detailed reporting of his trials and what his sympathisers said and did. There are also reports of his victims' views, which in many cases disagree with what Ned tells us. In the book, I will examine both sides of the coin to try to get as close as possible to the real story.

What is lacking in previous works dealing with the Kelly outbreak is a faithful account of the local community. The Kelly myth by removing Ned from the daily interactions of his community has done a great disservice to the rest of the people in north-east Victoria, who appear as no more than bit players in Ned's drama. The assumption is that the entire community with a few exceptions either passively or actively supported the Kelly Gang. Ned's story is more complex and a good deal more interesting than the superficial examinations of his life and times have so far revealed. To understand Ned's lawless life in its proper community context, the focus should be on complexity of behaviour, the variable nature of community relationships and the changing motivation behind both.

The sources for the life of Ned Kelly are well known and listed elsewhere. I have ranged more widely, drawing on records of the Police, Lands and Education Departments, Municipal and Regional Courts Proceedings, the records of local organisations (councils, churches and schools) and the local newspapers. The broader life of Kelly country is described and referenced in my published works:

'Ned Kelly's sympathisers', *Historical Studies*, October 1978, pp. 288-295.

'Fallout from Stringybark Creek', *Independent Australian*, November 1980, pp.13, 58.

'Our Ned: Getting it Straight', *Secondary Teacher*, May 1981, pp. 27, 28.

'Ned Kelly's World', *Royal Historical Society of Victoria Journal*, June 1984, pp. 29-34.

'Ned Kelly and Horse and Cattle Stealing', *Victorian Historical Journal*, June 1995, pp. 29-48.

And in my 1987 PhD thesis 'Selectors, Squatters and Stock Thieves:

A Social History of Kelly Country' available at the Borchardt Library, La Trobe University.

Due to the rearranging and re-cataloguing of public records in recent years, the file numbers I provided will no longer identify the item. The description I provide should still be adequate. Direct quotations from the documents are rendered in italics, with only occasional alterations to bad punctuation and poor grammar and with some statements being linked together when this gives a clearer account of what the person was trying to say.

The appendices which offer new information on matters long in dispute or not pursued are referenced. Ned's defence of his bushranging career was committed to paper in what is known as the Jerilderie Letter. It is drawn on and queried throughout this book. Appendix 5 reprints the letter in full with annotations that correct Ned's version of events.

Acknowledgements

No book is ever the work of just one person alone; there are others involved who deserve acknowledgement and recognition for the contributions they have made to its creation. Firstly I would like to thank my wife Joy, who not only made all of this possible by 'putting hubby through uni', but acted as draft editor, research assistant and devil's advocate with untiring perseverance and considerable skill. She suggested I write this book and has been there every step of the way in the good times and the bad with an encouraging word and unconditional support.

Dr John Hirst supervised my PhD thesis just on 30 years ago and is the editor of the current work. John is a tour de force in Australian history circles and an editor with formidable skill in honing in on the strengths and weaknesses of an argument and in skilfully shaping the text into a coherent and readable whole. It was through his advice and encouragement that I was able to find the style and the voice necessary to do justice to the historical enterprise undertaken here. Without John's able assistance neither my earlier work on the Kelly country nor the book itself would have turned out as they did. I feel privileged John agreed to act as editor and to write an introduction and I thank him for both.

My publisher, Dr Anthony Cappello, I thank for having faith in the Ned Kelly project and for agreeing to publish a critical work on Ned that does not pander to the popular Kelly myth nor seek to sell a book because of it. In more than 40 years of research, I have received assistance from librarians, archivists and all manner of people associated with preserving the historical record. Many went out of their way to locate obscure documents and other information and some facilitated access to archives that would have been difficult to access without their help. These people are the backbone of historical research and they deserve the respect and admiration of everyone who writes on historical topics.

I would also like to acknowledge the kindness and patience of the descendants of north-east families, who over the years welcomed Joy and myself into their homes to discuss Ned and their own families pioneering struggle to settle the land. Once trust had been established and Ned as a topic had been exhausted, they brought out and shared with us their family treasures; the Orange flag so lovingly brought from Ireland, the old faded photographs and the many humorous and tragic stories passed on within the family. These were very personal moments poignant and rewarding, particularly in the case of one Greta South family whose unbroken farming of the land for three generations was about to come to an end due to the only son's incapacity to take over from his parents. It was both a privilege and an honour to be taken into the confidence of these people and gain access to their families' private as opposed to conciliatory 'forgive and forget' public view of Ned and the Kelly outbreak.

Finally I would like to acknowledge Charcoal the cat who diligently sat on my knee throughout the writing of this book, occasionally walked across the keyboard and let me know when the current writing session had come to an end. To all of the above, I say a sincere and heartfelt thank you.

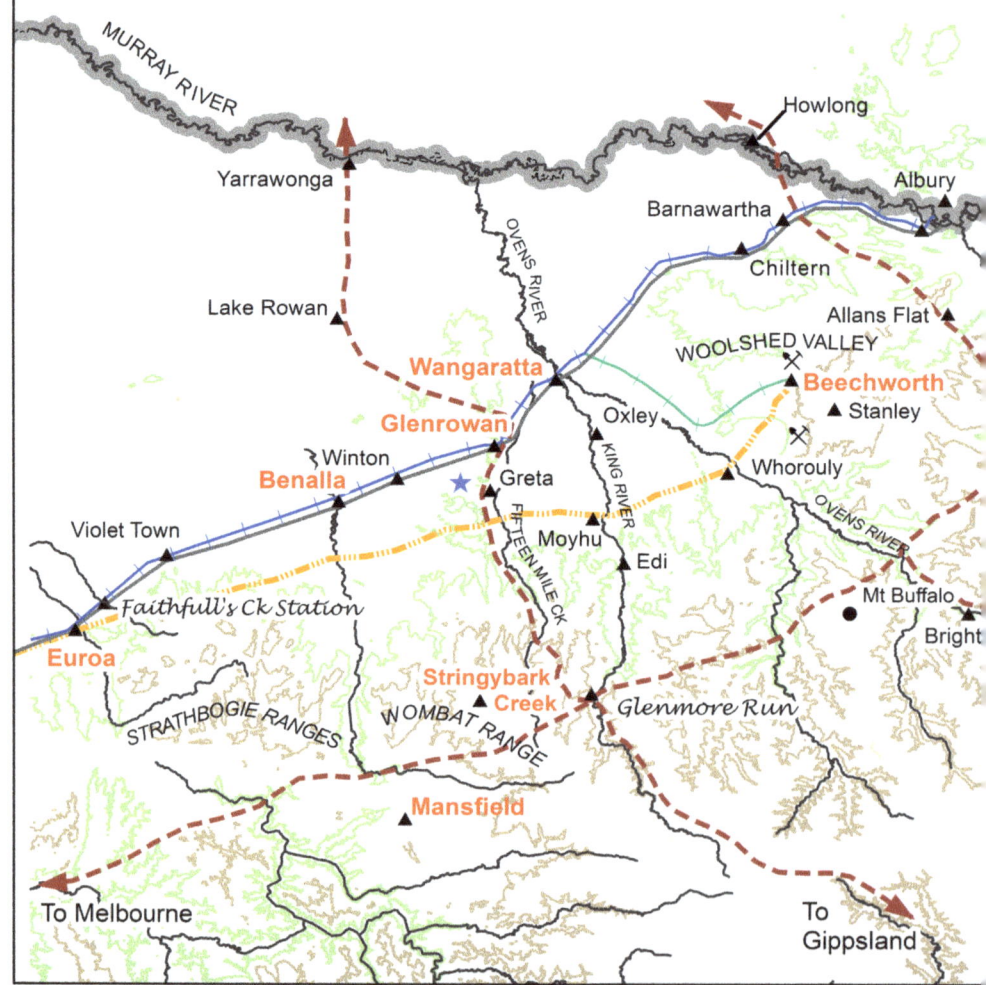

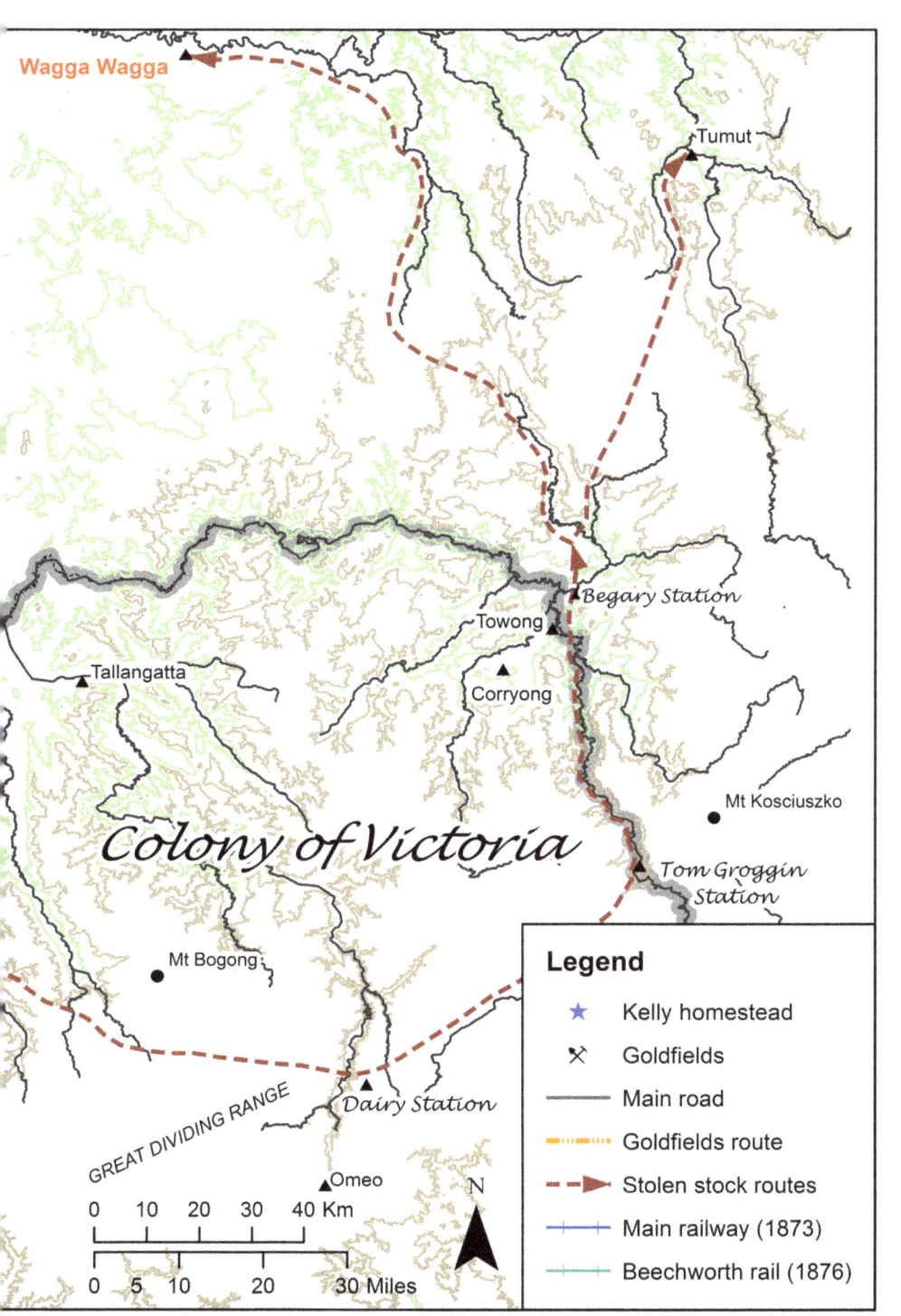

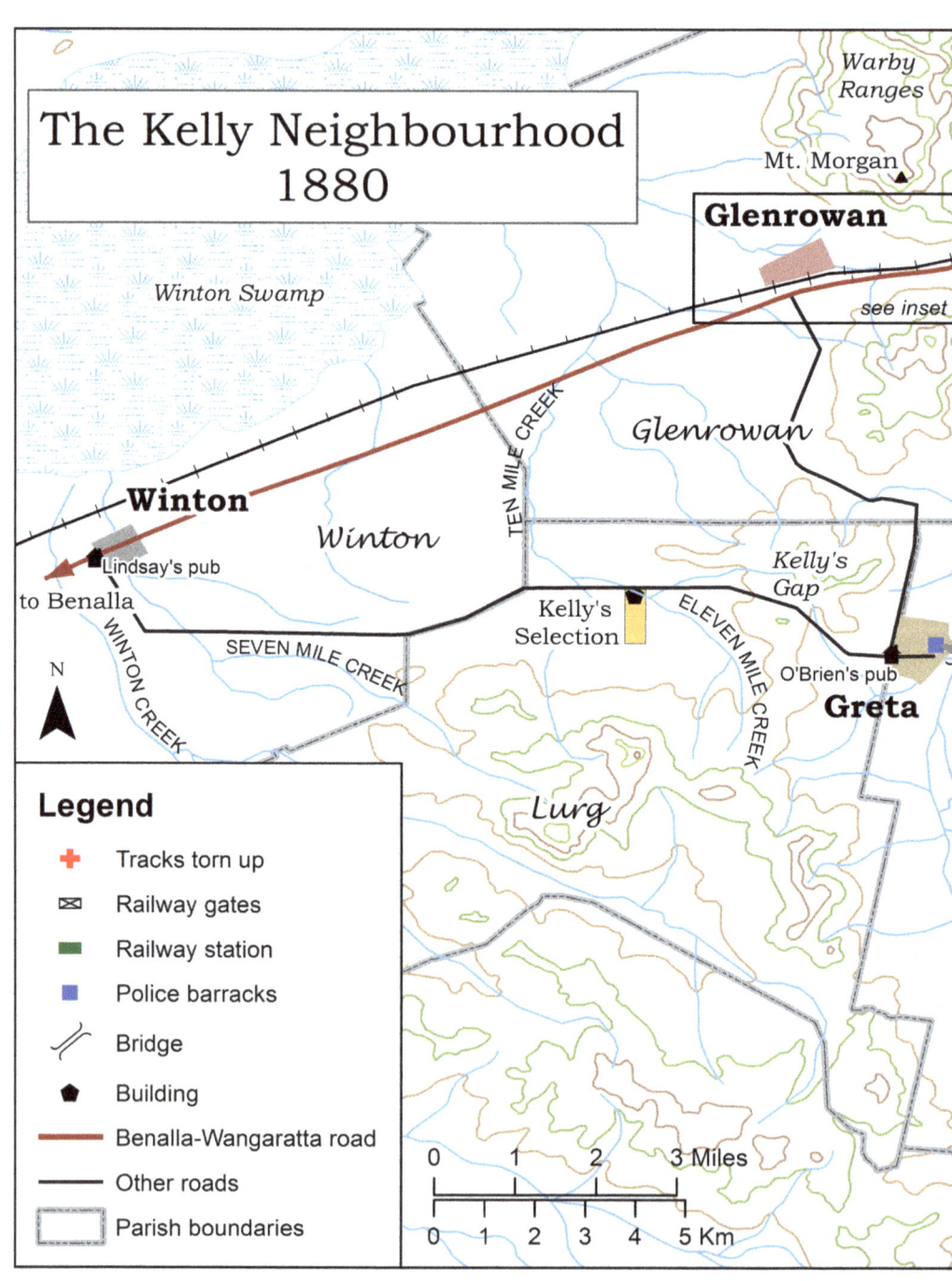

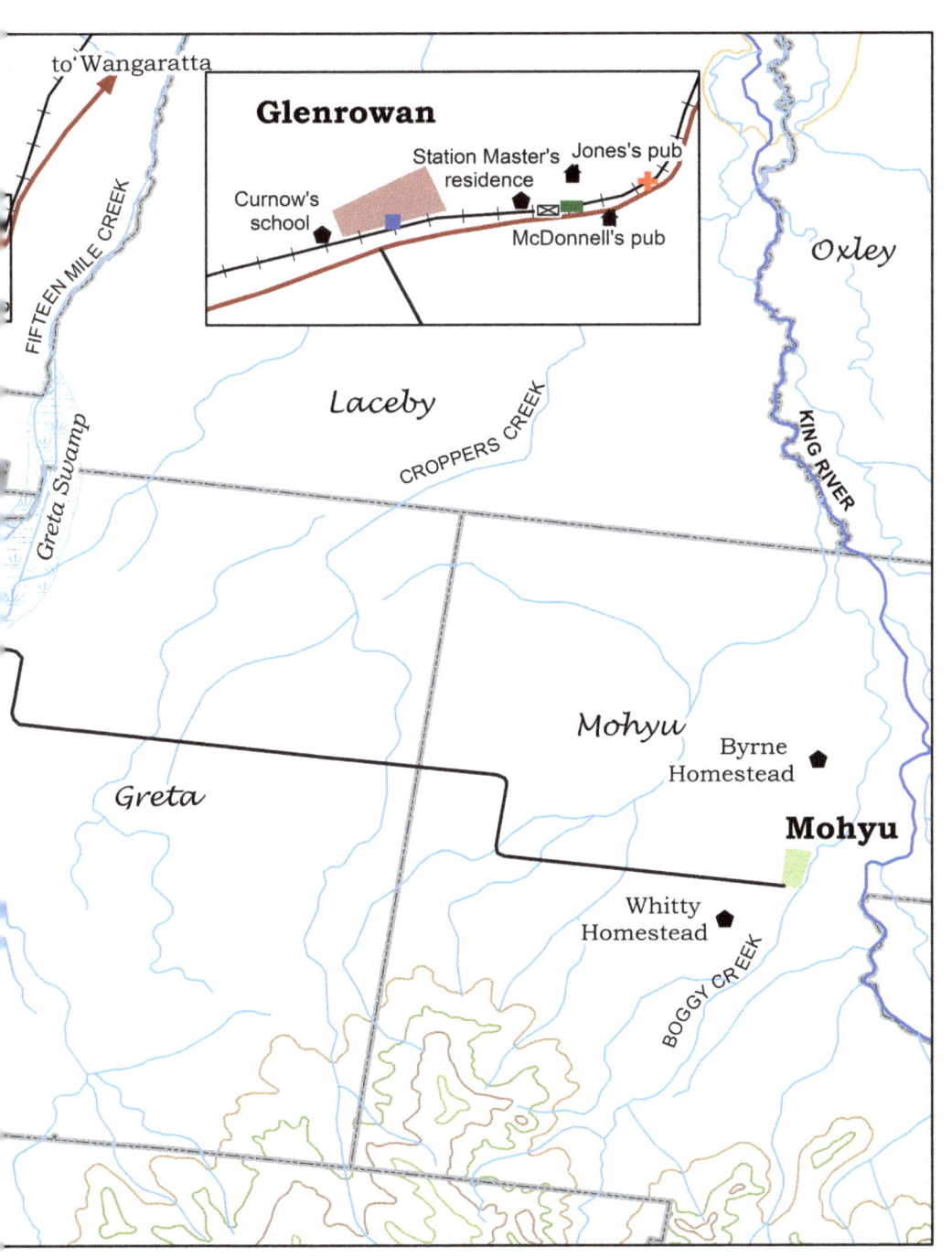

PART I:
Larrikin Thief

15-year-old Ned Kelly, at Kyneton, May 1870

1

Horse Stealing

I began to think they wanted me to give them something to talk about. Therefore I started wholesale and retail horse and cattle dealing.
Ned Kelly, The Jerilderie Letter (1879)

Larrikins can now be lovable; in Kelly's time larrikins were definitely not nice people. Spirited yes, but aggressive towards respectable people, free with crude suggestions to decent women, attackers of drunks, Chinese and the police — and involved in crime. With Ned Kelly and his larrikin mates in the Greta Mob it was serious crime: Ned boasted of his prowess as a horse and cattle thief. His complaint, shouted to the world, was that the police kept harassing him.

The thieving began as low scale. From boyhood Ned, his two brothers Jim and Dan and their cousins Tom and John Lloyd, were deft hands at stealing horses and cattle belonging to drovers who were 'overnighting' near the Kelly shanty at Greta. The livestock would disappear in the night and the next morning the Kelly boys and their cousins would suddenly appear with the animals quietly in tow to claim a reward and bask in the drover's gratitude. Sometimes, the 'lost' animals were not returned to their owners and an even greater profit margin was realised by the Kellys and their relatives and friends.

The Quinns, Ned's relatives on his mother's side, were bigger operators. In 1864 Ned's grandfather James took up a squatting run in the remote Upper King River Valley at Glenmore to escape from the police surveillance at Wallan, just north of Melbourne, where the family had been convicted of horse and cattle stealing. For a fee the Quinns offered safe haven away from the prying eyes of the police to livestock thieves and other district criminals.

The Quinns' pastoral run became the regional centre of a long established horse and cattle stealing network. Cattle stolen from Gippsland or even as far away as the Western District were driven over the Snowy Mountains high plains and down into the King Valley and Glenmore Station and then moved on into southern New South Wales.

Crossing backwards and forwards from Victoria to New South Wales gave protection to livestock thieves. Each colony was self-governing with its own laws and an autonomous police force. Although the police forces worked cooperatively, often they failed to share information and consequently would have been less likely to recognise brands of stolen animals from the other colony. The thieves and their receivers exploited this failing in intercolonial policing to their own advantage.

The squatters of the Upper King Valley petitioned for the protection of a police station soon after the Quinns arrived. Finally a station was opened just to watch over this one family. The Quinns responded with a 'match in the night'; they burnt down the police station's stables. The police station remained operational with the police patrolling across the routes of the livestock thieves. This encouraged Ned and his stepfather George King to think of livestock stealing in a different and grander way.

Instead as occasion offered rounding up large mobs, they developed a targeted 'fast track' thieving enterprise, a steal to order, rapid turnover business similar to today's 'chop shop' premier elite car stealing gangs. While still relying on an expanded kin and friendship network, and travelling along the older stock theft routes with some new ones added, this highly organised method of theft and disposal insulated thieves and receivers from each other and from the crime. The method instilled a heightened level of fear throughout the north-east in selectors and squatters alike. Everyone's stock was likely to be taken.

Aaron Sherritt, later to be shot by the Kelly Gang as a police spy, revealed to Superintendent Hare Ned's method of horse stealing. *He told me how he, Joe Byrne and Ned Kelly used to steal horses wholesale change the brands and dispose of them. They made raids on horses from about Wagga to Albury, took them on a back track to Melbourne, and on their return would pick up a number of horses in Victoria and take them over to Wagga or Albury for sale. One of the party used to act as the master and the others as his servants.* Altering and defacing brands was widespread. A branding iron dipped in scalding water or a smouldering cigar end were effective ways of effacing brands. Some thieves were craftsmen, erasing a letter or brand with little more than tweezers, iodine and a length of hoop iron.

Once stolen cattle were driven across the border, a long way from their owners, the thieves would release them and wait for them to be impounded. If animals in the pound were not claimed by their owners within twenty-one days, they were auctioned off at prices well below an animal's true market value. The thieves then 'bought' the animals they had stolen. Some pound keepers were in collusion with duffers and issued pound receipts on demand. With a pound receipt as legal proof of ownership, stolen livestock could be disposed of with impunity. Police found it difficult to break up duffing gangs operating under the protection of dishonest pound keepers. *Cattle are driven from either side of the Murray and left on someone's farm who may or may not be an agent of the thieves.*

The impounding is perfectly legal and cannot be got at except by some of the persons connected with the crime giving information.

A method of disposal which involved a greater degree of risk was the manufacture of bogus bills of sale. Ned issued them under the alias J. Thompson. To obtain the signature of a disinterested witness to a counterfeit bill of sale, stock thieves staged a well rehearsed charade. *They would make for some squatter's station where they were unknown, ask permission to put their horses into his stockyard on the pretence that they had met a stranger who wanted to purchase the mob of horses. The squatter would hear them making bargains about the price of each animal, they would ask the squatter to allow them to go into his office to draw up a receipt* [which he] *would be asked to witness.*

A counterfeit bill of sale written on the letterhead of a pastoral tenant and duly witnessed by him gave protection to stock thieves seeking to dispose of stolen livestock. Stolen animals were sold to squatters and selectors along the roadside or taken to remote country towns and sold by public auction. In the months before he took to the bush with the Kellys, Steve Hart made several journeys to New South Wales and visited the small town of Jerilderie with mobs of stolen horses, which were sold by the local auctioneer. This clever manoeuvre made it difficult for the police to prove complicity between duffers and receivers.

Professional horse and cattle stealing, which accounted for the vast majority of livestock thefts in the north-east, was the work of career criminals and those living on the fringes of this enterprise. Criminals and their hangers-on were not always the poverty-stricken wretches of popular myth. There was always the lure of 'easy' money and the thrill of illegality. Ned's network came unstuck with the arrest of the German settlers the Baumgartens, at Barnawartha along the Murray River, who were prosperous, ambitious farmers 'supplementing' their farming income through involvement in crime: in this case receiving horses stolen by the Kellys. As this case unravelled a warrant was issued for the arrest of Ned and Dan. The attempt to arrest Dan led to the Kellys moving from horse and cattle stealing to bushranging and outlawry.

No one can dispute Kelly's involvement in this trade. But his defenders say that there was a time from 1874 to1877 when he went straight, kept a regular job and only returned to the family business after police harassment. Of course having a regular job does not preclude a continuing involvement in crime. And the defenders have the odd notion that, if an habitual criminal is not successfully charged for a time, he must have been going straight. Actually, they might have got clever or got lucky. Kelly well knew the difference between doing crime and getting caught. To show that the police actually wanted crime to continue (to give them work) he said he had stolen *horses and cattle innumerable* and was never interfered with by the police. When he was interfered with, of course it was for things he had never done! Ned's uncle John Quinn, who was heavily involved in horse and cattle stealing for more than two decades, was never convicted of a crime though the police knew what he was up to.

In 1876, while he was going 'straight', Ned Kelly and his cousin Tom Lloyd junior were charged with stealing from Henry Lydeker a mare and foal. Lydeker was closely connected to Kelly's relatives the Quinns. He leased part of his farm to John Quinn for grazing and so was implicated in Quinn's horse stealing business for not all the horses to be grazed were honestly acquired. But the mare and the foal that were stolen were legally owned by Henry and were not grazing on the part of his selection leased to John Quinn, though they carried the Quinn's brand.

On the day before the horses went missing, Lydeker saw Ned and Tom, whom he knew by sight, acting *suspiciously* around his horses. Next morning when he discovered that his animals were missing, he reported the theft to the police and named Ned and Tom as the suspects. Warrants were issued for their arrest.

The mare and her foal were never seen again, prompting suspicion that the horses had been driven across the border and sold in New South Wales or, as was more commonly done with stolen animals when warrants were out, they were slaughtered, their brands removed and their remains either burnt or disposed of by the thieves down an abandoned mine shaft. A year later in 1877 when the Baumgarten case blew up, Ned and his fellow thieves burnt and partially buried the remains of stolen horses in an isolated bend of the Murray River. In the Lydeker case, the inability of the police to find any trace of the stolen animals or to discover the whereabouts of Ned, who had immediately gone to ground, explains why the Greta police took six months to serve the arrest warrant against Ned.

Tom Lloyd junior was never arrested because his uncle John Quinn brokered a settlement between Lydeker and Tom's family. They gave Lydeker a horse and a calf in compensation, and not it would seem the return of the stolen animals. One newspaper reporter described the settlement *as very like compounding a felony.*

Why Ned's family was not willing or able to broker a settlement deal with Lydeker remains a matter of speculation. Were they known to each other before this incident occurred? Almost certainly they were and their acquaintance may have related to livestock theft rather than being purely casual. Perhaps Lydeker and Ned had a previous bad history with one another.

The Oxley police were powerless to prevent Lydeker from coming to an out-of-court accommodation with the Quinns and Lloyds and despite Ned's unexplained exclusion from the Lydeker/Lloyd pact, they were just as powerless to compel Lydeker to press charges and give evidence against Ned in the ensuing court case. Without further compensation being offered or received, Lydeker did his best to undermine the police case against Ned. Throughout the courtroom proceedings, Lydeker remained uncooperative and even obstructionist in his dealings with the police and the court, to Ned's great benefit.

Several witnesses were called. There was testimony from some of *young Kelly's friends*, all of them Quinn clan associates, who in the past had demonstrated that they would swear to anything so long as it favoured the defendant's case. But without Henry's cooperation and his crucial eyewitness testimony as to who stole his animals and with the stolen animals having disappeared, the police case against Ned collapsed and not unexpectedly was dismissed *the evidence being inconclusive*. Ned was released despite his clear guilt in the theft and disappearance of Lydeker's horses.

The presiding Magistrate was far from impressed by Henry's reluctance to testify against Ned and by his all too apparent friendliness towards the accused. Most of all, however, he was annoyed by Lydeker's out-of-court deal with the Lloyds which brought a motion of *severe reproach* from the Bench. The police were unable to prove that Lydeker had compromised their case and there was nothing the court could do to compel him to cooperate.

Was this a case of criminal loyalties reaffirming themselves once the personal enmity of the moment had abated? Lydeker was not a man readily to give in to threats, whether they came from the police or the Quinns. It could be that the doubtful relations that Lydeker had as landlord to the thief John Quinn took some turn that put him into a new alignment on this case. These shanty friendships and business transactions were always unpredictable, fluctuating and capricious in nature. Sometimes collaborative, sometimes combative, today's friend invariably tomorrow's enemy until the trend reversed itself again. If we knew all about the inherently unstable relationships existing between John Quinn, Ned Kelly, Tom Lloyd junior, the Lloyds, and Henry Lydeker, we would discover why Ned could steal a mare and foal and not be convicted for it.

Personal agendas aside, honour among thieves is a perennial myth fostered most of all by thieves and criminals trying to convince themselves and others of a criminal solidarity, which was always conditional and unreliable in practice. When Ned Kelly's larrikin mate Wild Wright was confronted by the police with the choice between his own prosecution and that of a criminal associate, he shrewdly told Constable Scanlan that he would wait and see *how the case gets on* before *splitting* on his mate. Such about-faces by criminals in legal difficulty were and still are common when self-interest and a 'what's in it for me' attitude is at stake.

This case is a substantial blemish on Ned's so called 'going straight' years. The opportunity to go straight was in truth long gone. There was a moment when he was 15 that it might have happened. Young Ned's apprenticeship was not to an honest trade, but to bushranging and his master was Harry Power. Ned fell into this position through the Quinns, who provided a base for Power's operations.

Power and Ned, in traditional highway-man style, robbed travellers on the road. Kelly had been identified and the police arrested and charged him at Kyneton in central Victoria. But they found reasons not to bring the case to trial while they pumped Ned for information about Power. Ned was helpful (whether intentionally or not is unclear), but it was Ned's uncle John Lloyd who led the police rather reluctantly to Power's hideout high up on the range looking down the King Valley. Power was caught, tried and sentenced to fifteen years hard labour. As soon as the police were on Power's trail, they released Kelly, still without going to trial, and assisted him to get back to his family. Though it was Lloyd who had given most assistance to the police, it was young Ned who was known as the betrayer of Harry Power. The bushranger was convinced of Ned's betrayal and he never forgave nor missed an opportunity to belittle his former apprentice.

The two policemen who dealt with Kelly, Superintendent Nicolson who later led the hunt for him, and Sergeant James Babington were sympathetic to the lad and offered to help him. Six weeks after he returned home, he wrote asking for that help. To this poorly spelt message he added a heart-felt postscript:

> *Every one looks on me like*
> *A black snake send me*
> *An answer me as soon*
> *posable*

The help offered was to get Ned work on a sheep station in New South Wales, well away from his family and other bad company. But giving information to the police was not enough to break those bonds. Mrs Kelly opposed her son leaving and his fate was sealed.

2

Mrs Kelly's Selection

I don't know whether this criminal brood can be prevented from selecting. I suppose that selectors are not obliged to produce certificates of morality before getting the land they applied for.

Captain Standish, Chief Commissioner of Police, 1869

In Kelly country there were broadly two sorts of landholders, the squatters, the first land takers, and an incoming group of selectors. The squatters ran sheep and cattle over extensive ground; the selectors had small farms. Ned's mother Ellen was a selector. Ned thought of becoming one but did not carry through with it.

Mrs Kelly's husband, John 'Red' Kelly, former convict from Van Diemen's Land, died in 1866. In 1874 she married the American George King. According to J.J. Kenneally *George King was not liked in Greta and the local residents continued to refer to his wife as Mrs Kelly.* Ellen accepted the designation and publicly referred to herself as 'the widow Kelly' as if she had never married George King. Her son Ned did likewise *I am a widow's son outlawed.*

The selection held by Mrs Kelly was visited by Superintendent Nicolson of the Victorian police in April 1877 before Ned and Dan took to the bush. He reported *she lived on a piece of cleared and partially cultivated land on the roadside in an old wooden hut, with a large bark roof. The dwelling was divided into five apartments by partitions of blanketing, rags, etc. There were no men in the house, only children and two girls of about fourteen years of age, said to be her daughters. They all appeared to be existing in poverty and squalor.*

Six months after Ned's execution, the local crown lands bailiff wrote this assessment of the property. *The improvements on the selection are in my opinion of no value consisting of a slab house with a bark roof and post and rail fencing and some clearing and the value according to my estimation would be about £100. This selection has been gazetted forfeited* [for non payment of rent]. The forfeiture was rescinded and Mrs Kelly struggled on.

The undoubted poverty of the Kelly selection combined with the assumption that squatters were always oppressing the selectors produce in the Kelly literature a scenario where Ned can be seen as a social bandit and surrogate leader of a selector revolution. However, selectors were not disgruntled malcontents caught up in a rural culture of poverty; they were not abject farming failures. Mrs Kelly's selection is totally unrepresentative of the group.

The first attempts to settle small farmers on the squatters' extensive domains were abject failures. The Selection Acts of 1860 and 1862 were subverted by the men they were meant to ease out or supplant. Under the Acts, land in Victoria was resumed from the squatters, and then any person could take up a farm on this land and pay for it on time payment. However, if they had the cash they could buy the land straight away. So the squatters employed 'dummies' who selected land on their behalf, bought the selection outright with funds they supplied and then passed it over to them. By these means the squatters could become the owners of lands they had formerly leased. Any holder of a selection was meant to cultivate and improve it, but it turned out that it was impossible to enforce this requirement. The old system of buying land at auction continued and by this means wealthy men could continue to acquire land.

The liberals and democrats, who were responsible for passing the Selection Acts, did not give up and by 1869 they had passed laws that stopped the abuses and put the selector in a much stronger position. Ned Kelly came of age under this dispensation, something many authors overlook as they elaborate on the injustices of the land law. No one could now select land without their bona fides and suitability being scrutinised by a local land board. Buying land outright ceased. The selector in the first instance held a licence for three years; if all looked satisfactory he could then be given a seven year lease. Only when ten years were up could the selector become the owner of the land and throughout that time the crown lands bailiffs were checking that cultivation and improvement were occurring. That virtually eliminated the mass use of dummies by squatters; if any malpractice was detected the Minister of Lands could simply cancel the selection without taking the matter to court.

Previously selectors could choose land only after it had been resumed from the squatter and surveyed. From 1869 the selector at any time could enter the squatter's run and peg out a claim and then report his claim to the Land Office.

The members of the land boards and the crown lands bailiffs were appointed by liberal and democratic governments so that if these officials stretched the law it was to give the selector every chance. Even local councils, traditionally regarded as bastions of squatter power, had their fair share of councillors and mayors who favoured the political cause of selectors and safeguarded their interests.

The squatters were very much in retreat. They survived in the more remote country, but elsewhere their runs were diminishing or disappearing altogether. A selector with his survey pegs could arrive at any time. Some squatters were fighting this, not with the wholesale use of dummies, which was now impossible, but with members of their families taking up a selection. It might be in a key location on a creek or river so that the holder of this plot rendered all the land further back useless to anyone else. This was known as peacocking – which selectors could attempt as well. But all such applications now had to run the gauntlet of the land board. To protect his access to water a squatter might ask that a water reserve be declared which made this land ineligible for selection. But selectors could contest any moves of this sort and have their victories. A few squatters, seeing which way the wind was blowing, simply moved on.

Farming first became possible in the Greta area at the time of the gold rushes in the 1850s. The goldfields at Beechworth and smaller centres required flour and potatoes for the diggers and hay and oats for the horses. Likewise, stopping points on the way to the diggings needed the same supplies. At this time the squatters shifted from growing wool for the British market to running cattle to supply diggers with their steak. They were still running cattle in Kelly's time, which meant he had more valuable and biddable stock to steal. The local market diminished with the decline of gold mining but the arrival of the railway in the early 1870s gave selectors access to the wider market of Melbourne and the world beyond. The farming population continued to grow, which was one sign that farming on selections was not totally unrewarding.

In fact, the selection survival figures in the geographic centre of Kelly country are impressive: In Greta 79% of all selectors who took up land during the so called 'hungry seventies' survived the land selection process and obtained freehold title to their selections. In Lurg with its indifferent soil and sparse settlement where Ned's mother Ellen ran the Kelly shanty and some of his Lloyd relatives lived, 62%

of selectors who took up land in the parish between 1868 and 1880 survived their crucial first ten years on the land.

As significant as overall selection survival rates undoubtedly are, they may still disguise hardship and a sense of failure. The financial rigours of the selection process and the natural disasters of crop failure, flood and fire made life difficult for all selectors no matter what their financial position may be. Did selectors regard these practical realities of farming life through a glum prism of personal failure and despair or with a hopeful optimism that they would eventually succeed?

A tangible measure of whether or not selectors saw themselves as living on the edge can be glimpsed in mortgage rates, rent arrears and the necessity to seek employment off their selections.

Assuming that after three years of farming, the selectors told the truth on their lease applications, 58% were farmers without temporary employment off their selections; 15% were labourers employed on neighbouring farms or working for local squatters; the remaining 27% were self-employed tradesmen such as blacksmiths and carpenters or contractors tendering for government, council and private contracts. Seasonal occupations such as shearing and harvesting were not monitored in land selection records, but the probability is that struggling selectors and those in need of capital for farming improvements engaged in itinerant employment of this kind.

In Greta, Glenrowan, Lurg, Laceby and Moyhu less than half of the selector population (45%) mortgaged their properties to the banks or local moneylenders, while 55% never felt the necessity to do so.

Only a small percentage of selectors (10%) residing in the above land parishes regularly fell behind in their rent payments. Roughly half (48%) never fell into rent arrears and of those who did only 18% did so more than twice. Surprisingly, 60% of selectors never fell into rent arrears at all during the crucial three year licence period when conditions were at their toughest and cash scarce. These financial figures clearly indicate that selectors although not yet affluent or entirely confident in their ability to survive, were coping relatively well with the economic demands of farming their selections.

But even here selection failure was not outright farming failure. Ned's mother Ellen fell within the struggling 10% of selectors who were regular rent defaulters facing financial ruin and the forfeiture of their selections. Ellen was the quintessential poor selector and an even worse farmer. She struggled for more than two decades with chronic poverty, rent arrears and forfeiture. Yet she too survived the land selection process and in 1892 gained freehold title to her 88 acre property some 23 years after taking up the land in 1867, which was more than twice as long as the average period of time taken by selectors (10 years) to gain title to their land.

There was a small percentage of poverty ridden, struggling selectors like Ellen Kelly residing in the Greta and Lurg land parishes, some of them were respectable and most of them were not associated with either the shanty lifestyle or crime. They were few in number and their disastrous economic and farming lives were not at all representative of the more successful farming lives enjoyed by the majority of selectors. Yet authors all too readily accept Ellen Kelly and impoverished selectors like the unfortunate Dennis Kelly (no relation) who resided at Glenrowan as typical examples of selector life in the region. They were neither similar in their personal and community outlook, nor representative of anything other than sharing poor farming skills, a chronic lack of available cash and in Dennis' ill-fated case a continuous run of *bad health and bad seasons*.

Kelly always spoke warmly of his mother and he was enraged when she was sent to gaol with a babe on her breast. But Ned and his brothers Jim and Dan did very little to help out their mother or the Kelly family selection. The Kelly brothers rarely worked the selection and rarer still did they contribute money to its upkeep. What money they acquired they spent on themselves and their larrikin friends and only occasionally did they come to their family's assistance and then only in times of greatest need. If Ned had taken up a selection next to his mother's and worked them jointly that might have provided a viable farm, but his selection application lapsed when he failed to pay the small survey fee. Ellen's extended family, the Quinns and Lloyds, were of more help to her than her three wayward sons ever were. Ned's admirers make much of the fact that when he was momentarily flush with livestock theft money, Ned built for his mother a new sawn timber and bark hut with a verandah from which she could carry on her sly grog selling shanty business. The truth of the matter was starker still; the choice was to build a new house or abandon the selection entirely as the old ramshackle Kelly shanty was literally falling down about the family's ears.

Ellen's precarious financial situation and her farming failure as a selector was clearly of her own and her larrikin sons' making. The Kelly selection was not basically worked as a farm; it was on the Winton to Greta road and its chief business was dispensing sly grog, serving meals and providing board and sexual extras to its customers including miners on their way to the Beechworth goldfields. Even after Ned had robbed two banks, his mother's selection was not paid off. For the Kellys as a family, the shanty and larrikin lifestyle and the lure of crime and easy money always took precedence over hard work and the drab existence of the selector 'mugs' around them. The situation was to change little in the ensuing years. Even after gaining freehold title to the Kelly selection, Ellen and her son Jim remained marginal farmers and among the poorest landowners in the district.

Surprisingly, feminist historians with an interest in the Kelly women make no clear distinction between the unruly shanty behaviour and sexual promiscuity of Ellen Kelly, her daughters and her female friends and the more conventional morality based on decent behaviour of the majority of women living in the Greta, Glenrowan and Moyhu communities. Respectable selector women did not frequent the district's pubs and shanties nor did they freely grant sexual favours for money or presents. They were the moral compasses of their families and were far from being under the thumb of their husbands. These respectable women did not sit on Victorian pedestals; just as they did not inhabit a seedy shanty underworld of crime and debauchery.

In a recently published work on Ellen Kelly, she is portrayed as the quintessential rural selector woman greatly admired for her tenacity and perseverance in the face of police harassment, crushing poverty and the vagaries of bush farming life. Her flexible morals and her shanty culture lifestyle are extolled as representative and a shining beacon of womanly virtue and propriety, undermined of course by the cruel intentions and bad faith actions of others. It is as, if today, we would offer as a role model the proprietoress of a seedy motel on the edge of town, the haunt of the local crims and prostitutes renting its rooms by the hour. But the romantic illusions of respectable people today about disreputable people in the past knows no bounds.

3

Whitty and Byrne

Whitty and Byrne not being satisfied with all the picked land on the Boggy Creek and King River and the run of their stock on certificate ground free and no one interfering with them paid heavy rent to the banks for all the open ground so as a poor man could keep no stock.

Ned Kelly, The Jerilderie Letter (1879)

Whitty and Byrne, this duo of Irish Catholic go-getters, have been immortalised by Ned in his Jerilderie Letter. He denounced them as land monopolists and oppressors of the poor. They have come to stand for the oppression that the squatters visited on the selectors. But Whitty and Byrne were not squatters in the traditional sense. The squatters proper, those who held lands on pastoral lease, were in retreat. They were being replaced as large landholders and community leaders by a growing class of enterprising farmers with capital. They had bought land at auction sales in the 1850s and went on to expand their holdings by using the Selection Acts. Whitty and Byrne were among the most successful of these men. They had not used dummies to get more land; rather sons and other members of the family selected plots (which was perfectly legitimate). Ned was wrong to think the Whitty and Byrne patriarchs personally controlled all the lands that bore their name; their land 'empires' were family rather than individual concerns.

Once they were prospering, the rich farmers could buy up other properties as they came onto the market. The Whitty and Byrne partnership came into existence when they bid together for the right to lease the Moyhu lands held by the Union Bank. These were a relic of a past age; the property had been assembled by the Squatter Hugh Glass by the liberal use of dummies. Glass went broke and his property ended up with the bank. Whitty and Byrne won the tender for the lease and in turn rented out these lands for grazing to those who could pay. They held the lease for two years giving them temporary control over nearly two thirds of the entire parish. For the greater part of the 1870s, Whitty and Byrne's total landholdings fluctuated around the 6,000 acre mark, far below the 15,000 acres (which in pastoral terms was small) they jointly controlled for two years. Between 1877 and 1881 Whitty also leased a section of the much reduced Myrrhee run, when the run was in its final stage of decay. To this extent only was he a squatter.

The Whitty's landholdings were scattered throughout the parish and included some choice water frontages along the Boggy Creek. The Byrnes favoured a cluster settlement spanning both banks of the King River and parts of the Meadow Creek. The pattern of settlement adopted by the Byrne clan greatly discouraged selectors other than those related to the family, from selecting land adjacent to the clan's water frontages. Selectors who arrived in the parish later than the Byrnes naturally resented what they wrongly perceived as an elaborate family conspiracy to control the region's prime water frontage allotments. Despite the obvious disadvantage suffered by selectors who took up land adjoining the Whitty and Byrne water frontages, early arrival in the area and shrewd family enterprise, rather than a deliberate policy of peacocking designed to frustrate selection, accounts for the gradual accumulation by both families of so many choice water frontage allotments.

Selectors too developed a clustered family settlement. Confined by law to only 320 acres they used selection by different family members to accumulate more viable properties and to prosper. At all levels of society kin was a strong bond, a means of getting assistance to run properties and for support in times of trouble.

In Kelly's lifetime another large family enterprise was being assembled. The McAliece brothers Charles, Robert, William, Andrew, David and their brother-in-law James Shanks were active go-ahead men. They made their first money from gold digging and began to buy land while keeping up the mining to supply the capital for further purchases and improvements. Between them the McAliece brothers and James Shanks purchased and selected well over 2,500 broad acres and may have rented or leased considerably more land as was the custom at the time for all landowners to do. In the early to mid 1870s Charles McAliece and James Shanks selected the 488 acres lying between their original land purchases, consolidating their small but significant family-controlled piece of Hurdle Creek waterfrontage. There was nothing sinister or unhanded in how the McAliece brothers and James Shanks obtained their land. No dummying, no peacocking or any other of the usual array of methods employed by some squatters and some selectors to disadvantage and discourage others from settling near them.

The disputes over access to water could as readily occur between selectors as between large landholders and selectors. Selectors frequently petitioned the Lands Department against the application of a fellow selector to take up land with a water frontage. In August 1870, Michael English, a poor farmer with 12 children who had resided at Kilmore until his crops and livestock were destroyed by a bushfire, pegged out 167 acres of land at Greta bordering on the Fifteen Mile Creek. A petition signed by 32 Greta selectors claimed that this allotment was one of several which *contain the only permanent water in the neighbourhood and if leased a great hardship will be inflicted on the surrounding district.*

This protest was supported by the Oxley Shire Council which lobbied the Lands Department to have the land declared a water reserve. After months of local acrimony, a substantial portion of the water frontage pegged out by English was proclaimed a water reserve. The dispute, although settled legally, continued under a different guise for a further ten years. To annoy his neighbours, English refused to erect a fence between his selection and the water reserve and encouraged his dogs to drive off any livestock seeking to use it. After several years of complaint from selectors, the Lands Department took steps to compel English to fence his land, *to put a stop to future complaints, if not bloodshed!*

During the 1870s the Lloyds and the Barnetts, two leading Kelly sympathiser families, were engaged in bitter squabbling over water. William Barnett and Ned's uncle John Lloyd occupied adjoining selections of land. The Lloyds objected to the Barnetts taking up a water frontage allotment which effectively denied them easy access to creek water, so they commenced a campaign of harassment and let their stock wander into Barnett's wheat crop. Barnett, angered by Lloyd's repeated refusal to keep his livestock out of his crop, discovered some of Lloyd's horses in his wheat and decided to drive them to the pound. He was in the act of securing the animals when John Lloyd supported by son Tom arrived on the scene. The Lloyds were on horseback and easily rescued their livestock. Barnett, who was beside himself with anger yelled *If my horse was here you would not take the horses so easy.* John Lloyd replied, *You will not have your horse long!*

On the following day, Barnett took out a summons against Lloyd for *rescuing impounded horses.* The day before the case was due to be heard in court, Barnett discovered that his horse was missing. Suspecting foul play he tracked the beast to Lloyd's house, where he found a large quantity of fresh blood covering the ground. He then followed a clearly visible set of blood-stained tracks to O'Brien's stable adjoining Lloyd's property and discovered the mutilated body of his horse. The horse had been tied up with a length of rope and hacked to death with a tomahawk. When arrested by Constable Flood, Lloyd was dressed in a shirt and trousers caked with dried blood. He explained the bloody condition of his clothes by claiming that he had cut his finger reaping. He was found guilty. The judge took into consideration Lloyd's mature age and sentenced him to four years imprisonment with hard labour.

Prior to the arrival of large numbers of selectors in the region, sheep and cattle belonging to squatters wandered free and grazed the open range with little competition. Selection dramatically increased the livestock population and created intense competition for grass. Squatters were determined that selectors would not prosper by fattening their livestock on pastoral grass and whenever possible, impounded selectors' animals found trespassing on their runs. Selectors, restricted by the Land Acts to a comparatively small acreage in which to cultivate a crop and depasture their livestock, took advantage of pasture land wherever they could find it, even surreptitiously grazing their animals on land belonging to their neighbours.

To Kelly the worst offence of Whitty and Byrne was the impounding of stock that came onto their land. *If a poor man happened to leave his horse or a bit of a poddy calf outside his paddock they would be impounded. I have known over 60 head of horses impounded in one day by Whitty and Byrne all belonging to poor farmers. They would have to leave their ploughing or harvest or other employment to go to Oxley. When they would get there* [they would] *perhaps not have money enough to release them and have to give a bill of sale or borrow money.*

Although mass impoundings of the kind attributed to Whitty and Byrne sometimes occurred, they were not common. Single animal seizures were by far the most common form of impounding and were carried out by selectors and squatters alike. Everybody impounded trespassing livestock and no quarter was given as to whose animals they were; whether belonging to friend or foe they were driven to the pound. Mass impoundings, when they did occur, were usually carried out by squatters and large landholders simply because they had more grass to defend. Naturally selectors resented their livestock being impounded and felt aggrieved that squatters should insist upon strict compliance with the trespassing laws in a region where fences were still being erected.

But general hostility to squatters and large landholders was tempered in a small community by face to face dealings. The Quinns, Lloyds and the Kellys, as well as many of their horse and cattle stealing friends, considered Squatter Robert McBean to be an honest man who kept his word and was a good employer. He was prepared to employ them no matter what crimes they may have committed. Their high opinion was all the more remarkable since McBean was a Benalla Police Magistrate, who would frequently adjudicate their criminal cases, fining and sending them to gaol as necessary. When a McBean employee set fire to part of his run, it was the Lloyds who informed the squatter, a Lloyd who put out the fire and a Lloyd who reported the matter to the Greta police and gave courtroom evidence against a workmate. This happened on two separate occasions involving two different McBean employees. Spite was the motive in both cases and Ned's Lloyd relatives acted in defence of their squatter neighbour's property.

When McBean in a fit of anger impounded some of the Lloyd's cattle found trespassing on his run, Mrs McBean intervened, redeeming the animals from the pound and returning them to the Lloyds. She felt a respectable woman's compassion for a struggling family with many young children to support, whose chief breadwinner was away in gaol serving a long sentence for livestock stealing.

There were a number of hard men holding many acres, who vigorously protected their interests in stock and grass, and were not denounced by Kelly. In fact Whitty and Byrne are the only large landholders named in the Jerilderie Letter. In a document that is read as a manifesto of protest Kelly does not use the terms squatter and selector, which still had currency in colonial and local politics. Kelly hated this duo, who were not squatters, but it is doubtful that they were universally hated even by selectors. Members of the two families were elected to the Oxley Council for many years. A Whitty daughter Ellen had married into the Mason family of stock thieves and Kelly sympathisers. One of Kelly's relatives, William Tanner, gained the support of Whitty and Byrne when he was denied the right to select land; they assured the authorities (wrongly) that he was not a sympathiser of the Kellys.

Selectors wrote to newspapers about everything and often complained about bad treatment from squatters when it personally affected their own interests. I have not found one public complaint against either Whitty or Byrne in this regard. When their sons were elected to the Oxley Council, they tenaciously defended selectors' rights which largely were their own. Neither have I found a single instance of Whitty or Byrne supporting the squatters' side in political or personal arguments involving selectors.

It is always 'Whitty and Byrne' but it was about Whitty that Kelly obsessed most. What made Whitty distinctive? He was not a squatter, most of whom were English and Scots Protestants of some cultivation. Whitty was an Irish Catholic, who came to Australia as an assisted migrant, penniless and illiterate. He was a totally self-made man. At first he and his family of brothers and sons held land just north of Melbourne, using the takings of a hotel to feed into the farming business. Having prospered here they moved to the north-east and began the accumulation of property that so enraged Ned. James Quinn, the founder of Ned's mother's clan, arrived like James Whitty in the 1840s, and like him was a penniless Irish immigrant. He too moved from land just north of Melbourne to the north-east, where his wayward sons graduated from small crime to large.

Ned denounced Irish Catholics who joined the police for betraying Ireland. He could not denounce Whitty for making money, so he produced a rant to the effect that Whitty's money-making hurt everyone else — and perhaps hurt him, as he saw the different path that a poor Irishman could take.

In the Jerilderie Letter Ned absurdly blamed Whitty for turning him back to crime (which we have seen he had not in fact left). Whitty had lost his prize bull and Ned heard that Whitty was blaming him for it. He confronted the old man, ramrod straight, at the Moyhu races. Whitty said he had found his bull and had never blamed Kelly; it was his son-in-law John Farrell who had passed on this rumour. Ned continues *not long afterward I heard again, I was blamed for stealing a mob of calves from Whitty and Farrell which I knew nothing about.* Of course these rumours circulated because Kelly had done time and was well known as the leader of the lawless Greta Mob. But if his accusers got the wrong crime this was a total insult. These false accusations, Ned tells us, started him thinking: *they wanted me to give them something to talk about. Therefore I started wholesale and retail horse and cattle dealing.* And it was all Whitty's fault!

Ned proceeded to steal Whitty's horses and take them over the Murray River. When the receivers, the Baumgartens, were taken into custody, warrants were out for Ned and Dan's arrest.

4

Constable Hall's Farewell

He got James Murdock who was recently hung in Wagga Wagga to give false evidence against me. On Hall and Murdock's evidence I was found guilty of receiving and got three years.
Ned Kelly, The Jerilderie Letter (1879)

Edward Hall, Irish-born policeman, was the arresting officer in two cases that ended with Ned Kelly in gaol. Ned understandably did not like him. Ned's defenders have endorsed all his criticisms — and more.

Constable Hall is an easy target. He was grossly overweight and had difficulty in finding a horse to carry him. The *Ovens and Murray Advertiser* reported on the matter as follows: *as regards the obesity, it is quite certain that if Constable Hall has recently become somewhat stout of body, he has likewise shown himself to be stout of heart, and a man that will allow neither personal inconvenience nor danger to stand in the way of the performance of his duty.* He did not do policing by the book. If pushed, he would stretch the truth to gain a conviction. He could be heavy-handed in his arrest and treatment of prisoners. Yet in the eyes of Greta's respectable residents and his police superiors Hall was a good cop with an impressive conviction record during his time at Greta.

When he was transferred out of the district there was widespread praise for his work and a worry about whether anyone else could do so well. The *Benalla Ensign* said *the gang at Greta have always been kept well under by Hall and we shall see if the superior officer who recommended a change has acted wisely. We venture to think not and should not be surprised to see Hall back again in his old quarters.* The *Ovens and Murray Advertiser* was even more effusive, explaining that Hall was not being removed because of any personal misconduct but because horses kept 'breaking down' underneath him. *In the Greta district Hall has certainly shown himself to be the right man in the right place and considering the services he has rendered the respectable portion of the community, we should imagine that sooner than see him removed the squatters and settlers* [selectors] *in the neighbourhood would be quite willing to furnish him with re mounts for the next few years.*

At Greta itself publican O'Brien organised a collection of 20 gold sovereigns and a farewell dinner at his Victoria Hotel. A sumptuous meal was served, toasts were drunk to the policeman's health and sincere wishes were offered for a prosperous future. Ned's admirers wrongly assume that only the district's squatters appreciated Hall's policing endeavours against the Greta Mob and its allies in livestock theft. Most of the twenty sovereigns, a considerable sum of money, came from Greta's selector community and was not as the Kelly defenders allege a going-away gift from the North Eastern Stock Protection League. That body acknowledged Hall's policing achievements by a financial contribution of its own. Whitty and Byrne, who were influential members of the Moyhu chapter of the league, gave money but as private contributors not as league representatives. It was selectors who appreciated Hall's policing efforts the most, because predominately it was their horses and cattle that were stolen by the Greta Mob thieves.

Hall's police superiors felt so confident his sojourn at Greta had been successful in curbing the district's criminals that they downgraded Greta police station from a two to a one-man policing operation. This was an unwise move which they soon came to regret. Hall's removal emboldened Greta's stock thieves and despite some able police postings, and some rather less so, they were not to be brought under police control again until after the Kelly outbreak.

Ned Kelly could not allow that Constable Hall was genuinely popular. He thought he knew the reasons why O'Brien took up a collection and the reasons Hall needed the money. *Hall was considerably in debt to Mr. L. O'Brien and he was going to leave Greta. Mr. O'Brien seen no other chance of getting his money so there was a subscription collected for Hall. With the aid of this money he got James Murdock who was recently hung in Wagga Wagga to give false evidence against me.* Against this it can be said that O'Brien had no trouble finding subscribers to his collection and that Hall had already been rewarded for getting convictions against Ned and others from which he could have paid off his informer, though there is no evidence that he needed to. In any case, since he was about to leave the district there was no need to keep faith with any local informer.

Hall's policing methods did not depend on constant horse patrols. He made himself into a spymaster, controlling a network of police informers embedded inside the Greta criminal subculture and shanty community. Most of these people were involved in crime themselves and were the kinfolk or shanty friends of Greta's criminal ne'er do wells. Cultivated or coerced by Hall, they gave him the intelligence he needed. Honour among thieves was very much conditional and depended on advantageous circumstances.

James Murdock, accused by Kelly of giving false evidence against him, was one of Constable Hall's Greta informers and a good one because he was well connected to Greta's criminal community. *See

Appendix I The James Murdock Connection. He was married to Ann Maree Kershaw and his brother-in-law James Kershaw was married to Jane Graham, both prominent Kelly sympathisers. The Murdocks and the Kershaws were closely associated with the Kellys, Quinns and Lloyds participating in their shanty culture and larrikin/livestock stealing lifestyle. Neither family seems to have played an active part in the professional horse and cattle stealing ring, run by Ned and his stepfather George King, at least not as livestock thieves. (James was convicted on one count of horse stealing in 1873, but this was an amateurish crime, the only one of its kind attributed to him.) They may have occasionally acted as receivers, but more probably their role was as bush telegraphs for the thieves and the receivers.

Neither James Murdock nor James Kershaw pursued honest work beyond the bare minimum. The occasional slaughtering of other people's sheep for mutton was more their style of petty crime. Both men were shanty fringe dwelling opportunists ready to take advantage of any profitable situation that presented itself providing the price to be paid was not too high and gaol time was not involved. In comparison with hardened criminals such as the Quinns, Lloyds and Kellys, James Murdock and James Kershaw and their respective wives were inconsequential criminals, who could be relied upon to assist the more serious thieves and habitual criminals in committing or covering up their crimes.

Hall used James Murdock as his eyes and ears inside the Kelly shanty to catch them out in their criminal activity. Hall put constant pressure on Murdock to 'get the goods' on Ned. If Murdock wavered in his police informer duties, Hall ramped up the pressure further, going as far as prosecuting Murdock for his own crimes. In August 1870, Constable Hall arrested the Murdocks *for having meat in their possession for which they could not satisfactorily account*. Summoned before the Wangaratta Police Court in December 1870, James admitted to having slaughtered three sheep belonging to a local pastoralist. Murdock claimed the sheep had been given to him by Greta selectors Henry and Thomas Ainge, a story he made up when arrested by Hall and later had no option but to repeat before the Police Magistrate.

According to Henry Ainge's courtroom testimony, Murdock had *been splitting rails for me, working in the bush.* The brothers, who were neither criminals nor associated with the Greta shanty culture, denied giving any sheep to Murdock and in this they were supported by Greta selector William Canny and his daughter Maria. Murdock was convicted of the crime and sentenced to four months hard labour in Beechworth Gaol.

The police case against Ann Maree was harder to prove. Several prime cuts of a sheep's carcass had been found in her kitchen larder but, unlike her intimidated husband, Ann Maree remained silent and gave no explanation to either Hall or the court for the meat's presence. Against the odds Ann Maree was found not guilty and acquitted, when clearly she was guilty of receiving stolen meat and should have gone to gaol. Maybe Hall intervened behind the scenes and Ann Maree's involvement was judiciously overlooked. Her husband James was in gaol and Hall's policeman's message had been delivered; do your job properly or face the consequences.

Ned Kelly, as friend and foe, and through his family and their connections, was part of Hall's network. At first as a young man of 15, Hall seemed to offer him friendship. Ned had just returned home much troubled because he had seemingly betrayed the bushranger Harry Power. On one occasion, Hall asked Ned to help him deal with his troublesome uncles who were roaring drunk. Pat Quinn was a police informer while Jimmy Quinn was a chronic brawler and notorious basher of innocent people. Both were violent dangerous men. Hall asked Ned to provoke them into a fight, which would provide the occasion for despatching them to gaol. Ned was not coerced into cooperating with Hall and he probably saw the confrontation as no more than some larrikin fun or as a chance to retaliate against his uncles for some petty insult or perceived slight.

Ned had no trouble stirring up a fight. At the subsequent trial he reported *Trooper Hall said to me. 'I wish you would get up a row', he told me to insult the Quinns and Kenny* [a larrikin friend who earlier had been drinking with the Quinns]. *I run my horse up against James Quinn and nearly knocked him over. He asked why I did so. I said 'Find out'. James Quinn tried to get hold of me: I hit him and I also hit young Kenny.*

The irate Quinns and Kenny pursued Ned to the Greta lockup, where according to Hall: *Kelly threw himself off his horse broke the gate open and said. 'He is going to kill me'.* Ned it would seem was greatly surprised by the drunken ferocity of his uncles' pursuit of him. He knew he was in for a good thrashing and genuinely sought Hall's protection. To save himself, Ned rushed headlong into the backyard of the police barracks as Hall dragged the foul-mouthed and flailing Jimmy Quinn from his horse. Hall later said *I was in the act of handcuffing him, when on my knees* [Pat Quinn] *came up and said 'Let him go you dog'. He had a skull cracker with a stirrup-iron in his hand he struck me on the back of the head with the iron. I was stunned and attempted to get up when he struck me again. I was knocked insensible and bled profusely.* All the while, Jimmy Quinn partially subdued and lying on his back on the ground, repeatedly shouted out *Stave his head in! Stave his head in!*

Hall's injuries were severe and required several stitches leaving him with a three inch scar and a cautious attitude in his future dealings with members of the Quinn, Lloyd and Kelly clan. Ned watched in silence as his uncle Pat struck the policeman down and continued to pummel him on the ground. He neither came to Hall's assistance nor did he try to dissuade his rampaging uncles from bashing him further. Ned was either enjoying the spectacle or he feared his uncles' wrath if he intervened in the fight.

Before he passed out for a second time from the brutal assault, Hall wisely called out to the unarmed Constable Archdeacon to let the drunken trio go and the incident ended as rapidly as it had started. Ned told the court: *Constable Hall came with me to Wangaratta and advised me to swear out an information against Kenny,* who had played a lesser role in the Greta lockup brawl. On Hall's policeman's advice Ned did so, which clearly shows that the Kelly/Hall partnership continued for sometime after the row had reached its natural conclusion, indicating that the policeman's influence on young Ned was considerable despite everything that had happened. Hall used Ned to rope Kenny into the assault case, when he was no more than a spectator to the violent attack on the policeman.

By the time of the court case, however, Ned wanted to save face with his relatives by trying to distance himself from the policeman. He nevertheless gave damaging evidence against both of his uncles and told the court he wished to withdraw the charge against Kenny adding *I deserved to get all I received.* Kenny was acquitted of using threatening language. Jimmy Quinn was convicted of assault and sentenced to three months gaol and a hefty fine. Pat Quinn's crime was far more serious in the eyes of the law and he was sent to prison for four years for inflicting grievous bodily harm on Constable Hall.

Ned's partnership with Hall is generally dismissed in the Kelly literature as an example of a manipulative policeman taking advantage of a naive and inexperienced youngster to boost his Kelly clan conviction rate. Ned must have suspected Hall's motives and he went along with the policeman's request anyway. There was nothing naive or innocent in Ned's decision to help Hall entrap his relatives. Ned went into the fray with his eyes open and with a pride in himself as a flash bush larrikin, Harry Power's bushranging mate and a Greta criminal celebrity.

Constable Hall had his first success in putting Kelly away following the McCormick affair. After he had a dispute with a local hawker, Ned was party to a nasty revenge. He and his uncle John Lloyd, who may now have become a Hall informer, decided to send a pair of calf testicles to the childless Mrs McCormick suggesting her husband use them *to shag her better the next time.* John Lloyd who was functionally illiterate supplied the calf testicles while his nephew Ned wrote the offending note. Ned did not deliver the note and package himself but gave the job to his younger cousin Tom. This attests not only to Ned's strong guilt in the matter but is indicative of a deceitfulness and slyness of character that rarely if ever gets mentioned.

Soon after the note was delivered Ned and his uncle John arrived on the scene to jeer and savour the McCormicks' reaction. An altercation ensued, heated words were exchanged and Ned later said *my horse jumped forward and my fist came in collision with McCormick's nose*, as if it was no fault of his that he knocked the Greta hawker down. McCormick said *he jumped the horse upon me and knocked me down. I fell against John Lloyd and knocked him down.* Ned's uncle John Lloyd possibly upset at Ned's recklessness gave the lie to his nephew's improbable story when he testified in court that he *saw Kelly try to ride over McCormick*. With a stirrup iron in his hand, Ned angrily shouted at McCormick as he lay on the ground *Come on you old bastard and fight me!*

The truth is Ned deliberately launched his horse at McCormick saying *I will ride my horse over you and kill the whole bloody lot of you bloody wretches* and delivered a mighty blow *that caused* [McCormick] *to lose his equilibrium and fall prostrate* to the ground. When arrested by Hall Ned sulkily denied the assault but admitted to sending the offending note and parcel telling the policeman *he would do the same to him* if challenged. Brought before the Beechworth Circuit Court, Ned was sentenced to six months in Beechworth Gaol and placed on a twelve month good behaviour bond for the assault on McCormick and for sending an indecent note to his wife. He served four months of the sentence before being released.

It was around this time that Hall made a promise to Superintendent Hare that *Ned would not run long* assuring his superior that he was on an arrest and conviction mission to wipe the smile off the face of the cocky young larrikin. For this he had the assistance of his informer James Murdock who had been in gaol at the same time as Ned.

When they were both released from gaol, Ned tried at two meetings to persuade Murdock to join him in stealing several local horses, including Greta selector McMillan's prize draughthorse. Ned told Murdock that the Mansfield horse he was riding he would sell with the rest; clearly indicating that he knew before his arrest by Hall that the animal was 'lifted' demolishing Ned's claim to complete innocence. Murdock was wary. He was afraid that Hall and Kelly were in a secret partnership to catch him out agreeing to commit a crime, which would then allow Hall to 'pot' him. Murdock knew of the pair's earlier partnership and its consequences for Ned's uncles and he was not about to let himself be drawn into the same trap by Ned's bullying. Ned was later to claim that he had the same suspicion about a Hall/Murdock conspiracy when Hall used Murdock's report of these encounters to help 'pot' Ned.

The 'potting' of Ned was achieved by Hall charging him with receiving a mare known to be stolen. In the first instance the mare was not stolen but 'borrowed' from the Mansfield postmaster by Wild Wright a new acquaintance of Ned's. Wright had borrowed the Mansfield postmaster's horse on previous occasions and returned it, knocked up and the worse for wear. The postmaster, knowing Wright's character, did not report it, but after several weeks without a horse he did report the latest 'borrowing' to the police. The story goes Wright rode the horse when he visited the Kelly shanty, but when he came to return home the horse had wandered off. Ned gave Wright another horse and Wright said he could keep his until he returned. According to Ned, he did not mention that the horse was not his. Wright was as notorious for horse stealing as Ned – this was the larrikin bond between them – so the thought must have crossed his mind.

Wright was sentenced to 18 months gaol for borrowing the mare and Ned was given three years for receiving it. To Ned's defenders this smacks of a conspiracy to have the book thrown at Ned. The crucial distinction to be made here is between borrowing without permission and receiving, which legally implied theft. It's the difference in modern terms between joy riding for fun and car stealing for profit.

Ned was arrested while riding the mare by Constable Hall. The arrest did not go well. Kelly said he ended up on top of the portly constable digging his spurs into his flank. The spur raking was probably a dramatic touch added by Ned to show he was in control; however there is no supporting evidence for this claim. Hall fired a pistol at Ned's head, which fortunately misfired. Some onlookers came to Hall's assistance and Kelly was finally secured.

Hall claimed that he knew Ned was riding a stolen mare because it had been reported stolen and described in the Police Gazette. This was a lie for that notice appeared after his arrest of Kelly. The evidence that alerted him that the mare was stolen and that led to Ned's conviction came from James Murdock. He swore that Kelly had told him that the mare was stolen when he was trying to enlist Murdock's aid in stealing the Greta horses.

The defenders of Kelly are convinced that Ned was innocent and that he was convicted on the perjured evidence of a police informer who, as Ned claimed in the Jerilderie Letter, was later hanged at Wagga gaol. (In fact Ned was wrong about the hanging; it was Peter, James's brother, who was executed for murder.) These writers miss the wider significance of the James Murdock connection: that while Ned languished in gaol, Murdock was still welcome at the Kelly shanty and that five months after Ned's conviction he assisted Ellen Kelly in a case she had taken to court. She was claiming maintenance for a child fathered, she said, by William Frost, a boundary rider who had been a boarder at her shanty. Frost claimed that there were two other men who could be the father, but the evidence of Ellen's daughter Annie, her son-in-law William Skillion and Murdock's wife Ann Maree clinched the case for Ellen. She and her four helpers spent three days in celebration, drinking and riding furiously through the streets of Benalla.

There was no lasting stigma attached to the role of police informer. Ned's uncles John Lloyd, the betrayer of Harry Power, and Pat Quinn, the stirrup-iron basher of Constable Hall were constantly flip-flopping around in their personal loyalties. Both were police informers and neither man was shunned or banished from the Kelly family circle or those of their criminal friends because of it. It was hypocritical for Ned to denounce Murdock for engaging in secretive dealings with the police when he more than likely gave them information which assisted in Harry Power's capture and was himself active in Constable Hall's Greta spy network.

To understand Ned Kelly's world, the police and the criminals have to be seen as sharing a common life, in constant play with each other. The police had to catch the criminals and so wanted to be close to them; the criminals wanted to outwit the police and use them in their quarrels to damage each other. That fluid relationship was at the heart of the Fitzpatrick incident that sent Ned into the bush.

PART II:
Bushranger and Outlaw

19-year-old Ned in Pentridge Gaol, January 1874

5

That Bloody Fitzpatrick

> *I have heard from a trooper that he never knew Fitzpatrick to be one night sober and that he sold his sister to a chinaman, but he looks a young strapping rather genteel* [fellow] *more fit to be a starcher to a laundress than a policeman. To a keen observer he has the wrong appearance or a manly heart. The deceit and cowardice is too plain to be seen in the puny cabbage hearted looking face.*
>
> Ned Kelly, The Jerilderie Letter (1879)

Ned complained to Constable McIntyre during the Stringybark Creek police murders *that Bloody Fitzpatrick is the cause of all this!* glossing over Ned's central involvement in the Fitzpatrick Affair for he was the one holding and firing the gun which wounded the policeman. Against the evidence, Ned claimed he was not there when the shooting happened and generally his admirers have followed suit.

Constable Alexander Fitzpatrick rode out to the Kelly shanty on 15 April 1878 to see his girlfriend Kate Kelly and to arrest her brother Dan for stealing Whitty's horses. A policeman who thought he could combine these purposes was always going to be in trouble. It led him to scheming and deceitful behaviour very similar to the shrewdness and cunning of the Kellys themselves. Fitzpatrick was not a 'Kelly style' criminal in a policeman's uniform; he was a larrikin, as his superiors described him when they sacked him, but he had some respect for law and order.

Fitzpatrick was two years younger than Ned and also a first generation Australian having been born on the Victorian goldfields. His youthful exuberance, his sexual adventurism and his fondness for pub and shanty good times were seen by the Kellys as making him one of their own.

Alexander Wilson Fitzpatrick was born at Mount Egerton Victoria in 1856, the third son and fourth child of gold rush emigrants, Charles and Jane (nee Neilson) Fitzpatrick. Alex grew up in a turbulent goldfields atmosphere amongst honest and dishonest diggers, overstretched police resources, shanty and gin mill loafers and a variety of petty criminals preying on the law-abiding and the gullible. It was here he probably picked up his 'live fast' larrikin proclivities, which were later to stand him in good stead with the Kellys. In the twelve months before joining the police force Alex, who was working as a boundary rider, fathered an illegitimate child with Jessie McKay whose family resided at Meredith. The McKay family sued Alex for the child's maintenance and the twenty-year-old Fitzpatrick suddenly found himself in need of a better income, preferably somewhere well away from the scene of his recent misadventure.

Through his work as a stable hand at the Bayview Hotel or more likely through his friendship with Frankston solicitor Theodore Savage, Fitzpatrick made the acquaintance of Charles Alexander Smyth a prominent lawyer and part-time County Court Judge, who as Chief Crown Prosecutor was to prosecute Ned for murdering

Constable Lonigan. An improbable friendship to be sure, but Smyth apparently liked Fitzpatrick and he agreed to use his influence with Police Commissioner Standish to get the young man appointed to the police force. Around the time he began his probationary training as a police constable at the Richmond depot in Melbourne, Alex got into more romantic trouble. He promised marriage to Theodore Savage's daughter Annie. The romance continued to blossom even after Alex was sent to north-east Victoria in August 1877.

In December 1877 while Alex was on leave and back in Frankston, Annie became pregnant and Alex had to be persuaded to live up to both his marriage proposal and upcoming parental responsibilities. In July 1878 Alex and Annie were married in the Presbyterian Church at Mornington and spent their honeymoon at the Savage family residence at Frankston.

In 1879 Fitzpatrick was posted to Sydney to watch the trains in case the Kelly Gang attempted to flee the country. He may at this time have crossed the line from flash larrikin to petty criminal when he became sexually involved with Edith Graham, a servant girl who was involved in a bitter dispute with her Sydney storekeeper employer. The elderly storekeeper had given her gifts, promised her other gifts and offered her marriage in order to get young Edith to remain in his employ. A breach of promise dispute ensued and Fitzpatrick became mixed up in the argument when he distracted the storekeeper while Edith removed some goods. Whether the goods taken were promised to her is not known. The storekeeper pressed charges against Edith for theft of his property. Fitzpatrick paid for Edith's solicitor fees and the storekeeper accused him of assisting her to steal his goods. It is more likely, however, that Fitzpatrick allowed himself to be manipulated by the scheming Edith which was the conclusion drawn by his police superiors.

According to one trustworthy Glenrowan source, Fitzpatrick and Kate Kelly were romantically attracted to one another in the months leading up to Fitzpatrick's 15 April 1878 visit. Kate's mother Ellen and her elder brother Ned raised no objection to the budding romance and may even have encouraged it. The harsh accusations only came after the 15 April falling out. Ned and Fitzpatrick were larrikin friends sharing an interest in fast horses and shanty good times.

In 1922 Joseph Ashmead wrote a small unpublished manuscript which he titled *The Thorns and the Briars: The True Story of the Kelly Gang*. Ashmead was a respectable Glenrowan selector's son and a reliable conduit for Greta and Glenrowan rumour. He was not a larrikin or a criminal confederate of the Kellys. He was a staunch Primitive Methodist churchgoer whose father was a leading light in the Greta Primitive Methodist church. Ashmead watched with mounting curiosity and a vicarious interest the Kelly family's reckless doings and a flowery account of the romance between Fitzpatrick and young Kate was included in his book.

Fitzpatrick reports in his Beechworth deposition that during the fateful 15 April visit Kate was very upset at his wounding. *Miss Kelly was in the house while the firing was going on; she sat down and cried.*

Nothing in Fitzpatrick's history indicates his sexual approaches to women were unwelcome. He made two girls pregnant and captivated others with his young man's charm. Kate, his latest conquest, was just 14 years old but she was a toughened observer all her young life of the shanty debaucheries and permissive sexual encounters of her female relatives and would have been sexually aware beyond her years.

The rooky policeman Fitzpatrick started mixing with the Kellys soon after his arrival in the north-east.

As a sign of the trust and friendship developing between them, Fitzpatrick was instrumental in persuading Ned to *bring in* his brother

Dan and his cousins Tom and John Lloyd junior who were wanted to face court over a ruckus the trio had caused at Davis Goodman's Winton store. Ned would deal with and deliver the boys only to Fitzpatrick, which greatly chagrined Inspector Brooke Smith who had also spoken to Ned. Fitzpatrick had *taken care of* Ned following his Benalla arrest for drunkenness and rowdy behaviour in September 1877. Fitzpatrick was later to say Ned appreciated that *he never pressed the charge against him* and the friendship grew stronger.

Ned's combined Cameron and Jerilderie Letter version of the Fitzpatrick Affair reads as follows. *On the 15th of April Fitzpatrick came to the Eleven Mile Creek to arrest* [Dan]. *He went to the house and asked was Dan in, Dan came out. He asked Dan to come to Greta with him as he had a warrant for him for stealing Whitty's horses. Dan said all right they both went inside Dan was having something to eat his mother asked Fitzpatrick what he wanted Dan for. The trooper said he had a warrant for him Dan then asked him to produce it he said it was only a telegram sent from Chiltern. Dan's mother said that Dan need not go without a warrant. The trooper pulled out his revolver and said he would blow her brains out if she interfered. She told him it was a good job for him Ned was not there or he would ram the revolver down his throat. To frighten the trooper Dan looked out and said Ned is coming now.* [Dan] *slapped Heenan's hug on him took his revolver and threw him and part of the door outside and kept him there until Skillion and Ryan* [Ned's brother-in-law William Skilling aka Skillion and his cousin Joe Ryan] *came with horses which Dan sold that night. The trooper left and invented some scheme to say that he got shot.*

A warrant had been issued for Dan Kelly's arrest for horse theft, published in the Police Gazette but not yet distributed to all police stations. The matter of the legality or the illegality of arresting Dan without a paper warrant was mentioned several times at the Police Commission in 1881. The answer was always the same: no paper warrant was needed in the circumstances described.

In his Beechworth trial deposition Fitzpatrick said *Sergeant Whelan had informed me there was a warrant out for Dan Kelly*. But in all his other versions of what happened he tells a different story. Before the Police Commission in July 1881 he said *I noticed in the Police Gazette that there was a warrant issued by the Chiltern bench for the arrest of Dan Kelly. I drew the attention of the sergeant to this warrant. He agreed with my arresting him and he told me to be careful*. Fitzpatrick was to say the same thing slightly differently many years later. *I remarked to the sergeant if I see Dan at the Eleven mile Creek on my way to Greta, I'll arrest him and take him along with me. He said 'Be careful how you go about it. They are a bad crowd'.*

A similar warrant had been issued earlier for Ned's arrest but he had successfully gone to ground. By chance just two days before his visit Fitzpatrick had seen Dan and his cousin John Lloyd at the Cashel races and he suspected that Dan would be staying at his mother's shanty. Sergeant Whelan advised the rooky policeman that caution should be exercised in Dan's arrest, but whether it was wise for Whelan to have encouraged the inexperienced Fitzpatrick is debatable. Whelan was aware of Fitzpatrick's fraternising with the Kelly family and he may have decided to make use of the relationship to bring about Dan's arrest. Whether he agreed to Dan's arrest or not, Whelan acting on orders from Beechworth sent Fitzpatrick to Greta to take charge of the police station.

Superintendent Nicolson had instructed the police never to go to the Kelly home alone because *if there were two constables together bad characters are always afraid to proceed to extremities with them*. Fitzpatrick was aware of this twelve-month-old police stricture and he knew the practical reason behind it. Being a part of the Kelly family's circle of shanty friends he saw himself as a special exception to this sensible instruction and he paid it no heed. When asked by a Royal Commissioner why was there a need to be careful, he replied *they were known to be dangerous characters and likely to resist.* The reason he gave for going alone was *I knew I was capable of taking Dan Kelly away if he resisted.*

According to Fitzpatrick's Beechworth trial deposition: *On 15 April last I left Benalla about 2.30 pm stopped at Lindsay's* [Winton pub] *on the road. Had lemonade & brandy did not stop anywhere else got to Kellys between 4 and 5 pm. On first occasion stopped about an hour. Was talking to Mrs Kelly all that time. Her daughter was there. I* [returned] *again about ¼ of an hour* [later]. *I had no warrant but saw by Police Gazette that one had been issued.* Elsewhere he describes his arrival at the Kelly shanty as follows: *Had occasion to pass the house of Defendant Kelly. I dismounted and went in saw Mrs Kelly and 3 children* [five children were present] *stayed about an hour.*

Traditional narratives overlook this hour-long friendly visit and take up the story only when Fitzpatrick returned to the house some fifteen minutes later after talking to 'Brickey' Williamson on a nearby hill. The previously cordial atmosphere suddenly disappeared and became hostile and sullen when Fitzpatrick revealed that he was there to arrest Dan. Fitzpatrick said of his return visit *they all showed me bitter dislike from the time that I rode up* and his true intentions became known. This is why Ellen Kelly called him *a deceitful little bugger.*

Combining several statements Fitzpatrick's account continues. *I left and went up the hill in the direction of a sound of chopping. Saw Williamson spoke to him, saw 2 horsemen stop in front of Kelly's hut; went down and saw Skillion. I went to the house, saw Dan Kelly. Told him I wanted to arrest him as there was a warrant issued for his arrest on* [a] *charge of horse stealing. He said I suppose you'll let me have something to eat I've been out riding all day. I allowed him to eat, he went inside and I followed him. I had not been inside more than 10 minutes, before Mrs Kelly went up to the girls and whispered something to them. They ran out to the back hut. I know now that the old lady had given them a message to carry to Ned.* [It] *was just getting dusk. Mrs Kelly said you won't take him out of this tonight. Dan said 'Shut up that's all right'. Ned then came* to the doorway [and] *fired a shot at me. Mrs Kelly rushed at me with a* [fire] *shovel, she struck me on left side of helmet. Ned fired again and the ball lodged in my left wrist. I turned round to draw my revolver and found it was gone. Dan had snatched it. Ned remained in the same position with his revolver pointed at me. I slewed round and took hold of the muzzle of his pistol and turned it off me and said 'You cowardly wretch, do you want to murder me? In the struggle his pistol went off a third time.* [Williamson and Skillion were present and both had revolvers.] *Ned said 'that'll do boys'.* [He] *said to Skillion 'you bugger why did you not tell me who was here'. He said 'if I had known it was Fitzpatrick I would not have fired. If it had been any of the other buggers they would not leave here alive'. My wound was bleeding and I fainted. When I came round Ned said to me I'm sorry that this happened it will get me into trouble, I'll get it pretty heavy.*

If Fitzpatrick's version of the conversation between Ned and Skillion is correct, then Ned may have been genuinely surprised when he discovered it was Fitzpatrick and not one *of the other buggers.* The conversation is a clear indication that Ned's friendship with Fitzpatrick was genuine and different from the relationship he had with other police.

Many years later Fitzpatrick added more detail to what happened when Ned arrived on the scene. *Just at this moment Ned Kelly rushed in revolver in hand. 'Out of this you* [bastard] *he exclaimed and he fired a shot at me. The bullet went through the left sleeve of my jumper. As I backed out I tried to draw my revolver, Dan who was sitting at the table jumped up and prevented me. Two more shots were fired at me. One of Ned's bullets struck me on the left wrist and the bullet entered just on the edge of the knuckle bone. Almost at the same moment Mrs Kelly hit me on the head with a shovel and I went down unconscious.*

After Ned's wounding of Fitzpatrick the shanty's occupants were faced with a quandary: Do they release or kill Fitzpatrick? The stakes were now much higher and the second option would make the problem go away permanently. According to Williamson a conversation took place between Joe Byrne (aka Billy King) and Dan Kelly. *Dan and King had some talk about what they would do with him. King was for taking him with them and Dan for letting him go.* Williamson said of Billy King he is *a mate of the Kellys* [and] *has been stopping at Kelly's since last year.* [He] *was in Kelly's house when Constable Fitzpatrick was fired at* [and] *wanted the Kellys not to let Fitzpatrick get away alive and said that in place of being shot through the arm, he should be shot through the heart.* Williamson warned the police Joe Byrne *is a man that would fire on any one that would attempt to arrest him, he is a dangerous man.*

There is some debate in the Kelly literature concerning the identity of Billy King; Williamson however was quite clear in his identification of Billy King as Joe Byrne both inside the Kelly shanty and later *up on the range* when the Kelly brothers made their escape. If Joe had his way Fitzpatrick would have been taken into the bush and murdered, his body disposed of and nobody would have been any the wiser or so the shanty criminals would have thought.

Ned's brother-in-law William Skillion may also have been a far more violent character than has previously been thought. According to Fitzpatrick, as he was regaining consciousness he heard Ned say Skillion had earlier wanted to *give a pill to* [shoot] a passing *Benalla Cove* [policeman] and was only prevented from doing so by Ned's intervention. This was the usual shanty bravado. Ned said of Sergeant Steele who kept a close watch on the Greta Mob's livestock stealing activities *I've got a pill for him yet*. Fitzpatrick pretended he heard neither remark as the grog was brought out and the Kellys convivially did their best to make their latest problem go away.

Fitzpatrick was held prisoner by the Kellys from dusk to 11 o'clock before he was allowed to leave. Ned or Fitzpatrick removed the bullet from the policeman's injured wrist with a razor or Fitzpatrick's penknife. The bullet was only superficially embedded under the skin and Fitzpatrick said he cut it out himself, while Ned held his hand steady. Elsewhere it is claimed Ned removed the bullet and Ellen bandaged the wound. Amidst friendly grog-fuelled banter, Ellen threatened the wounded policeman with violence *from their many friends* if he reported the matter. According to one eyewitness source, *Fitzpatrick shook hands with everyone and declared the whole thing would be forgotten*. Fitzpatrick knew if he said otherwise his life would be in jeopardy.

Ned with Williamson and Dan trailing behind escorted Fitzpatrick away from the Kelly selection and left him on the road near the Winton pub. Ned promised the injured policeman *a few hundred pounds* after the Baumgarten case was over if he said nothing about what happened. Ned departed and Fitzpatrick reached Lindsay's Winton pub still being stalked by Williamson and Dan. David Lindsay later testified that Fitzpatrick was sober when he arrived sometime after 11 pm. Given Fitzpatrick's six hour stay at the Kelly shanty it would be surprising indeed if he wasn't drinking during this time; however the visit was long enough for him to get over the worst effects of any intoxication before he reached Lindsay's pub.

Fitzpatrick fainted while dismounting from his horse and was helped inside by David Lindsay and his brother Richard. His wrist was bleeding again and was tightly rebandaged. He was given some food and a reviving *lemonade and brandy* or two. He told David Lindsay *Ned Kelly had shot him and that Williamson and Skillion were there*. If Fitzpatrick was drunk and lying about Williamson and Skillion's presence, he must have made up his alcohol-inspired conspiracy story as he rode with Ned towards the Winton pub. If he was sober as David Lindsay claims, there is every possibility he was simply telling the truth as he believed it to be. In either case there was little if any time for the injured policeman to concoct a complicated tale of attempted murder when all he had to do was point his finger at Ned alone.

A wounded Fitzpatrick set off accompanied by Richard Lindsay for a harrowing night time ride to Benalla. At 2 am Fitzpatrick and Lindsay roused Sergeant Whelan from his bed in the police barracks, with the startling news that Ned Kelly and several of his friends had attempted to murder him. Dr. Nicholson was called to attend to Fitzpatrick's wrist wound. Nicholson remarked Fitzpatrick was *pale* and *smelt of brandy*. This is not surprising considering Fitzpatrick's ordeal and the efforts of the Lindsays to fortify him with alcohol for his midnight ride to Benalla.

Knowing that horse stealing warrants were out for both of the Kelly brothers and with Fitzpatrick wounded and likely to talk, Ned and Dan decided to flee. Skillion and Williamson assisted them and accompanied by Joe Byrne they made their escape. *Skillion and I were told to take the horses up on the range and wait there till they came. We waited there about an hour when Dan and King* [Byrne] *came up and took the horses and started* [for their Bullock Creek hideout near Mansfield]. *Skillion and I then started for home.* Six months later, the Kelly Gang ventured out from their fortified hideout and shot and killed three policemen at Stringybark Creek.

The day after the attack on Fitzpatrick, Ellen Kelly, William Skillion and Brickey Williamson were arrested and brought before the Benalla Police Court where they were remanded to appear at the next Beechworth Circuit Court to answer a charge of attempted murder. Ellen was arrested with a two-day-old baby at her breast and protesting she had not seen Ned for the last four months.

Ned and Dan could not be found but a £100 reward was offered for their apprehension. Later the Kelly brothers were to offer to surrender if their mother was released from gaol. This was an offer from notorious criminals on the run; an offer the authorities could not legally or morally accept. Although with hindsight, it may have prevented everything else that was to follow.

Immediately following the Stringybark Creek police murders, Williamson, who did not hold with murder, began to distance himself from the Kellys and gave the first of several prison statements he was to make to the police. Captain Standish the Police Commissioner told the Police Commission that Williamson *entirely corroborated every word of Fitzpatrick's evidence and he gave me some considerable information* [as to where the Kellys may be hiding] *and volunteered to assist me in every kind of way.*

Commissioner Standish was clearly gilding the lily with the statement that Williamson entirely corroborated every word of Fitzpatrick's evidence. But the significance of Williamson's several statements is that much of what he told the police and prison officials was consistent with Fitzpatrick's account and damaging to Ned and his friends. Some truth, some lies and minimising his own role in the incident was Williamson's strategy. Williamson described what happened inside the shanty when Ned arrived. *Soon after this Ned Kelly rushed round the corner of the house to the door and fired two shots at Fitzpatrick. Ned cut the bullet out and Mrs Kelly dressed the wound. I asked how Fitzpatrick was. Kate Kelly said he was in great pain. Ned had made it all right with him.* Williamson says that just before Ned appeared on the scene he took *two of Mrs Kelly's children in my arms and went out of the house to quiet them.* This could mean that by the time Ned had arrived to fire at Fitzpatrick the atmosphere inside the Kelly shanty was volatile and unpredictable. The fact that Williamson describes Ned as rushing round the corner of the house to the door seems to suggest that he was outside the house comforting the Kelly children when Ned arrived and set the row in motion.

Williamson claims to have stepped between Ellen Kelly and Fitzpatrick when the fire shovel assault was imminent, knocking the shovel from Ellen's raised hand as she about to strike *I stepped between them and took it from her and threw it behind the fire.* This intervention seems to be entirely fictitious. It was not mentioned by Fitzpatrick in any of his accounts of the shanty fight and it disagrees with what Ellen Kelly said. The same is probably true of Williamson's comforting of the Kelly children which had the alibi benefit of removing him from the house while Ned went about his business of shooting at the policeman. In both cases Williamson makes himself out to be an innocent bystander reluctantly participating in order to prevent further trouble.

Williamson was already inside the shanty when Fitzpatrick was wounded or he entered soon after through the partitioned-off bedroom with Joe Byrne; the pair having removed a section of bark sheeting from the back of the hut as Ned came through the front door. Fitzpatrick says Skillion having come to the hut door as Ned entered *was beside Ned all the time with a revolver in his hand but he did not use it*. Fitzpatrick has Williamson coming into the kitchen from the bedroom pointing a revolver at him. Williamson claims to have restrained Joe Byrne who also had a revolver from making his presence known. Fitzpatrick may have been mistaken or he lied about some of this. But there is no question Williamson was an eyewitness to the fight inside the shanty or that he allied himself with the Kellys at this time against Fitzpatrick.

Williamson gave a clear example of how Ned pressed his friends to get himself clear of trouble. *Fitzpatrick promised to say nothing about having been shot, but if there was any noise about it I was to say that Fitzpatrick was standing talking to me, when he saw two men on the next range and started away to try and arrest one of them when the other man fired from behind a tree at him*. Williamson who was afraid of Ned said *I should never be able to think of that story and had better say I knew nothing about it*. Williamson goes on to say *though I might have interfered I thought it better not to do so, as I might have made matters worse.*

In a similar vein Fitzpatrick recounts Ned dictating a fictional story he was made to write down verbatim in his police notebook and which was later read out in court. Ned said *you had better say you went up to arrest Dan he was in company with Williamson. I was putting the hand cuffs on him. I had my revolver out it went off and shot me.* This story was totally unbelievable given that a 45 calibre bullet from a Webley revolver fired at close range would have shattered the wrist rather than leaving a minor flesh wound. Ned then *asked me did I know Whitlow* [the pound keeper], *I said no. He said say this: Two men rushed from behind a tree as you were arresting Dan describe them as two big men one of them like me and they'll think it's my brother Jim and Whitlow and then say I heard one of them sing out Oh! Whitlow you've shot him.*

Whitlow may be synonymous with Robert Ellis alias Whitnell a Greta Mob associate and named by Kelly either because he had fallen out with him or knew he was many miles away from Greta at the time of the incident. Ned implicated his brother Jim because he knew Jim had an unbreakable alibi. He was in gaol in New South Wales serving a prison sentence for horse stealing at the time of the Fitzpatrick Affair. This was a typical Ned Kelly performance designed to misdirect his pursuers by sending the police off on a wild goose chase diverting attention away from the real culprit, Ned himself.

Williamson's evidence has been described as ingratiating, self-serving and an attempt to obtain a sentence reduction for his role in the Fitzpatrick Affair. While there is some truth to this, it is not the whole truth. Williamson had turned against his former friends and told much of the truth of what happened during Fitzpatrick's visit, while occasionally lying to make himself appear innocent. The Kellys were no longer his shanty friends, death threats were made while he was in prison and following his early release in October 1882 *for service rendered to Police*. Williamson moved to Mullengandra in New South Wales to escape the death threats and wrath of the Kelly sympathisers.

At first glance Fitzpatrick's claim that Ned tried to murder him when he fired three shots at close range and only succeeded in wounding him in the wrist seems ludicrous. *I was about 1 ½ yards* [away] *when* [the] *first shot was fired. I lost my revolver after 2 shots had been fired.* Ned denies he fired a gun at Fitzpatrick. [I] *would never attempt to fire into a house full of women and children while I had a pair of arms and a bunch of fives at the end of them that never failed to peg out anything they came in contact with.* Yet the evidence suggests Ned did confront Fitzpatrick with a revolver and shot at him when he was no more than an arm's length away with Ned's family present in the same room.

The antiquated weapon Ned fired at Fitzpatrick was an underpowered, small calibre, Colt percussion pocket revolver, capable of firing undersized pointed bullets. In all Ned fired three shots: one which missed its target, one passing through Fitzpatrick's jumper sleeve and one which lodged in the policeman's wrist. There is some confusion about the order in which the shots were fired. Perhaps the first shot was a warning directed over the heads of those present and the second and third shots did the wounding and the damage to the policeman's jacket in the confusion and chaos that followed.

As for trying to murder Fitzpatrick, Ned had the opportunity to murder him at any time. Ned's purpose was not murder but to scare Fitzpatrick with a sudden eruption of violence. He may have accidentally shot him when Ellen was wielding the fire shovel and Dan was putting *Heenan's hug* on and relieving the policeman of his service revolver. The shot through the sleeve of Fitzpatrick's jumper may have occurred while he was wrestling with Ned over the pocket revolver. Fitzpatrick's wounding was probably unintentional and came about in the chaotic three-pronged attack on the policeman. Ned's claim that he was careful with guns around other people is invalidated by his irresponsible behaviour on numerous occasions.

Fitzpatrick clearly underestimated the Kelly family's wrath and he did not realise that Ned was close enough to home to intervene in Dan's arrest. Ned may have felt that Fitzpatrick's previous friendship, his courtship of Kate and his leniency towards himself and the family would mean that if he frightened the policeman enough, he would agree to leave without taking Dan with him. Fitzpatrick admitted while under cross examination at the Benalla Police Court pre-trial hearing of Ellen, Williamson and Skillion that *he was acting perhaps, as an amateur constable on this occasion.*

There is controversy surrounding the precise nature of Fitzpatrick's wrist wound, with some later accounts denying that it was a bullet wound at all. Fitzpatrick told the Police Commission the first shot fired missed and *grazed the bark behind my back and lodged in it.*

Searching inside the Kelly house at the time of Ellen's arrest, Constable Flood found a homemade bullet mould and he cast two bullets from it. One of these was *a small pointed ball* similar in shape and size to the wound sustained by Fitzpatrick. A piece of partition bark which Fitzpatrick said had been struck by a bullet was found to have been removed and replaced with another greener sheet of bark. The Kellys had overlooked the bullet mould but cunningly replaced the bark partition sheet. Ned probably took his small pocket revolver with him, while the other firearms said to be present were stashed away to hide them from the police.

Doctor John Nicholson the Benalla doctor who treated and

dressed Fitzpatrick's wounded wrist described having *examined his left wrist* [and] *found two wounds, one a jagged one and the other a clean incision. They were about an inch and a half apart; one was on the outside of the wrist and the other near the centre. They might have been produced by a bullet that is the outside wound.* Also he says he *could not swear* [the wound] *was a bullet wound but it had all the appearances of one.*

A later statement by Nicholson is more definitive. *I examined the wrist, there appeared to be a bullet wound. The bullet had apparently entered at the outside of the wrist in the end of the bone that curved upwards in a slanting direction and lodged in the back of the wrist under the skin. The entrance wound was slightly elongated in the course of the bullet. At the exit end* [the centre of the wrist] *there was a clean incision a little more than half an inch in length, none of the deep structures were injured.* [The wound] *could not have been produced by the first bullet, the second* [or third] *one could have caused it.*

Kelly's defenders dismiss Fitzpatrick's wrist wound as self-inflicted and superficial. They claim Nicholson confronted Fitzpatrick in a Beechworth street denying that he could have been wounded by a bullet. Both statements are false and attributable to a dubious biased source. Nicholson's assessment of Fitzpatrick's wrist wound has been misrepresented in the Kelly literature. It is clear from the totality of his testimony that Nicholson regarded Fitzpatrick's wound as having been made by a bullet that lodged itself under the skin and was removed before he examined the policeman's injured wrist. He concluded *the wounds are consistent with Fitzpatrick's statement.*

Other supporting evidence for the firing of bullets comes from Fitzpatrick's memo of the 24 May 1878 to the Chief Commissioner of Police requesting *reimbursement of the cost of a new uniform jumper as the one I wore on the occasion of the affray with the Kellys at Greta was destroyed having been shot through the sleeve and otherwise damaged and has to be kept for evidence against them.* Fitzpatrick's claim was approved and he was granted 25 shillings to replace his damaged police jumper. His dented helmet and his bullet torn jumper were produced as courtroom exhibits at the Beechworth trial of Ellen Kelly and her co-accused. They have long since disappeared but his reimbursement request survives to tell the story.

Following his Glenrowan capture, Ned confirmed in a Benalla cell interview with Constables Kelly and McIntyre that he had indeed shot Fitzpatrick. *Yes, it was I that fired at him* adding *I almost swore after letting him go, I would never let another go.* By this time more serious events had overtaken the Fitzpatrick Affair and Ned had nothing to lose by admitting the truth.

Some months after the Fitzpatrick visit, the trial of Ellen Kelly, William Skillion and Brickey Williamson for attempted murder eventually got underway at Beechworth. The courtroom was packed. The accused were defended by the Melbourne barrister John Bowman, paid for from the proceeds of the Kelly Gang's gold fossicking and whiskey-making at their bush hideout. Bowman alleged that Fitzpatrick was at the Kelly shanty illegally to arrest Dan; he was drunk, throwing his weight around and intimidating the women and children. The fractious atmosphere soon erupted into violence when the drunken policeman began waving his revolver around. Fitzpatrick was disarmed and in the process he was hit with a fire shovel and sustained a wrist wound; he fainted and when he came round Ellen roughly bandaged the wound. Everything that happened was Fitzpatrick's fault and his fault alone. Ned was not there and neither was Skillion (nor in this version) was Brickey Williamson. To hide his own culpability Fitzpatrick falsely reported that the Kellys had tried to murder him.

Ellen's fire shovel assault is often downplayed in the Kelly literature as an insignificant attack, but the fire shovel used was a formidable heavy metal weapon. Fitzpatrick's helmet was severely dented and he was knocked unconscious by the force of the blow. The police helmet worn at that time consisted of a cork filled frame covered by a hardened outer shell and was capable of withstanding a moderately severe blow. Ellen claimed she *knocked Fitzpatrick down with a shovel which glided off his head and striking his wrist caused the wound which he said was done by a bullet.* The second part of Ellen's statement was not believed by anybody including her defence counsel who surprisingly had allowed her to make the claim. None of the other witnesses supported Ellen's version of the fire shovel incident and the Judge and Jury disregarded it as an obvious falsehood.

In the Jerilderie Letter Ned claims that at the time of the Fitzpatrick Affair he was *400 miles from Greta.* During the Euroa bank raid, Ned told his captives *Fitzpatrick is an infernal liar* and said *he could prove he was 15 miles away at the time Fitzpatrick was shot in the wrist.* That would place Ned much closer to Greta than his Jerilderie Letter statement reveals. On this occasion, a month before the Jerilderie Letter was delivered, Ned undermines his own alibi and puts himself within the vicinity of his mother's Greta shanty when Fitzpatrick came to visit.

If we accept that Ned's Euroa statement is likely to be more truthful, it matches nicely with his cousin Joe Ryan's courtroom alibi for Ned. According to Ryan, Ned with Joe Byrne as his companion were returning from nearby Winton after completing some horse trading business there. On oath Ryan swore *I bought a horse from Ned Kelly on the 15th* [the day of Fitzpatrick's visit] *and gave £17 for it.* Ryan gave into evidence a bogus bill of sale of the same fraudulent kind the Kellys were constantly manufacturing and distributing. In Ned's mind, the bogus bill confirmed the false miles-away alibi. But Ned could easily have engaged in Winton 'horse dealing' and confronted Fitzpatrick at Greta on the same day. An inconvenient truth, he unwittingly revealed by his 15-miles-away comment made at Euroa.

Joe Ryan played a further defence witness role during the Fitzpatrick Affair trial. With Frank Harty, a fanatical Kelly sympathiser who declared *Ned Kelly is the best bloody man that has ever been in Benalla. I would fight up to my knees in blood for him!* Ryan gave testimony that Skillion was in their company four miles away, when Fitzpatrick said he was at the Kelly shanty with a revolver in his hand. Crown Prosecutor Chomley accused Ryan and Harty of lying and providing false alibis for both Ned and Skillion, but surprisingly no further action was taken against either of them.

Sir Redmond Barry, who presided over both the Fitzpatrick Affair and Ned's capital case trials, knew that criminals regularly provided one another with false alibis and false documentation. Barry dismissed Ryan's bogus bill of sale for the manufactured sleight of hand it was and said he disbelieved Harty and Ryan's evidence and directed the jury to do likewise. Judge Barry was right in his overall assessment of what criminals do when facing prosecution. Ironically, although some lawbreaking chicanery was involved, Joe Ryan was probably telling something fairly close to the truth when he provided his Winton 'horse dealing' alibi for Ned.

According to both Ned and Brickey Williamson, Ryan and Harty assisted in the Kelly brothers' escape to their Bullock Creek hideout following the assault on Fitzpatrick. Ned tells us that *Skillion and Ryan came with horses which Dan sold that night.* Williamson states *Ned came out and told me to run into the yard some horses and to tell Skillion to go to Harty's – a farm about four miles away and bring two more horses.* It is unclear why Dan would be selling horses in the middle of the night, but as he and Ned were going into hiding they may have needed some ready cash. What is clear is the involvement of Ryan and Harty in Ned's getaway plan as willingly accomplices.

J. J. Kenneally's 1929 fiercely partisan account of the Kelly outbreak places Ryan and Skillion inside the house with Fitzpatrick and the Kelly family for several hours after the shanty brawl had subsided. One of Kenneally's principal sources was Tom Lloyd junior (Ned's cousin and the unofficial fifth member of the Kelly Gang) who told him, Ryan and Skillion came to the house around 7 pm and were still there some four hours later when Fitzpatrick was released. This oral history testimony, biased as it is, serves to identify both men as active participants in the Fitzpatrick Affair.

During the trial the prosecution heard whispers that Kate had been sexually assaulted by Fitzpatrick and they requested that the defence put Kate and her younger sister Grace on the stand to substantiate or deny the rumour. Fitzpatrick would hardly have supported the prosecution's request, if he had any reason to think he would be compromised by the Kelly girls' testimony. If the sexual assault claim was true, Kate and Grace's evidence would have discredited Fitzpatrick's unprovoked assault story and damaged the prosecution's case irreparably. Neither was called as a defence witness and the prosecution made no further mention of the matter. The defence had missed a golden opportunity to allege police provocation and put two witnesses on the stand to prove it.

Ned's defenders tell us Kate was not called as a witness because the Kelly family wanted to protect her reputation and save the young girl from any embarrassment. When measured against a serious charge of attempting to murder a policeman, a young girl's reputation and her courtroom embarrassment seems a lame excuse indeed. The more probable reason was that Kate stubbornly refused to testify or perhaps the reason was to keep her romance with Fitzpatrick from being publicly aired in court. Such an admission would have undermined and destabilised the defence's case, revealing the Kelly family's friendly relationship with the larrikin policeman right up to the moment they fell out with one another.

Although they refrained from making sexual assault a central plank in the defence case, the Kellys and their friends orchestrated a campaign of rumour and innuendo around the sexual assault claim to curry public support for the accused and denigrate Fitzpatrick's character. It did not seem to worry the Kelly camp that Kate's as well as Fitzpatrick's reputation would be tarnished by this story. On the day of the Jerilderie bank robbery in February 1879 a newspaper described an interview conducted with Kate Kelly in these terms. *She was in the house alone when Fitzpatrick came in and he commenced in a violent manner to behave improperly. Just then her brother Ned came to the door and caught Fitzpatrick in the act attempting an outrage. Ned fired his revolver and this was how Fitzpatrick came to be shot in the wrist.*

Many years later Fitzpatrick was to put forward the best evidence of his innocence. *One of the proofs that I acted the straight part came from Ned himself. When he stuck up the bank at Jerilderie the question was put to him while he was talking with some of the townspeople; 'What about Fitzpatrick?' Ned answered, 'If he had done what they say he did the country would not have been big enough to hold him'. Ned Kelly clearly meant that if I had molested his sister Kate he would have shot me no matter where he found me.* Even more uncompromising are Ned's words after his capture. *That is a foolish story, if he or any other policeman tried to take liberties with my sister, Victoria would not hold him.* Fitzpatrick is allowed the final word. *In the name of commonsense was it likely, when I told them that I had come to arrest Dan that they would permit me to be even friendly towards Kate Kelly!*

The sentencing of the three accused of attacking Fitzpatrick occurred on the 12 October 1878, just two weeks before the 26 October Stringybark Creek police murders. Heavy gaol sentences were handed down: Ellen Kelly with a babe in her arms received three years; Skillion and Williamson each received six years hard labour. Judge Redmond Barry is alleged to have said *if your son Ned was here I would give him fifteen years!* Another account records the sentence as twenty-one years. There is no convincing evidence to support either claim and Barry's alleged remarks although unfounded are accepted as an integral part of the Kelly myth.

In a published letter written in May 1928, Brickey Williamson described an emotional Fitzpatrick with *a handkerchief to his eyes* escorting him back to his cell following the sentencing. *Well Billy* said Fitzpatrick *I never thought you would get anything like that.* Williamson went on to speculate. *I was released after the* [Police] *Royal Commission, whether Fitzpatrick had anything to do with that I don't know.* Despite everything that had happened this reveals Williamson's not unfriendly relationship with Fitzpatrick, as well as attests to Fitzpatrick's apparently genuine regret at Williamson's harsh sentence.

Mentioned but glossed over in traditional accounts of the Fitzpatrick Affair, is the significant fact that Fitzpatrick was invited inside the Kelly shanty as a family friend and spent an hour talking to Ellen and Kate while waiting for Dan to arrive home. It would be surprising indeed, if some spark of romance or flirtation between Fitzpatrick and Kate was not present during this first visit. Whatever happened in that convivial hour was not objected to by Ellen or Fitzpatrick would not have waited around for Dan to come home. Ellen later sent the Kelly children to fetch Ned and would probably have warned Dan before he arrived home, if she had known that Fitzpatrick was waiting to arrest him. Fitzpatrick declares that no brandy was drunk (he says nothing about other alcoholic beverages) which is scarcely believable in a shanty where grog was on offer twenty-four hours a day.

Fitzpatrick had visited the Kelly shanty many times in the past always on the friendliest of terms without the slightest trouble occurring. On the more volatile second visit of the day, he agreed to let Dan have his supper before taking him to the Greta lockup and he foolishly allowed Mrs Kelly to abuse him. Both are a clear indication of the policeman's relaxed attitude in a familiar shanty situation that was rapidly deteriorating into antagonism and aggression. If Fitzpatrick had taken his prisoner into custody and immediately proceeded to Greta as was normal police procedure, the Fitzpatrick Affair would never have occurred and the Kelly outbreak would have taken shape in a different fashion but always with murder or attempted murder somewhere in the mix.

Many years later Ellen Kelly would recount her own version of what happened on that long ago April day. Fitzpatrick she said *came over to our place and said he was going to arrest Dan. He started the trouble. He had no business there at all they tell me, no warrant or anything. If he had he should have done his business and gone. He tried to kiss my daughter Kate. She was a fine good looking girl. Kate and the boys tried to stop him. He was a fool. They were only trying to protect their sister. He was drunk and they were sober. He stayed there to make trouble and there was trouble.* Here Ellen admits that 'the boys', her sons Ned and Dan, were present (not Jim who was in gaol in New South Wales at the time) but of course she blames Fitzpatrick for everything.

From stories he heard later Jim Kelly said Fitzpatrick pulled Kate onto his lap. If such familiarity occurred, it would have taken place during Fitzpatrick's earlier visit before he had announced his intention to arrest Dan. Perhaps by this time Kate and Fitzpatrick's romance had reached the stage, where it was acceptable for the policeman to act in such an openly flirtatious manner with young Kate. It is surely too much of a coincidence that Ned just happened to burst through the shanty door with a revolver in his hand as Fitzpatrick was taking unwanted liberties with his younger sister. Fitzpatrick and Ned both deny it ever happened and on this occasion we should perhaps take them at their word.

The several versions we have of the Fitzpatrick Affair have different people present inside the Kelly shanty at the time of the affray. It is acknowledged by all that Ellen, her younger children and Dan and Kate were present at the time of Fitzpatrick's return visit. The Kellys disingenuously claim Ned, Williamson, Skillion and Byrne were not there. Williamson from his Melbourne prison cell disputes this and puts the whole group at the scene. Fitzpatrick places them all there except for Byrne whom he may not have seen. Many years later Williamson said *I pulled Burns* [Byrne] *back in the dark when he was going into Fitzpatrick's presence*, belatedly confirming Joe Byrne's presence.

Fitzpatrick has been accused of all manner of treachery and betrayal. Of faking his wrist wound by enlarging it with a penknife. Of creating a bullet hole tear in his police jumper. Of inventing an assault and an attempted murder story to cover his groping of young Kate. Of lying about Ned, Williamson and Skillion being present at the time of the assault. He has been vilified, pilloried and portrayed in the worst possible light in the Kelly literature as the sole villain of the piece when clearly he was the set upon victim, regardless of the policing or personal reason behind his visit.

In his defence Fitzpatrick was to claim. *I have been grossly misrepresented; at that time I was a young fellow, 19* [actually 22] *years of age. The stories that were circulated about me were of a ridiculous description. They are entirely false, but were believed by people who at that time were ready to believe anything against the police. It was entirely to the interests of the Kellys that I should be misrepresented.* Fitzpatrick was made the scapegoat for Ned's violent temper and his precipitous attack aided and abetted by his family and friends on a policeman whom he liked and regarded as a friend.

There was a chemistry to the relationship which Ned and his family intuitively picked up on. Fitzpatrick's character failings and his unorthodox conduct as a policeman made him attractive to the Kellys who welcomed him into their shanty culture netherworld. They thought they could do so on their own terms, controlling and manipulating him to their advantage. Fitzpatrick thought he could use the relationship to further his policeman's career, while having some fun along the way. The relationship finally exploded in violence and rancour when competing interests came into conflict.

Kelly's defenders deny that Ned and Fitzpatrick were friends but clearly such was the case. They deny there was a romantic attachment between the larrikin policeman and young Kate Kelly when there obviously was one. They accept the Kellys' version of what happened dismissing as lies and fantasy Fitzpatrick's version of events. By far their greatest failing, however, is that Ned's admirers do not comprehend the context in which the Fitzpatrick Affair was played out. What came before had the greatest bearing on what happened on the day of Fitzpatrick's visit. There was a significant history between the participants that set the tone and course of the day's events; beginning with a friendly welcome, erupting into violent confrontation and ending in a temporary reconciliation that soon fell apart.

If Ned and Fitzpatrick had not been friends there would have been no Fitzpatrick Affair as we know it. The battle lines would have been clearly drawn from the beginning. Fitzpatrick's mission to arrest Dan may well have ended in murder. That Fitzpatrick lived to tell the tale was a consequence of his larrikin bond with the Kellys and his lack of professionalism as a policeman.

6

Murdering Police

I was deceived by Kelly who notwithstanding his promise to spare the men's lives if I could induce them to surrender, neither gave me an opportunity to explain nor them to learn the position they were in.
Constable Thomas McIntyre

The police murders at Stringybark Creek have been particularly susceptible to Ned Kelly myth-making. At this remote bush site in the Wombat Ranges near Mansfield, Ned and Dan Kelly, Steve Hart and Joe Byrne shot and killed three policemen: Sergeant Michael Kennedy and Constables Thomas Lonigan and Michael Scanlan. A fourth policeman Constable Thomas McIntyre escaped on Kennedy's runaway horse and lived to tell the tale. It was on McIntyre's evidence that Ned was later hanged for the murder of Constable Lonigan. The police had been sent into the bush to arrest the Kelly brothers for their attack on Constable Fitzpatrick at the Kelly homestead six months earlier. They were seeking to discover the whereabouts of the two fugitives when the Kelly Gang fired upon them from ambush.

Ned said he shot the police in self-defence because they came into the Wombat Ranges not to arrest but to shoot him and his brother Dan. In a letter sent to the Acting Chief Secretary Sir Bryan O'Loghlen in late January 1879 and allegedly written by Ned, the bushranger protests his innocence and bemoans his fate. *I take this opportunity to declare most positively that we did not kill the policemen in cold blood as has been stated by that rascal McIntyre. We only fired on them to save ourselves and we are not the cold blooded murderers which people presume us to be.* The Kelly myth accepts Ned's version of the Stringybark Creek police murders and exonerates him of any wrong doing.

All of the participants in the Stringybark Creek police murders were either Irish born or of Irish ancestry. The four policemen were native-born Irishmen who had emigrated to Victoria as young men. The four members of the Kelly Gang were native-born Australians whose parents were Irish. They were all Catholic; the policemen were religiously divided: Kennedy and Scanlan were Catholic, McIntyre and Lonigan were Protestant. Lonigan had been baptised and raised as a Catholic but in 1868 while still in Ireland he converted to Protestantism in order to marry.

Like tens of thousands of other Irishmen, Kennedy, Scanlan, McIntyre and Lonigan emigrated to Australia seeking a better life for themselves far removed from the economically and socially diminished lives they left behind in Ireland. Kennedy and McIntyre had previously served in the police force in Ireland and they pursued this calling in their colonial lives. Lonigan had no connection to Irish policing and upon arriving in the colony, he engaged in farming then served six months in the Colonial Artillery Corps before seeking employment as a police officer. Scanlan studied at the Dublin Agricultural College with the firm intention of farming the land. However his plans changed and on arriving in Victoria he became a storekeeper before *putting on the jacket.*

The greater part of Kennedy's ten years in the colonial police was spent in the adjoining police districts of Jamieson and Mansfield whose rough bushland he had come to know well. He established a strong reputation among Mansfield's lawbreakers for tracking down and getting his man, a professional perseverance which engendered respect from even his toughest criminal enemies. Kennedy's disruption of the across-border stolen livestock trade received praise from his police superiors and financial reward from New South Wales and Victorian pastoralists.

Michael Scanlan spent some time stationed at Mansfield police station with Kennedy before being transferred to Mooroopna. He was an expert bushman with a good knowledge of the Stringybark Creek area and *every part of the country lying between there and the King River*. He was called back to Mansfield to serve under Kennedy on a scouting patrol to apprehend the fugitive Kelly brothers.

Thomas Lonigan did not have an unblemished record in the police force. On one occasion he was fined two shillings and sixpence for assaulting a drunken prisoner who when taken into custody continued to vigorously resist and mouth off. Of lesser consequence, he was reprimanded for playing cards while in uniform. In general however Lonigan was judged by his police superiors to be a very steady and well conducted police officer. He was a well liked community policeman who would tolerate no nonsense from larrikins and livestock thieves. Lonigan's reputation has been unfairly tarnished by several generations of Kelly defenders who criticise him for grabbing Ned by the privates, which was the nineteenth century equivalent of the modern day use of a Taser Gun. Ned was violently resisting and Lonigan brought him under control in a most painful fashion. Lonigan was recruited from Violet Town to be a member of the Kelly search party because he was the only one of the four policemen who could recognise Ned on sight.

Thomas McIntyre, the only policeman to escape the Kelly Gang's clutches, had served in the Irish police but he had also been trained as a schoolmaster (which explains his clear reporting style). In Australia he taught for four years in New South Wales and then joined the Victorian police. From 1877 he was stationed at Mansfield where he was well liked by the townspeople as a thorn in the side of the larrikin show-offs and shanty thieves. He was particularly good at dealing with larrikin madmen such as Wild Wright who liked to get drunk, pick fights and bash people. He had years of experience in calmly and firmly dealing with potentially dangerous situations, an attitude of reasonable behaviour he adopted to good effect at Stringybark Creek when questioned by Ned. By all accounts McIntyre was not much of a bushman; his assigned duty was to cook, tend the campfire and carry out other camp functions, which is what he was doing when Ned shouted 'bail up'.

Ned's admirers charge the police with carrying excessive weaponry and with an alleged plot to kill Ned and his brother Dan rather than arrest them. They allege that the police parties carried leather body straps with which to bring the dead bodies of the Kelly brothers back to town. Well provisioned, meticulously prepared and with murderous intent, the police went in search of the poorly armed and ill-prepared Kelly brothers.

Part of the evidence for this claim is Ned's Jerilderie Letter in which he accused the police of coming into the Wombat Ranges with the intention of shooting him down and then crying surrender. The basis for Ned's belief has never been properly canvassed, but seems to be based on bush rumour and innuendo. The one specific piece of evidence available suggests that Ned heard about an angry remark made by Constable Anthony Strahan, the Greta policeman at the time, to the effect that he would shoot Ned first and then call upon him to surrender. This remark was made in the heat of a frustrating argument with Ned's flip-flopping, police informer uncle Pat Quinn. It was never official or unofficial police policy, merely an argument clincher for Constable Strahan, who was being seriously messed around by Pat Quinn over the whereabouts of his two fugitive nephews.

Ned is at pains to point out in the Jerilderie and Cameron Letters that he failed to recognise those he shot at Stringybark Creek because he either didn't know his victims or he believed them to be somebody else. Behind Ned's 'misidentification' and 'stranger' justification statements lies a shifting of blame and responsibility, that is only too evident in all of his proffered excuses justifying his actions. It was a very strange defence; so had he known and recognised them he would not have shot them?

Ned said when he shot Lonigan he had mistaken him for Strahan but the mistaken identity claim seems doubtful, as the Kelly brothers had watched the police camp from close quarters, probably for many hours prior to bailing them up. Strahan was the local Greta policeman, who had close contact with the Kelly family. So is it likely that Ned would have failed to recognise him?

When told of Lonigan's identity after he had shot him, Ned said *I'm glad of that for the bugger gave me a hiding in Benalla one day*. Ned was referring to the famous Benalla boot maker's shop fight, in which Lonigan took hold of Ned by the privates in order to subdue him and where it is alleged, that Ned said *if ever I kill a man Lonigan, you'll be the first!* A policeman who had literally had him by the balls --- his face would not so easily be forgotten!

Ned also claims in the Jerilderie Letter to have heard that Lonigan had *blowed* [boasted] *before he left Violet Town that if Ned Kelly was to be shot he was the man who would shoot him*. Both Ned and Lonigan's rumoured threats against each other although colourful, are questionable and were probably never uttered.

Ned tells us he mistook McIntyre for Constable Ernest Flood, an old Kelly enemy and the father of Ned's deceased sister Annie's illegitimate child. Contrary to the Kelly myth, the affair between Flood and Annie was consensual and not a seduction by Flood. While he was away in gaol serving time for his involvement in the Mansfield horse borrowing incident, Ned claims that 29 of his legitimately acquired(?) horses *the best the land could produce* were stolen by Constable Flood *who when I came out was shifted to Oxley*. From the time of his release from gaol in February 1874, until the Stringybark Creek murders in October 1878, Ned never confronted Flood over this horse theft or the childbirth death of his sister Annie, despite the fact that for part of this time, Flood and his family remained nearby at Oxley.

As to the leather body straps with which the police were to cart the dead bodies of the two Kellys into Mansfield *in a mass of animated gore* as Ned graphically describes the anticipated circumstance in the Jerilderie Letter, there is good reason to believe that neither police search party was equipped with them.

Police sources claim there is no record of such leather body straps or other specially made restraints being used in connection with police work in the 19th century. If they had been available, they would have been useful for moving the dead bodies of Kennedy, Lonigan and Scanlan to Mansfield for burial. In fact lengths of rope borrowed from a sawmill and not leather body straps were used to accomplish this grisly task. Contemporary newspaper woodblock prints clearly show Lonigan and Scanlan's dead bodies tied to the side of a horse with hessian bags and ropes.

In a prison letter to the Governor composed shortly before his execution, in which he explained his intentions at Stringybark Creek, Ned said *I believe John Martin, a wild dog poisoner and boundary rider gave information to the police of me and my brother's presence in the Stringybark*. He mistakenly thought that because of this information, three not two police search parties had been dispatched with *thirteen in number* and they *were to meet at Stringybark to search for me.*

Ned was expecting a large party of police to converge on his Stringybark Creek hideout, some of whom he said were prepared to shoot him down pretty much on sight. Why then did he and his companions not use their prodigious bush skills to simply melt away into the dense bush? Better still, why did they not make for the New South Wales border and relative safety?

They knew the countryside and its hideouts well from their horse and cattle stealing raids and could have received help and assistance from their extensive network of intercolonial livestock thieves. They had been able to operate as horse and cattle thieves relatively unhindered by the police in the past. So why would their fugitive status make their plight any different now?

Ned may well have believed that his life and that of his brother Dan were in danger and devised his Stringybark Creek strategy with that in mind. But the indications are that any fear he had was greatly exaggerated and later became a convenient excuse to exonerate himself and his larrikin gang from the aggressive, pre-emptive course of action they adopted. He was a clever self-publicist with a shrewd understanding of how to fashion and manipulate public opinion.

During the Euroa bank robbery, he said *I did not wish to kill any of the* [police], *but only to take their arms.* He told his Jerilderie pub captives, that his plan was to deprive the police *of their arms and horses and let them tramp it back to Mansfield.* He was of course, putting a sympathetic gloss on his motives for the benefit of his captive audience.

In the six months the Kelly brothers had been on the run, they spent their time at Bullock Creek making sly grog for their mother's shanty, prospecting for gold, heavily fortifying their miner's cabin hideout and on daily target practice. The hideout was within a mile and a half of the Stringybark Creek police camp and was surrounded by trees with targets drawn on them. Many of these trees displayed bullet holes. There were signs that homemade bullets had been fired into the trees, dug out, refashioned and fired again.

Ned tells us the fortified miner's hut was set in twenty acres of ground cleared for growing mangle and barley for the purpose of distilling whiskey and had two miles of fencing and a house. Ned and Dan knew of the hut's existence, because they had earlier used it as a secure remote bush location for 'planting' stolen livestock.

The 'house' was composed of thick logs with loopholes and a cut-up ship's metal ballast tank covering the door. It was designed to withstand the strongest assault. A newspaper reporter who visited the Kelly hideout soon after the police murders described *the evident pains taken by the Kellys to improve themselves as marksmen. In every direction we saw trees which were marked with bullets, from five to fifty having been fired into each, at ranges varying from twenty to a hundred yards.*

Ned himself needed little practice and he took the lead from the outset of the Stringybark Creek encounter in shooting the three policemen. He was immensely proud of his prowess as a crack marksman and of his single shot, crooked-barrel old carbine of which *the stock and barrel were tied together with a waxed string, which covered three or four inches,* that he took to Stringybark Creek. When engaged in a lengthy conversation with McIntyre, Ned said *I will back it against any rifle in the country. I can shoot a kangaroo at 100 yards every shot with it.* Judging from the deadly results he achieved with the old battered weapon, Ned's reputation as a crack marksman was no idle boast.

Ned tells us in the Jerilderie Letter *we only had two guns, if they came on us at our camp they would shoot us down like dogs.* Between the Fitzpatrick Affair in April 1878 and the Stringybark Creek police murders in October of the same year, the Kelly brothers' hideout was visited by their larrikin friends, who would have brought with them provisions, information about the police and one would think weapons as well. It is simply implausible to believe that Ned and Dan were unprepared for a confrontation with the police. Are we seriously meant to believe that Ned would have neglected to beg, borrow, steal or even purchase firearms, with which to protect himself and his brother?

Ned's admirers accept his Jerilderie Letter claim of self-defence. Despite Ned knowing of the police parties scouring the bush for him and his brother. Despite his hearing rumours of alleged police threats to shoot him and then cry surrender. Despite the addition to his gang of Steve Hart and Joe Byrne, who the police knew nothing about. And despite his having six months to adequately prepare and arm himself and his comrades, for what was always going to be an inevitable, violent clash with the police. Poorly armed, poorly provisioned and living frightened in the bush! How could this possibly be the case?

Either Ned was prepared and knowingly carried the fight to the police or he dithered in the bush, without a serviceable plan to put into effect. The former shows him to be a most dangerous and well organised criminal leader, the man we know from his horse and cattle stealing days with the Greta Mob. The latter has Ned doing nothing at all, just watching and waiting for something to happen. This seems entirely uncharacteristic of his earlier and his later behaviour. So which is it to be? Ned the criminal leader with weapons and a master plan or Ned the procrastinator, indecisive with only two guns and waiting patiently about?

Ned's account of the Stringybark Creek police murders reads as if his victims were the cause of their own demise. According to Ned nothing was his fault, as he was forced against his will and better judgement into shooting the policemen, or else *lie down and let them shoot me*. Yet it was he and not they, who unleashed the bloody fury of Stringybark Creek and it was his unsuspecting police victims, who died surprised and bewildered as a consequence.

The Stringybark police detail left Mansfield carrying their four regular police service revolvers with 18 rounds of extra ammunition and two borrowed rifles, also with extra ammunition. One rifle was an old shotgun fowling piece borrowed from the Mansfield vicar the Reverend Samuel Sandiford. The other was a state-of-the-art Spencer repeating rifle which none of them had used before. This rifle was borrowed by Sergeant Kennedy from a gold escort guard the day before the police party set out in search of the fugitive Kelly brothers.

McIntyre says of Kennedy's prowess with a weapon. *I did not look upon Kennedy and Scanlan as experts with firearms; during the sixteen months I was stationed with* [Kennedy] *I had never known him to fire a shot*. Hardly it would seem, a party of police going into the bush, combat ready.

The Spencer repeating rifle which was only issued to police gold escort guards, was perhaps the 'over armed' item that Ned's defenders complain of. As it turned out the repeating rifle which was strapped to Scanlan's back, was never used as he was shot before he could reach it. None of the policemen knew how to use the rifle and Ned found he could not use it either and quickly cast it aside.

In the Jerilderie Letter, Ned said he asked McIntyre why the police *carried Spencer repeating rifles and breech loading fowling pieces*. McIntyre says Kelly asked him only about *long firearms* not specific rifles. If Ned knew a patrol was coming from Mansfield then he could have been forewarned about the Spencer repeating rifle. On balance however, it is doubtful that Ned knew about the Spencer repeating rifle beforehand, as Kennedy had borrowed the weapon close to the eve of his search parties' departure. Is this 'armed to the teeth' complaint by Ned and his latter day defenders, an 'after the fact' excuse for shooting the police?

Suppose for a moment that the police plan was officially or unofficially to shoot the Kelly brothers down and then call upon them to surrender. Why didn't the police hierarchy supply the four policemen with a rifle each, as well as their service revolvers? After the murders McIntyre said, that *for an expedition against men like the Kellys revolvers were comparatively useless, and that the police ought to have breechloaders.*

In addition to be being adequately armed with rifles, the police should have been sharpening their firearm skills long before they ventured into the bush. Instead Sergeant Kennedy had to run around borrowing rifles at the last moment, to supplement his party's regular service weapons. Even such a basic item of search party equipment as their tent was not provided by the police department and had to be borrowed from within the Mansfield community. Borrowing a state-of-the-art rifle the day before the patrol was due to leave for bush duty, seems like a hurried last-minute addition to its weapons cache, rather than a calculated plan to murder the Kelly brothers.

The police department's stringent budget cut-backs at the time and the fact that the police force as a whole was inadequately trained to use firearms, left the Mansfield policemen vulnerable to the crack shots the Kellys had become. The police had to pay for their own ammunition if they wanted to use it for practice. Understandably weapons drilling on the firing range was at the bottom of a policeman's list of priorities.

The police were at a further disadvantage. They were hampered in the drawing of their Webley service revolvers by the need to undo a metal stud and lift the flap on their holster case before they could access their weapons. Unlike American Wild West or Hollywood movie holsters, those used by the Victorian Police were a wet weather fully-enclosed type of holster case. The need to unbuckle the flap proved to be a significant drawback for both Lonigan and Kennedy in an ambush situation where the Kelly Gang had their rifles aimed and ready to fire.

The police were tasked with searching for a notorious on-the-run criminal and his less dangerous brother. One brother was suspected of being armed with at least one revolver (the same revolver allegedly used against Constable Fitzpatrick) and both were expected to offer some kind of violent resistance when cornered. The level of police weaponry officially supplied was wholly inappropriate for these dangerous circumstances.

The weapons described by McIntyre as being used by the Kelly Gang may not have been state-of-the-art weapons, but they were still serviceable and suitable for the task at hand. Dan Kelly carried *a single-barrelled fowling-piece, an old cheap gun of common bore;* Hart carried *I believe it was a double-barrelled gun;* Byrne had an old-fashioned gun *with a large bore*, which he later exchanged for the police fowling piece. Ned's weapons were his crooked-barrel old rifle and the revolver he had used during the Fitzpatrick Affair. The gang brought with them an unknown quantity of homemade ammunition, which was probably far in excess of their actual need and had Lonigan and McIntyre's weapons when they attacked Kennedy and Scanlan.

Despite knowing of Ned's notorious criminal reputation and his willingness to employ violence, the police greatly underestimated what might happen once the Kellys were confronted in the bush. Yes, there was an awareness of the danger posed by the Ned Kelly threat, but there was also a professional awareness of their own competency as experienced policemen. Not exactly overconfidence, but an everyday faith in their own ability to handle any situation that arose. It was only a matter of time before the fugitive Kelly brothers were located and taken into custody. Shooting them down was not an option the police ever contemplated or seriously believed would be necessary and they paid the price for their misjudgement with their lives. According to McIntyre's Police Commission testimony, the policemen never expected to be attacked. They mistakenly believed that the Kellys *would defend themselves; but not that they would attack us*. Ned expressed surprise when McIntyre told him that they did not keep guard on their camp overnight, and his questioning of McIntyre shows he was convinced that the police already knew of his general whereabouts.

The Mansfield police party spent their first day (Friday 25 October) travelling to Stringybark Creek and arrived there at around 2 pm. They set up camp and rested for the remainder of the day. Next morning Kennedy and Scanlan set out to scout the area for any sign of the Kellys. They left at 6 am and returned at around 5:20 pm probably exhausted, to run into the Kelly Gang's ambush in their camp. If Kennedy had prior knowledge of the Kellys' whereabouts, why did he wait until the next morning to look around? Why did he divide his police party in two? Why was no guard put on the police camp? Kennedy who was a proficient bushman, the equal of Ned Kelly in bush-tracking skills, simply had no idea that the Kelly hideout was so close to the police camp.

Stringybark Creek was no more than a secondary destination for the Mansfield police party. The rugged bush around the Glenmore run formerly leased by Ned's relatives the Quinns and the place where Harry Power was captured seemed a far more likely site for a Kelly hideout to be located. The Mansfield police party plan was to stop over at Stringybark Creek on their way to the Hedi (Edi) police station, where they were to join up with the Greta police party sometime later in the week. Together both police parties would scour the King Valley searching for any sign of the Kelly brothers' hideout.

The Kellys came to Stringybark Creek armed, prepared and ready for battle, wearing their larrikin finery with their trademark bush hats with the chinstrap fastened under their noses. Ned was wearing a red sash borrowed from Steve Hart. (At Glenrowan, he was wearing a green silk sash under his armour.) The symbolic statement made by the distinctive larrikin style of dress, was something like: 'We are the Greta Boys! Don't mess with us!'

The fact that the gang dressed themselves in the trademark trappings of bush larrikinism rather than normal bush working clothes clearly shows that they knew in advance of a police presence along the Stringybark Creek and donned larrikin battle dress to confront the adversary. This was entirely lost on the respectable living Constable McIntyre, who was unaware of the nuances of the Greta larrikin dress code and he commented on the novelty and strangeness of it all.

Ned's Stringybark Creek battle plan was to make a pre-emptive attack against one party of police to disarm them, take their horses or worse, before the others arrived to increase the odds against him. There was nothing ad hoc or spontaneous about his decision to attack Kennedy's party.

At around 5 o'clock in the afternoon, McIntyre was boiling a billy of tea. Lonigan was sitting on a log watching the fire crackle. Both of them were waiting for Kennedy and Scanlan to return to camp. All of a sudden from a nearby spear grass thicket, came a shouted command *Bail up! Hold up your hands!*

On turning quickly round, McIntyre said, *I saw four men standing in the rushes each of them armed with a gun which they held at their shoulders presented in our direction. The bushrangers were in a line two or three yards between each other.*

Taken completely by surprise and seeing Ned Kelly's gun pointing directly at his chest. McIntyre, who was unarmed, threw out his arms horizontally. Lonigan reacted quickly, jumping up from the forked log he had been sitting on and started to run.

McIntyre tells us *Ned Kelly shifted the muzzle of his gun to the right and without taking it from his shoulder shot at Lonigan who had started to run putting his hand down as if to get his revolver, he had no time to open the case and must have been looking over his right shoulder when he was shot in the right eye by Ned Kelly. The whole affair occurred so quickly that Lonigan did not run more than four or five paces before he was shot.*

Ned tells us something different *Lonigan ran some six or seven yards to a battery of logs instead of dropping behind the one he was sitting on, he had just got to the logs and put his head up to take aim when I shot him that instant or he would have shot me.*

McIntyre admits that he was facing the bushrangers and did not actually see Ned's bullet hit Lonigan, but says he distinctly heard and saw the fatal shot fired and the sound of Lonigan's body hitting the ground. *I took a hasty glance around when Kelly fired and saw Lonigan fall heavily he said 'Oh! Christ I am shot!', made several plunges, breathing stentorously, after which he remained quiet.*

Ned's account of Lonigan's death is concerned with showing that Lonigan had reached the safety of *a battery of logs and put his head up to take aim when I shot him that instant or he would have shot me.* This is the legal and moral basis of his self-defence case, that he had shot Lonigan in a fair stand up fight and only in fear of his own life.

Ned's brother Dan makes an interesting observation that supports McIntyre's account, which has Lonigan running when the fatal shot was fired. Dan said *he was a plucky fellow, did you see how he caught at his revolver?* Dan then moved his hand down to his hip in the same way as Lonigan had done, which he could only have seen if Lonigan was running away and trying desperately to draw his revolver.

Kelly always endeavoured to make it appear that he was defending himself when he shot the Police, wrote McIntyre, *but always admitted his was the attacking party. He incurred no more danger in shooting Lonigan or Scanlan than he would have done in shooting two kangaroos; he simply gave the men no chance to injure him, and might have shot them down without challenging them, as they scarcely had time to realise their danger until they were shot.*

After shooting Lonigan, Ned rushed up to McIntyre with his revolver drawn and pointed directly at him, demanding to know the location of the policeman's firearms.

Ned went over to Lonigan's dead body removed his revolver and made his way back to where McIntyre stood. He inquired of McIntyre who it was he had shot and when told said, *'What a pity the Bastard tried to run!'* It is significant that Kelly used the word *'run'* not *'fight'* in describing what Lonigan was doing when he shot him.

Ned then engaged McIntyre in a lengthy questioning, which was to last for nearly 20 minutes until Kennedy and Scanlan returned. As Ned carried on his conversation with the subdued Constable McIntyre; Dan, Steve and Joe feasted on the policeman's billy tea, tinned ham and freshly baked bread.

I thought you were Flood, Ned said, *and it is a good job for you that you are not, because if you had I would not have shot you but roasted you upon the fire. You buggers came here to shoot me, I suppose* Ned said, challengingly. McIntyre denied the charge and the conversation turned to the promise Ned had extracted from him to *leave the force*, if Ned was to set him free.

McIntyre had good reason to be fearful of arousing Ned's anger. *During the time they had me a prisoner Kelly threatened not less than a dozen times to shoot me and several times pointed his rifle at me*. Many years later reminiscing on the Stringybark Creek encounter, McIntyre wrote. *Kelly many times afterwards said that he intended to shoot me and expressed great regret that he had not done so. He told me himself, that if he had thought there was any chance of my getting away he would have shot me at once.*

McIntyre pleaded with Ned not to shoot Kennedy and Scanlan when they returned to the camp. To keep his captive passive and cooperative, Ned said that if McIntyre persuaded them to surrender, he would not take their lives. *I could have shot you half an hour ago, when you were sitting on that log* he said and added *we don't want their lives, only their horses and firearms.*

At this moment Kennedy and Scanlan were seen approaching the camp with Kennedy riding slightly in front of Scanlan. Both policemen suspected nothing and the bushrangers had taken cover, as McIntyre went forward to explain the situation.

As McIntyre stepped towards Kennedy's horse, Ned shouted out *Bail up, hold up your hands!* Kennedy smiled and put his hand on his revolver case, thinking that Lonigan and McIntyre were playing a joke. As soon as Kennedy's hand touched the tip of his revolver case, and before McIntyre had time to speak more than a few words, Kennedy was fired at by Ned. Ned only missed Kennedy because he had to fire over McIntyre's head.

Too late, McIntyre called out for his colleagues to surrender. Kennedy rolled off his horse and fired at least one shot in Ned's direction and hurriedly made for the cover of a tree, where he continued to discharge his revolver at his attackers. Seizing the moment, McIntyre mounted Kennedy's bolting horse and hunched over, trying to get his foot in the stirrup, he rode off under a hail of Kelly Gang bullets. Dan seeing him slumped over thought he had been shot and let out a triumphant shout.

Scanlan fared no better than Lonigan. He was in the act of dismounting, when he heard the challenge to bail up and saw the shot fired. Letting go of the reins too soon he ended up on the ground. Desperately trying to unsling the Spencer repeating rifle he lost his balance again and while on his hands and knees, trying to regain his feet and control over the tangled rifle, he was shot under the right armpit.

McIntyre describes the fatal moment of Scanlan's death. *I saw the blood spurt out from the right side as he fell. At this time a great number of shots were being fired by Kelly's party.* Scanlan did not utter a single word nor did he rise again; he just collapsed backwards onto the ground his eyes bulging.

Michael Scanlan was an intensely introverted and lonely man. McIntyre said of him *his manner was silent and his appearance was rather troubled*. Like Lonigan, who it is said had farewelled his wife and children twice before setting out to join the Stringybark Creek patrol, Scanlan allegedly had a premonition of his death, promising his dog to a friend in Shepparton if he did not return. These stories may have been invented to add further drama and tragedy to a community tale already mythologised.

One of the saddest things to record concerning Constable Scanlan's death is that nobody ever came forward to claim his personal effects. Many months later his personal possessions were put up for public auction and were sold for a pittance. Of Lonigan's pregnant widow Maria and her four children we know very little, except that she was said to have been prostrate with grief for weeks.

McIntyre never forgave Ned for his duplicity in shooting at Kennedy and Scanlan, before he could deliver his timely warning to surrender. *I was deceived by Kelly who notwithstanding his promise to spare the* men's lives, if I could induce them to surrender, neither gave me an opportunity to explain nor them to learn the position they were in.

For his part, Ned denied responsibility and blamed McIntyre for Kennedy and Scanlan's deaths. *McIntyre is the man most accountable, because he told them a falsehood when he said they were surrounded therefore placing them in a wrong position.* It was not McIntyre's fumbling attempt to warn his police comrades which caused their deaths. Ned did not give him enough time to alert them to the danger they faced, before he commenced firing at Kennedy.

Without a weapon, there was nothing McIntyre could have done to assist Kennedy and he knew by this time that if he remained he was surely a dead man for the murderers would not leave alive the only eyewitness to their crimes. Ned called him a coward for running away to support his denigration of the police, but he did not repeat the charge to McIntyre's face when they met up in a Benalla prison cell after Ned's capture. On the contrary he took it back and McIntyre left the encounter well pleased, but the accusation dogged him for the rest of his life.

With Lonigan and Scanlan dead and McIntyre escaped into the bush, the four murderers went after Kennedy as he moved from tree to tree. The gun battle quickly became heated and noisy with bullets hitting the trees in all directions as Kennedy, despite his hopeless situation, fought on. The pursuit covered a distance of nearly a mile (Ned wrongly says a quarter of a mile), before it came to a bloody and violent end.

Ned wrote *upon seeing McIntyre gallop away, Kennedy continued to fire at us without effect as we sheltered ourselves. We let him fire about five shots from his revolver he remaining nearly in the one position, and standing. A shot was fired by one of my mates, after which he started to run.*

What Ned is telling us here, is that at the beginning of the chase Kennedy was doing all of the shooting, while the Kelly Gang meekly sheltered behind trees. He says nothing of the nature of the running gunfight and mentions nothing about other bullets being fired by Kennedy during his break for freedom. Yet when McIntyre asked Kelly after his capture: *Did Kennedy fire many shots at you?* Ned replied, *Yes, he fired a lot*.

Ned's admission and the fact that the trees along Kennedy's escape route were said to be liberally peppered with bullet holes suggests that the gunfight must have been a good deal livelier, with many more bullets fired on both sides, than Ned's sparse account acknowledges.

The Kelly Gang sheltering behind trees barely firing their weapons. Patiently waiting for Kennedy to empty his revolver before commencing the pursuit. Kennedy given his chance to shoot his ambushers without them firing a shot. A policeman who according to Ned was a crack marksman. Just how believable is any of this?

As the gunfight and pursuit reached its climax, Kennedy fired one final shot at Ned. Ned said *I thought I was done for as he fired and the ball grazed my ribs, I immediately fired* [shooting Kennedy] *in the armpit*. Ned later told his Faithfull's Creek captives that he had shot Kennedy in the right shoulder causing him to drop his revolver. But he also said that he mistook Kennedy's blood-stained hand raised in surrender for a revolver when he had none and he immediately fired at him. Kennedy then fell to the ground 'badly' wounded.

As Kennedy plummeted to the ground, he most probably heard Dan Kelly shouting hysterically at Ned *to finish the Bastard off!* Ned hesitated and the terrible moment passed with Kennedy lying wounded, feeling vulnerable and completely exposed to his attackers and whatever fate awaited him.

With Ned's approval, Henry Perkins, a trusted Kelly sympathiser, related the details of Kennedy's death to a newspaper reporter, who published it as a pamphlet. In the Perkins's account, Ned gives a highly colourful and most surreal account of Kennedy's death. He describes himself as being greatly distraught at Kennedy's impending death, offering the dying man his gun saying: *Here take my gun and shoot me*. Kennedy is supposed to have compassionately remarked *No, I forgive you and may God forgive you too*. It was then that the wounded Kennedy began to plead for his life to be spared. The best Ned would allow Kennedy to do was to put together a hastily written note for his family. Then Ned reports that he *put the muzzle of my gun to within a few inches of his breast*. Kennedy said *let me alone to live as long as I can, for the sake of my poor wife and family. You surely have shed blood enough*. Ned said *I fired, and he died instantly, without a groan.*

Evidence for the existence of the note rests with the policeman's diary, found near the burnt-out police tent, from which several pages had been ripped. McIntyre says *on my return to the site of our encampment, the following night, this book was found close to the place where our tent had stood. It had some stains of blood upon it but no writing. There were four pages torn out of the front, if Kennedy wrote to his wife it would have been upon one of those missing pages. This book was carried by Kennedy in his breast pocket, and how it came to be at the tent can only be surmised.*

Ned failed to carry out his promise to deliver to Kennedy's widow the scrawled hand-written note her husband had written in the final moments before his death. The note seems to have completely disappeared. After his capture Ned adamantly maintained that no note had ever been written, suggesting that if there was a note he would have delivered it. Ned's own 'sympathiser' newspaper account clearly refers to a note written by Kennedy to his wife.

Ned later covered Kennedy's body with his police service cloak as a mark of respect, it is said by his modern day sympathisers, for the death of a brave man. Scanlan and Lonigan's dead bodies apparently deserved no such respect or recognition and when found were uncovered and soaked with rain.

Ned, we are told, admired Kennedy's pluck in fighting to the bitter end and that was the reason why he honoured Kennedy's bravery in this particular way. Yet, the incident could just as easily have been triggered by his lingering guilt at having shot an unarmed man, as it was a public recognition of Kennedy's courage.

When the fighting was over, Ned allowed himself the luxury of indulging in a victor's sympathy, for those he had earlier killed without compunction or compassion. Even if Ned did feel a genuine sorrow and sympathy for bringing about Kennedy's death, how does that mitigate or excuse this murder?

Ned's 'sympathiser' account of Kennedy's 'mercy killing' is no more believable than what he recounts in the Jerilderie Letter, where the emphasis is not on Kennedy or his family but on Ned's supposed reluctance to act to put an end to Kennedy's suffering.

We only have Ned's account from which to construct Kennedy's death. By his own admission, Ned tells us he took a shotgun and placed it to within a few inches of the policeman's breast and pulled the trigger. There is forensic confusion as to whether Kennedy was shot in the side of the head as well. Kennedy's autopsy revealed *there was a large wound in the centre of the sternum, caused, it was supposed, by a charge of shot fired at a very short range. It passed completely through the body, coming out of the back.* Sub-Inspector Henry Pewtress who led the search party which recovered Kennedy's body said *it presented a frightful spectacle. He had been shot through the side of the head, the bullet coming out in front, carrying away part of the face.*

The Mansfield Police Station Occurrence book describes the presence of four bullet wounds on Kennedy's body. *There was found on the body a bullet wound directly under the right arm, which was probably given when Kennedy held up his arms* [in surrender]*, one on the right cheek, one on the left temple and one on the chest.*

Doctor Samuel Reynolds conducted autopsies on Lonigan and Scanlan but only did a visual examination of Kennedy's body. He does not mention a temple wound and the animal predation he describes seems to have been primarily associated with the loss of one of Kennedy's ears. Is the temple wound, therefore, a mistake and not to be taken seriously? Ned's armpit shot was, according to Ned, the shot that brought Kennedy down. The cheek wound was no more than a minor wound and most likely occurred sometime during the tree to tree fight.

We cannot know one way or the other, precisely what occurred during Kennedy's dying moments. Except to say perhaps that Kennedy's death was not the straightforward, compassionate affair described by Ned.

Of Kennedy's death, Ned said *the sergeant never moved from the spot where he fell, but complained of the pain he felt from the bullet wound. I should say we were with him nearly two hours trying to get what information we could out of him. He always endeavoured to turn the conversation in the direction of his domestic affairs, his home, his wife and family, and very frequently of the little one he had recently buried in the Mansfield Cemetery, to whom he seemed very much attached.* William Fitzgerald, a captive of the Kellys at Euroa, confirms Ned's long interrogation of Kennedy. *Kelly told me he had spoken to Kennedy for a long time after the sergeant had been wounded.*

Two hours of trying to get what information we could out of him sounds more like a heartless interrogation of a suffering man, stretching well into the night-time (sunset was at 6:48 pm) with murder waiting at the end. It could also be speculated that if Kennedy was physically able to compose and write a note to his family and was alive after Kelly's questioning of him for nearly two hours, he may have been able to survive his wounds.

At the time of his death, Kennedy was pleading for his life to be spared and rather than convey the wounded policeman back to the police camp, where he could at least have been made comfortable, supplied with shelter, food and water, Ned made the decision to bring Kennedy's life to an abrupt end. If as he believed other police search parties were making their way to Stringybark Creek, then Kennedy's life may have been saved.

From Kennedy's still warm body lying before him on the ground. Ned stole his gold fob watch and other personal possessions. Dan Kelly, Steve Hart and Joe Byrne were also guilty of looting the policemen's dead bodies. Scanlan's gold ring and his Geneva hunting watch and chain were stolen, probably by Joe Byrne. When Byrne was shot and killed at Glenrowan, he was still wearing Scanlan and Lonigan's signet rings. Scanlan's ring can be clearly seen on Byrne's little finger in the latter's famous Benalla death photograph.

During the Euroa bank raid, Ned proudly displayed to his Faithfull's Creek captives Kennedy's gold watch, telling them he had shot the dead policeman in a fair stand-up fight. His intention he said was to return it to Kennedy's widow. He never did so and it was not until 14 years later that the watch found its way back to Mrs Kennedy, obtained from a Kelly relative through a third party for an extorted cash reward.

Kennedy's widow Bridget was left to raise, Mary nine years old, Roseanna seven, Catherine six, Laurence five and John two. She was still mourning the death of James who had died a year earlier aged 11 months. She did not have the comfort of her husband's last words. Newspapers accounts speculated: *Mrs Kennedy so far has not received the letter said to have been written by her husband and the belief is, that if there is anything in it which would in any way destroy the gloss the ruffians choose to put on their actions she never will.*

In his official report describing the Stringybark Creek crime scene, Sub Inspector Pewtress expressed his personal disgust and anger at the looting of the three dead policemen's bodies. He described the bodies of Kennedy, Lonigan and Scanlan with *their pockets turned inside out.*

McIntyre escaped from the drama of Kennedy's battle with the Kelly Gang, with bullets whistling past his ears and Dan Kelly maniacally shouting out *Shoot the Bugger! Shoot the Bugger!* and then letting out a wild yell of delight when he thought McIntyre had been shot. *After this remark* McIntyre said *a great number of shots were fired but none of them hit me.*

McIntyre's escape was, he tells us, *an impulsive one and not premeditated.* Kennedy's frightened horse plunged its way through the thick bush, subjecting him to many cuts and bruises from the dense foliage. The fleeing policeman was struck by an overhanging tree branch, which knocked him senseless. *I saw blood, tasted it and smelt it* he recounted, as he was thrown from the saddle to the ground. He later suspected that Kennedy's horse had been wounded during the wild fusillade of shots and that was the reason why the animal was so quickly 'knocked up' and had to be abandoned.

Fearful and terrified that he was being pursued by the gang and utterly exhausted by his ordeal, he sought shelter in a wombat hole. McIntyre was later to say that he regretted telling the story of the wombat hole, as it became the predominate media-image plaguing the rest of his life. Proof of this is found in Ned's mocking reference to wombat-headed policemen in the Jerilderie Letter and Ned's post-Glenrowan comment: *This is better than a wombat hole, eh, McIntyre*. Even among the police the joke was uttered as a clear insult to McIntyre. When seeking to rejoin the police force in 1879 to go in search of the Kelly Gang, ex-constable Flynn said *I will not take* [to] *a wombat hole and leave my comrades in action.*

McIntyre scribbled in his notebook a hurried message. *Ned Kelly, Dan, and two others stuck us up today while we were unarmed. I am hiding in a wombat hole until dark. The Lord have mercy on me. Scanlan tried to get his gun out.* He wrote this brief note not just out of fear as has been suggested by Ned's admirers, but as a written record of the ambush murder of his police colleagues, in case he did not make it back to Mansfield.

McIntyre battled severe fatigue and serious injury from his frantic ride and heavy fall. His feet were swollen and badly chaffed from rubbing inside his waterlogged boots, one of which he had to take off and carry. He was not cowardly, creeping barefoot through the bush, as Ned's admirers sarcastically claim.

Luckily McIntyre had a compass and was able, in his injured and worn out state, to make his way into Mansfield to raise the alarm. *About 9 am on Sunday morning I felt thoroughly done in, and fearing that I might never reach Mansfield I made another entry in my Police book to the effect that I had been travelling all night, and I was weary and sick, I was lying on the bank of a creek.* Resuming his journey, McIntyre *got to Dueran station at noon seeing nobody about I was just going in when I saw a number of horses and amongst them two horses that looked like troop horses belonging to our party. Thinking that the Kellys had stuck up the station, I left and made for Mansfield. I reached Mr McColl's farm house on the outskirts of Mansfield around 3 pm.*

From there a neighbouring farmer named Byrne took McIntyre into Mansfield by wagon.

Within a few hours of reaching Mansfield, still utterly exhausted by his ordeal, McIntyre accompanied Sub Inspector Pewtress's rescue party and returned to the scene of the bloody crime he had just fled. Pewtress had many more civilian volunteers than he could readily accommodate. He later said *the townspeople turned out in a praiseworthy manner and it was only the shortness of firearms to equip a larger party which prevented many others from joining us.*

A search party consisting of 12, nine civilians and three policemen including McIntyre, set out for Stringybark Creek late in the evening of Sunday 27 October. The search party travelled for many hours along darkened bush tracks until they reached Monk's Sawmill. *Monk at once prepared to accompany us* [with his two mill hands who also volunteered], *without the slightest hesitation or consideration of the danger he incurred himself, or of the reprisals, which might naturally be expected to his family and property situated in an isolated position, for thus assisting the Police.* Monk would later pay a heavy price for assisting the police on this occasion.

After travelling by moonlight through the bush, the search party soon arrived at the scene of the murders. Ned and his mates had obliterated the camp site and it was only after the burnt-out tent was identified that McIntyre could orientate himself and they then quickly found Lonigan and Scanlan's bodies lying where the Kelly Gang had left them.

Straightaway they began an unsuccessful search for Kennedy. *It was after midnight and a drizzling rain was falling.* McIntyre thoroughly exhausted by his herculean exertions collapsed. *I threw myself down on the wet ground and slept.* At daybreak a further fruitless search was made to find Kennedy, before a decision was made to return to Mansfield with Lonigan and Scanlan's bodies. The gravest fear was held for Sergeant Kennedy and further search parties were sent out in the days that followed to discover his fate.

Little has been said concerning the serious nature of McIntyre's injuries and the emotional trauma he was to suffer for the rest of his life because of them. His physical wounds were extensive and would later turn his entire back an ugly shade of black and blue and leave a multitude of scars that he would carry with him to the grave. His badly injured feet and heels recovered, but were never quite the same as before.

Sub Inspector Pewtress said of McIntyre's exhausted condition after the recovery of Lonigan and Scanlan's bodies: *McIntyre is very ill and suffered great pain whilst with me.* McIntyre's health deteriorated from that time on. He had pleurisy during Ned's Beechworth committal hearing in August 1880 where he spent time in Beechworth Hospital to recover his strength. He was also unwell during Ned's Melbourne trial in October 1880.

McIntyre had a long history of health problems prior to his encounter with the Kelly Gang, but it was Stringybark Creek and its aftermath specifically, that led to his being discharged from the police force in September 1881 for *bodily infirmity*. In his retirement McIntyre spent time writing poetry, much of it about the Kelly Gang and his life as a policeman. Family members said his encounter with the Kelly Gang blighted the rest of his life.

Lonigan and Scanlan's bodies arrived at Mansfield shortly after 1 pm on Monday 28 October and the following day autopsies were performed on both bodies. It was not until Thursday 31 October, five days after his death, that Kennedy's body was found in dense bush, quite some distance from the police camp, still partially covered with his police service cloak.

Kennedy's body was conveyed to Mansfield in the same manner as the other two policemen's bodies. His body was so badly decomposed with more than half of his face missing and his chest so severely damaged from a close range shotgun blast that it was deemed advisable not to let his widow and children view the body before burial. A brief examination was carried out and Kennedy was buried the next day within sight of the graves of his police comrades, Lonigan and Scanlan. The regional and Melbourne press reported that Kennedy's funeral was attended by nearly all the people of Mansfield and great sympathy was expressed for his widow and children. If any Kelly sympathisers were in attendance they prudently kept a low profile and remained silent while the mourners were assembled.

A marble and granite memorial funded by public subscription and costing £800 was erected at Mansfield: *To the Memory of the three brave men who lost their lives while endeavouring to capture a band of armed criminals, in the Wombat Ranges near Mansfield, 26th October 1878*. Hundreds attended the Mansfield dedication ceremony, as the impressive cenotaph was unveiled by Police Commissioner Standish on 22 April 1880.

Kennedy's police party went in search of Ned and Dan not out of spite or malice, but because the Kelly brothers were fugitive criminals, notorious horse and cattle thieves who some months earlier had fired on a policeman. There were warrants out for both crimes and the police had a legal duty and a moral right to seek out the offenders. Ned would not accept this; he had no sense that the police as an instrument of government had reason to catch him. For him there was no such thing as 'fair cop, guv'nor'. He had the grandiose conceit of thinking he had the right to destroy those who sought to arrest him — so long as he staged a fair fight. He did not stage a fair fight. Even by Kelly's own perverse standards he stands condemned of murder at Stringybark Creek.

7

Going Public

Move and I'll shoot you. I'm Kelly. Put your hands up!
Ned Kelly at Jerilderie, 1879

Within the space of two months in the summer of 1878-79 the Kelly Gang carried out two daring bank robberies which netted them over £4,000, twice the size of the reward currently offered for their capture. For years Kelly and his mates had stolen horses from rich and poor. Now he presented himself as a bushranger who robbed only from the rich and was a champion of the poor. He was courteous to the ladies and fair-minded and honourable in dealing with captives. His model for these exploits was Ben Hall, the New South Wales bushranger who had amazed the world by taking captive the whole town of Canowindra. As a bushranger Hall had actually robbed from everyone who had something worth taking. This did not prevent him acquiring a Robin Hood image from those who did not know his methods and lived at a distance.

In Sydney and Melbourne it was easy for bushrangers to become heroes. Kelly played to the popular image; his robberies of the banks at Euroa and Jerilderie were very much public performances. Though they netted him ample funds (which went to the poor only if they were his relations and sympathisers) these robberies were as much the opportunity to present his case to the world. The people he held captive had to listen at tedious length to his criticisms of the police and the justifications for their slaughter. At Euroa he organised for a letter of self-justification to be posted to Donald Cameron a Victorian MP. At Jerilderie he came prepared with a much longer apologia for his life, which he wanted published immediately as a pamphlet, the press kit of the day.

During the Euroa bank robbery the outlaws stuck up the Faithfull's Creek homestead and used it as an overnight base of operations from which to launch a daring raid on the National Bank at Euroa the next day. Joe Byrne was left behind to guard the gang's considerable tally of prisoners, while Ned, Dan and Steve set off to rob the bank. Ned drove a hawker's wagon and Dan a spring cart, both commandeered from the prisoners, and Steve rode a station horse. These were very confident, slow moving bank robbers. Neither Ned nor Dan brought with them a getaway horse in case it all went wrong. Wild Wright and Ned's relatives the Lloyds were seen in the township in the days leading up to the robbery and they may have been near at hand to offer a means of escape if escape was needed.

Arriving at Euroa's National Bank around closing time, the outlaws emptied the bank safe of its cash without any difficulty. A cavalcade consisting of the hawker's wagon, the family buggy of Scott the Bank Manager, and the jaunty spring cart conveyed the bank manager, his family, servants and the bank staff to Faithfull's Creek homestead to join the other prisoners, where *tea was served and speeches were made*. This was accomplished without anyone in the town being aware of the bushrangers' brief visit.

The Jerilderie bank robbery, also an overnight raid, was conducted from the locked-down premises of the police station and later the

Royal Mail and Albion Travellers Rest Hotels. Many hostages were detained at gunpoint, while the Bank of New South Wales next door to the Royal Mail pub was robbed. Bank Manager John Tarleton was taken prisoner in his bathtub, forced to dress hurriedly and to open the bank's safe emptying its contents into a sugar bag. Samuel Gill, the town's newspaper proprietor, got wind of what was happening and escaped into the bush before he could be prevailed upon by Ned to publish the rambling Jerilderie Letter manuscript. Reluctantly Ned handed over his manifesto — *a little part of my life* — to the bank teller, Edward Living, who promised to oversee its publication. Instead he passed it on to the Victorian Government.

For these performances the gang threw off their standard Greta Mob uniform. At Euroa they dressed as country gentlemen with suits acquired from a hawker almost certainly a sympathiser, who happened to arrive at Faithfull's Creek Station soon after the gang. Once in possession of their new outfits the gang *made Mrs Fitzgerald* [the housekeeper] *give them water, a comb and a hairbrush. She brought them a bucket of water from the creek and they performed their toilet carefully.* At Jerilderie they wore the uniforms of the police they had captured and locked in their own cells. One policeman, Constable Henry Richards, was kept out and he was obliged to escort the outlaws around the town introducing them as reinforcements to assist in the capture of the Kellys. How better to make their case that the police were cowards and nincompoops! Joe Byrne even had the audacity to have some of the gang's horses shod by the local blacksmith at New South Wales government expense.

When the gang had finished their business they departed with great éclat showing off their horse-riding skills. Henry Dudley a Faithfull's Creek prisoner said of Ned *he maintains his seat* [in the saddle] *sometimes resting his legs at full length along the horse's neck and at others extending his whole body till his toes rested on its tail, dashing along at full speed in view of the prisoners.* When they departed from Jerilderie, Dan and Steve (or some other combination of Kelly Gang members, the sources are contradictory on this point) rode up and down the main street of the town exuberantly calling for a return to *the good old days of Morgan and Ben Hall!*

On the surface of these stage-managed events, it appeared the bushrangers were acting alone. There were however Kelly sympathisers present behind the scenes helping the outlaws on both occasions. Those held captive knew there were *strangers* in their midst. Without their assistance particularly during the Jerilderie raid, which lasted for more than a day and a half and involved a considerable number of townspeople, the task would have been difficult to accomplish. The situation at the Faithfull's Creek homestead during the Euroa bank robbery was similar but far more contained and controllable. Although Kelly sympathiser spies were relatively few in number their presence was greatly magnified in the minds of the captives.

The atmosphere at the homestead near Euroa and the pub at Jerilderie appeared friendly and sociable on the surface but actually was strained, tense and far from relaxed with both sides warily viewing each other, awaiting an opportunity to act or react. The captives, as captives always do, played a friendly game of 'wait and see' and wisely placated their captors. This has been misinterpreted in Kelly histories as sympathy and support. Just as circumspect in their behaviour were the *strangers*, watching and waiting for dissent and defiance to emerge, and not becoming involved in the conversations taking place between the outlaws and their captives. The history books might find evidence of sympathy for the Kellys; the bushrangers certainly did not take it for granted.

On both occasions some of the captives thought of striking back, but they were deterred more by the presence of the strangers than the bushrangers who were at least clearly identifiable. At Faithfull's Creek *among those who might otherwise have been in favour of some bold step, there was knowledge that the storeroom contained strong sympathisers with the Kellys as well as bone fide prisoners and it was suspected the outlaws friends were lurking near the station.* In the Jerilderie pub in hushed whispers Bank Manager John Tarleton and Constable Richards devised a plan *readily acquiesced in by others; a rush was to be made on Hart in the passage by some; others were to slam the half door leading into the bar and thus prevent Dan Kelly from firing into the room.* Dan became suspicious of the whispering among the prisoners or he was warned by one stranger of *over half a dozen who it afterwards transpired were undoubtedly sympathisers with the outlaws* [who] *gave a signal of what was going on.*

The presence of the strangers helps to explain why the captives were so obedient to the outlaws' demands that they make no move for hours after they had left. They were still being watched. At Faithfull's Creek the *strangers* played their part when they all left the storeroom. *The sympathisers* [who] *had been in confinement mounted their horses and under the pretence of looking for tracks kept riding around the station in every direction together with the scouts who had been watching all day. It was for the sole purpose of baffling the trackers when daylight came.* By the time police trackers arrived to pursue the outlaws, the Kelly Gang had disappeared into the safety of the Strathbogie Ranges and the direction of their escape was impossible to detect.

So fearful were some of the Jerilderie captives of *the outlaws' sympathisers roaming of the town* after the Kelly Gang departed promising to return if the alarm was raised too soon, they took extraordinary precautions against the outlaws' return. While others rode to nearby towns to convey the news of the audacious bank robbery, four of the Kelly Gang's released prisoners barricaded themselves in the post office with *four double barrelled shotguns and a good supply of cartridges.* [Constable] *Richards* [who] *held the belief the outlaws intended to return and had spies in the town managed to secure a revolver and cartridges. With these arms they took up their positions in the post office.*

The Reverend John Gribble, a man of sterner mettle, tried to convince some of the pub prisoners to arm themselves and go in pursuit of the bushrangers. They were *laughing and talking over their amusing adventure* in the street and were not at all inclined to confront those who just a short while earlier had held them captive at gunpoint. Gribble persisted; it was he said their *honest duty to protect the town and if possible capture such desperate outlaws*. If the townspeople failed to do their duty, *we shall be branded by the whole country as cowards*. The reply Gribble received was typical of hostages released from an ordeal in which their lives were placed at risk by unpredictable and aggressive gunmen; they were relieved and agitated men who that day wanted no more trouble. *Why should we interfere with them unless they interfere with us. They came to stickup the bank, they have stuck it up and that is all they did.*

When charming the ladies and acting the role of the gentleman bushranger, Ned was an impressive figure favourably commented on by all who fell under his charismatic spell. He could however in an instant change from affability to fury. One moment he was sentimentally reminiscing about his mother, the next he was threatening someone with his fists or a revolver. When roused to anger Ned presented a terrifying appearance to his Jerilderie prisoners. *His aspect was perfectly demoniacal, his face became distorted with the violence of his passion and the veins in his forehead stood out in strong relief until he looked horribly ferocious, his eyes in a frenzy rolling.* Henry Dudley a prisoner at Faithfull's Creek was slow to obey Kelly's commands and gave him cheek. Ned *shouted in a threatening manner presenting a revolver at my head. 'I'll shoot you dead on the spot if you give me any cheek!'* Dudley promptly submitted, *I smell the* [gun] *powder now* he later said, and he was cheeky no more. At Jerilderie, Bank Manager Tarleton described Joe Byrne's reaction to a Chinaman who refused to obey his orders. *As we passed in* [to the hotel] *I saw Byrne hit the Chinese cook a tremendous blow under the ear because the Celestial refused to go into the parlour when ordered to bail up. After the blow the Chinaman went in as meekly as a lamb.*

At Jerilderie Ned threatened to shoot Constable Richards and Storekeeper James Rankin. Ned said to his pub audience, *I'm going to shoot Constable Richards before I leave* and pointed his revolver directly at the policeman's chest. To Rankin who had run out of the bank as it was being robbed and unwisely sought safe haven inside the Royal Mail Hotel, Ned said as he entered the pub *Get out here you fat bastard, I'm going to shoot you!* and presented his revolver squarely at Rankin's head. Yet Richards and Rankin courageously stood their ground and refused to be cowed by Ned's shouting and gun waving.

On both of these occasions there is little doubt the bushranger was playing to the assembled gallery of onlookers rather than seriously intending to carry out his threat. The same is true of a threatening encounter at Faithfull's Creek homestead, which was clearly choreographed for the occasion. Ned enacted a violent sham argument with James Gloster, the hawker who supplied the bushrangers with a new set of clothes. Ned and Dan threatened to shoot Gloster. *Put a bullet through the bloody wretch!* Dan called out with his gun pointing squarely at the hawker's chest as Gloster walked towards his wagon to retrieve his revolver. How forgiving would Ned have been to a recalcitrant adversary whose express intention was to defy him not with words but with a loaded revolver?

What makes this confrontation appear stage-managed was that Ned's angry bellowing with his revolver pressed firmly against Gloster's cheek so very quickly subsided. Ned allowed himself to be dissuaded from shooting Gloster by the pleas of William Macauley the station overseer. *Ned Kelly at last said he would let him off this time and praised his own moderation by saying that not one man in one hundred would have dealt so leniently with him after the manner in which he had behaved.* Throughout his career as a bushranger, Ned enjoyed the public spectacle of threatening to shoot those who even mildly defied him. He enjoyed a great deal more appearing to give in to the wishes of onlookers pleading for him to spare the lives of those he threatened, playing the magnanimous bushranger with death in one hand and forgiveness in the other.

One woman, key to his success at Jerilderie, he controlled not by charm but blood-curdling threats. Mary Devine was wife to Constable Devine locked in the cells by Ned. To while away the time until the bank opened, Ned read to her several pages of the Jerilderie Letter. Mary listened without comment; she dutifully went about her household work while Ned read of the grave injustice done to his mother. When asked two days later what was in the document, she *could not remember anything about it*. The Kelly literature describes Mary Devine as being friendly and sympathetic towards Ned. Yet, as Ned and his companions left to rob the bank, the bushranger warned her not to go outside the house under any consideration until he returned. *If his orders were disobeyed,* he said, *he would burn the house down over her head.* Mrs Devine was terrified by this threat. So frightened was she that Ned would return she refused to hand over the key to the lock-up where her husband and several others including a Justice of the Peace were incarcerated until several hours after the Kelly Gang had departed from Jerilderie. *The poor woman had not recovered from the terror of the outlaw's threat* and feared for her husband and her family's lives. She did not want her husband George who was already bedridden from a severe rupture injury to go *chasing Ned Kelly*.

Despite all the threats no blood was spilled at Euroa or Jerilderie. The captives who knew of the Kellys as murderers of policemen were relieved to be alive, pleased to have been at the centre of momentous events, and fascinated to have made the discovery that criminals can appear to be nice. The charm offensive worked, more on the women than the men. Men of any social standing were humiliated to find themselves in the power of men such as the Kellys. Their manhood required them to make some stand against them. The women had no qualms about falling under the sway of handsome, courteous and charming bushrangers.

At the Euroa bank when Ned forced his way into the private residence, Robert Scott bravely protested. *I said to him 'Kelly, if you go [in] there I'll strike you, whatever the consequences maybe'. Hart presented his revolver at my head and Kelly passed through.* Later while travelling to Faithfull's Creek homestead, Ned and Bank Manager Scott calmly discussed the encounter. *I asked him what would Hart have done if I had struck you when you were going into my private residence?* Ned replied, *he would have shot you dead on the spot.* Inside the private residence was Mrs Scott who was quite beguiled by Ned and said of him. *He was a much more handsome and well dressed man than she had expected and by no means the ferocious ruffian she imagined him to be.* The male captives in reporting on their experience were more aware of the bushrangers' power and how it was maintained even while they acknowledged gentlemanly manners.

The Euroa bank robbery although successful, was in many ways a dress rehearsal for the better executed and more flamboyant Jerilderie undertaking. At Euroa Ned decided as an afterthought to send a letter to Donald Cameron. He dictated it to Joe Byrne at the Faithfull's Creek homestead on the night before the robbery. For Jerilderie this document was rewritten and greatly expanded in a dramatic and emotively-crafted style. Ned sent the Cameron Letter through the post while he vainly sought to have the Jerilderie Letter published during his visit to the town.

At Euroa Ned removed a few bank securities and title deeds from the bank safe. *Mr Scott the manager asked Ned to give them up as they would be of no use to him. This Ned refused to do and announced his intention of burning them.* If they were burnt, it was done privately. At Jerilderie Ned seized title deeds, securities and bank ledgers and burnt them on the spot, though strangely without assembling a crowd of onlookers or haranguing his pub prisoners as to the wickedness of banks. Ned's only assistant in the arson was a local jockey by the name of Henry Teffen brought there by the bushranger to start and tend the fire. This was strange behaviour indeed for a garrulous and publicity seeking bushranger. Did Ned fear an adverse crowd reaction to the burning of legal documents many of which directly related to Jerilderie residents? *The banks as a rule* Ned wryly commented when removing documents from the bank's safe *are crushing the life blood out of the poor struggling man.* That was a stock thing for a bushranger to say, but it was not clear whether the documents the bank held represented an asset or a burden to the strugglers.

Within a few days of the Euroa robbery, Bank Manager Robert Scott wrote to the bank's head office in Melbourne listing the few securities and title deeds that had been stolen. Scott's letter suggests that selectors who were not wealthy men were the only bank customers to suffer loss from Ned's mishandling of the bank's securities. They lost the title deeds to their properties, while other bank customers were granted a financial boon by having their promissory notes disappear. In his letter Scott specified that only a small number of title deeds and promissory notes valued at less than £100 were involved. *The securities taken are: – O'Brien's Crown Grant 160 acres Kialla, John Foy's*

Crown Grant a half acre Violet town, G. G. Walls lease 69 acres Kialla and Bills No. 393-A. Palmer due 7 months £20, T. Walsh due 8 Feby £20, G. M. Walls 3 months £25 and Pat Kean 5 months £29 5 shillings 4 pence. No squatters were disadvantaged nor were their pastoral properties in anyway affected. Neither did Kelly sympathisers holding selections of land benefit from Ned's ad hoc and poorly carried out removal of Euroa bank documents.

Ned and his gang knew much more clearly what they were about when they seized the contents of safe deposit boxes and took watches off their captives. They were collectors of watches for their value and as trophies. During the Euroa bank robbery Ned dramatically displayed Sergeant Kennedy's stolen watch. At Faithfull's Creek Robert MacDougall, a troublesome prisoner who had contemplated a mass escape, pleaded with the bushranger not to take his watch because it was a keepsake from his recently departed mother. Ned handed it back saying *No, I will never take it from you.*

Maybe Ned was utterly genuine in his sentimentality, remembering his own mother who was serving a three year sentence in Pentridge Gaol for her part in the Fitzpatrick Affair. However not to be denied his bushranger booty, Ned stole the watch of William Macauley the station's overseer, while Joe Byrne took the gold watch of Robert Scott the Euroa bank manager. At Jerilderie Reverend John Gribble asked Ned for his watch to be returned. It had been taken by Steve Hart and *in a towering rage* Steve obeyed Ned's orders to give it back. Ned said *when you touch a man for a watch, go for a good one!* Out of a safe deposit box at Jerilderie, Ned took an inexpensive and possibly damaged watch which belonged to the deceased daughter of Mrs Edward Maslem. *Mrs Maslem's distress was very great. She even went so far as to insert advertisements in the North East Victorian newspapers appealing to the outlaws to return the watch to her; but the watch was never returned.* Despite Ned's much touted love and reverence for his own mother's wishes, this mother's plea went unanswered.

Within five days of Ned's capture at Glenrowan, Charles Cox the Jerilderie proprietor of the Royal Mail Hotel, where the Kelly Gang had held the majority of its captives, travelled by train to Melbourne at the request of many Jerilderie residents and the widow Maslem herself, to obtain permission from the Chief Secretary to visit Ned in the Melbourne Gaol. Despite a near total embargo on visitors, Cox's request was granted. In a brief conversation with Ned, Cox was blunt. *All I want to know is what you did with the jewellery you took out of the bank at Jerilderie belonging to Mrs Maslem especially an old watch valueless for ordinary use, but which was a heirloom in the Maslem family and they greatly desire to remain in possession of it.* Ned replied *I can't tell you. It was taken away but I don't know what became of it.* Was the precious family treasure simply discarded as valueless and thrown away? *Mr Cox,* it was duly reported by the Melbourne press, *left without having found a clue to the stolen jewellery.*

At both Euroa and Jerilderie there was a lot of waiting around, time that Ned filled by giving his captives an account of his life and justification for killing the police. Ned's pub address to the Jerilderie captives differs in some respects from the same story he told at Euroa just two months earlier. Ned tightened up some parts, omitted others and brought in additional information that did not always gel with what he had said earlier.

There was consistency in Ned's account of what led him to a life of crime and eventually to bushranging, a fantasy view of himself he probably half believed and desperately wanted the public to believe. There was also half truth and straight-out lies to mislead his pub audience into believing that he had no choice other than do what he did. Ned hadn't spoken to crowds before and this was crowd pleasing stuff, vehemently attacking his police enemy and denying responsibility for any of it.

At Jerilderie, according to Schoolmaster Elliott's account, Ned said the police *were a low lot of lazy loafing scandals, always ready to swear a man's life away.* [They] *were constantly formulating false charges against his family. Constable Flood was one of the worst offenders. Fitzpatrick was a low, drunken blackguard.* Carried away by his own rhetoric, Ned spoke of Fitzpatrick putting a revolver to his sister Kate's head demanding sexual favours. At Euroa Ned made no mention of sexual assault; after his capture at Glenrowan he made it very clear that nothing like this had happened.

Ned spoke angrily of Detective Ward and Constable Hayes threatening his sisters with drawn revolvers and *shoving the girls in front of them into the rooms,* while searching for him and his brother Dan following Fitzpatrick's shooting. With police anger at a premium following the wounding and alleged attempted murder of a police officer, some of what Ned presents here in the worst possible light is very likely true.

It is Ned's Jerilderie pub account of the Stringybark Creek murders that differs most markedly from what he said elsewhere. Ned and his brother Dan *were peacefully pursuing the vocation of fossicking in the gullies with their two mates.* [They] *came across the* [police] *camp and prepared for flight. While his mates were getting things together for a move,* Ned decided instead they would *seize their arms and ammunition.* The bushrangers had decided to flee rather than confront the police? No mention of this is made in either of Ned's letters, nor spoken of at Euroa or any time later. This was a sop to the Jerilderie pub captives.

In contradiction to Constable McIntyre's account of four armed bushrangers, Ned told his Jerilderie audience he was the only one of the gang who carried a weapon, his crooked-barrel old rifle that *could shoot around corners.* Lonigan *jumped up, rifle in hand and made a dash for a tree.* This is the only time Ned refers to Lonigan with a rifle. McIntyre says Lonigan was reaching for his revolver and not a rifle. There was no mention of him coming up from behind a log as there was in other accounts. In this version he made a dash for a tree. According to pub witnesses to Ned's rant, he said little about Lonigan's death *except that he brought about his own end.* Blame the victim was Ned's standard ploy.

Ned claimed *I could easily have shot Constable McIntyre for he passed within a dozen yards.* If he could so easily have shot McIntyre, why didn't he? Because the policeman had surrendered and been promised his life? Ned later said he would have shot McIntyre without hesitation, if he thought the policeman harboured even the slightest thought of escape. Ned wanted disingenuously to show his Jerilderie captives his compassionate side.

The performance at the Jerilderie pub shows how unreliable Ned was in giving an account of his doings. He could not even stick to the script which Joe had written out and he had brought to Jerilderie to be printed. Naturally enough he shaped his words to please his current audience, something which should be remembered by those who take the Jerilderie Letter as holy writ.

The Cameron and Jerilderie Letters are historical truth only in so far as they are Ned's words and are not taken as an accurate description of the events and people he treats. We should not be misled by the wonderfully evocative words Ned uses in describing the police, Whitty and Byrne and the unhappy plight of the convict Irish into believing that what he writes as invective is in fact historical truth. Always in his public utterances Ned has a clearly defined propaganda purpose in mind, portraying himself as an innocent victim driven to crime and bushranging by unwarranted police harassment. Amidst the humour and the pathos of Ned's letter writing, we should not lose sight of what it is he is actually saying and why he is saying it. Historical truth lies not in Ned's distorted characterisation of people and events; but in the hidden meaning behind the veil of Ned's misrepresentations. Some of which he no doubt believed or came to believe was a truthful reflection of what he saw around him.

Ned's contemporaries were not taken in by his letters. Superintendent Hare considered the document *as a tissue of lies from beginning to end, a wandering narrative full of insinuations and complaints against the police of the type familiar to all who have experience of tales which men of the criminal stamp are in the habit of telling; it is as impossible to prevent these men from lying as it is from stealing.* As a policeman Hare had considerable experience of criminals and their lying ways.

William Elliott the Jerilderie schoolteacher read the letter in its entirety before the bank teller, Living handed it over to the Victorian Government. Living supplied from memory to the editor *Mr Gill a synopsis which appeared in the Jerilderie Herald.* Like Superintendent Hare, Elliott was far from impressed with the Jerilderie Letter's self-serving arguments. *To judge by reading between the lines, one would be inclined to think that the leader of the outlaws was a bit of a fanatic or rather a dreamer. With his ambition there must also have been a lot of Don Quixote about him. One might conclude that he is a desperate man, driven to desperation by imaginary wrongs and* [he took] *up arms against the community. To sum up, the greater portion* [is] *little better than emanations of wild fancies from a disordered brain. Some critics might have been more severe and class the lot as a pack of rubbish.*

In the weeks following the Jerilderie robbery 'Ned Kelly's Letter' as it was called in the newspapers was published in an abridged version, not word for word but based on Schoolmaster Elliott's memory of what it contained. Editorial comment was mostly scornful and distrustful of Ned's version of events and the letter was dismissed as self-serving invective. Referring to the letter *The Argus* commented, *an account is given of the terrible tragedy at Mansfield, but it is obviously a string of falsehoods and it would be improper for any journal to publish it.*

There seems have been little if any letter correspondence from the public either supportive or condemnatory concerning what was said, merely a newspaper reader's beguiled interest in Ned's controversial words. In 1930, the letter was published in full as 'Kelly's Manifesto' in the *Register News-Pictorial* as part of a newspaper serialisation titled 'The Kellys Are Out!' In 1948 Max Brown published the Jerilderie Letter as an appendix in *Australian Son*.

As for the Cameron Letter, Police Commissioner Standish called it *a tissue of falsehoods* and counselled the government: *It is inadvisable that publicity should be given to such a production.* This view was accepted. Apart from a few brief references to the contents of the letter published in Ned's lifetime, it remained largely unknown until published in 1929 in J.J. Kenneally's Kelly book.

The regional and city newspapers reported in full the drama of the Euroa and Jerilderie bank robberies. The bushrangers were scandalous and exciting news and everybody wanted to know more. Editorial comment was scathing in its criticism of the bushrangers and the sympathy for them generated by their attention-grabbing deeds. *Every day the gang is at liberty is a public misfortune. It allows a spurious sympathy to spring up, the adventures of the bushrangers cloaking their crimes and tempting the thoughtless to forget the abhorrence in which they should hold the habitual thieves, whose criminal instincts hardened by impunity have led them on, step by step, until they developed into wholesale murderers.* But of course by their reporting the newspapers encouraged the admiration and sympathy that they deplored.

The growth in sympathy was exactly the effect that Ned Kelly sought. He was already making his own legend. The threats, intimidation and dissembling required to produce this effect are still hard for modern Australians to contemplate.

The success at Euroa and Jerilderie depended on threats not being carried out. If these daring robberies had been other than bloodless the label of murderers would have stuck more firmly to the gang. Because they were known murderers, their captives took their threats seriously. They knew the four outlaws were dead men walking. Another murder would not add to their punishment, which would be on the scaffold. It was nevertheless a fine line for Ned Kelly to walk between threat and reassurance. He had the self-control, despite the rages, to carry it off and good luck on the day for there were a hundred ways things could have gone very wrong.

It was Dan Kelly who was the greatest threat to the enterprise. *The prisoners* [were] *all united in declaring that Dan Kelly had a most villainous cast of countenance. The younger Kelly is one of those tyrannical ruffians whose sole delight is in inflicting cruelty for the purpose of enjoying the agonies of his victims and more than once Ned Kelly had to interpose his authority to prevent bloodshed.* Ned had to put a very firm stop to Dan's suggestion of *having a lark with the women.* Predatory sexual behaviour was alright among the Greta Mob; it would have been death to the image of gentlemanly bushrangers, which for the moment was what the gang presented themselves to be.

For the next 16 months the gang remained at large. The police looked foolish and incompetent, while the outlaws appeared invincible. Actually the police were pressing the outlaws far more than has generally been realised. It was a costly business to remain safe. The bushrangers had to pay dearly for protection, information and provisions. They ran dangerously short of money, became distrustful of many of their sympathisers and frustrated by the police search parties and numerous police spies constantly nipping at their heels. They had to leave the colony, which they knew would result in their capture, or do something sensational.

8

Operation Massacre

Come on you bloody cocktails! You can't hurt me, I'm in iron.
Ned Kelly, 28 June 1880

The armour that the Kelly Gang wore at Glenrowan has become iconic. No other bushrangers decked themselves out in this way. The armour became Ned's symbol even more definitely when the artist Sidney Nolan depicted Ned as only armour. All four sets of armour survive. Ned's armour is in the State Library of Victoria, Steve and Dan's in the Victoria Police Museum and Joe's is presently in private hands.

The armour was not used for the purpose it was intended. The armour was to have protected the gang while they slaughtered a trainload of police and anyone who was travelling with them. These would be the dazed survivors of the wreck of their train that the gang would engineer. After 16 months hiding in the bush, a massacre is what Kelly planned for his reappearance into the public eye. He had threatened it in the Cameron Letter *Remember your railways* and in the Jerilderie Letter *I will be compelled to show some colonial strategem which will open the eyes of not only the Victorian Police, and inhabitants, but also the whole British Army*. He wanted a bloody spectacle *wholesale and retail slaughter*.

When he was on death row Kelly in a petition to the Governor declared: *It was not my intention of upsetting the train for the purpose of killing the police.*

To the people he held hostage soon after taking up the railway line he was quite clear about his intentions. They reported:

They had come to Glenrowan in order to wreck the special train of inspectors, police and black trackers which would pass through Glenrowan to Beechworth [and they] *were going to send the train and its occupants to hell.*

Ned told us that they had come there to settle with the black trackers and that he would be on the spot when the train ran over the culvert and would shoot all who were not killed.

I was talking a long time with Joe Byrne and it was him told about the rails being torn up and that they came here to kill the police and black trackers. What they wanted to do was bad.

I expect a train from Benalla with a lot of police and blackfellas. I'm going to kill them all.

They stated that they would shoot down all those who escaped death from the wrecked train and if any civilians were in the train, they should share the same fate, as they had no business accompanying the police.

Ned had a particular hatred for the Aboriginal trackers, even though they had not succeeded in tracking him down. He was conscious of their great skill and his hatred might not have been strongly racial; he hated them the more because they were effective enemies.

* * * * *

Just over a year after the Jerilderie hold-up, a strange series of farm thefts occurred throughout the Greta-Glenrowan area. Mould boards from selectors' ploughs began to disappear. The robberies were reported to the police, who were as mystified as everybody else as to their purpose. Before he relinquished control of the police hunt for the Kelly Gang, Superintendent Nicolson had his suspicions from information provided to him by his network of police spies that the outlaws were planning *some sort of outrage*, but the intelligence he received was sparse and disjointed. His successor Superintendent Hare received a crucial clue as to the bushrangers' preparation for another public appearance, yet he dismissed both the police spy and his information as useless gathered from Nicolson's redundant spy network which he was in the process of dismantling.

A police spy known as the 'Diseased Stock Agent' who in reality was Daniel Kennedy, a former Greta schoolmaster turned hotel manager and selector, was the police spy in question. *See Appendix II Diseased Stock Agent. Kennedy was appalled by the Stringybark Creek police murders and throughout 1879 and the first six months of 1880, he passed on a steady stream of information to the police picked up as community gossip and rumour concerning the comings and goings of the bushrangers. He was one among several police informers who just before the Glenrowan battle cryptically reported that *feed is getting scarce* and another Kelly Gang appearance was imminent. On 20 May 1880 the Diseased Stock Agent reported to Hare. *Missing portions of cultivators described as jackets now being worked and fit splendidly. Tested prior to using and proof at ten yards.* Here was the vital clue behind the mysterious mould board thefts and their extraordinary use. The stolen ploughshares were fashioned into protective armour. Superintendent Hare was blind to the information he received and he did nothing to follow it up.

Where the idea of Ned's ploughshare armour originated has been canvassed in many directions but no satisfactory answer has emerged. Some say he got idea from his favourite book Lorna Doone. Although it is doubtful that Ned was much of a book reader, armour is not mentioned in the book beyond a brief reference to *leathern jerkins, long boots and plates on breast and head*. This seems too ambiguous and fleeting a reference to have inspired the armour. Ned may have followed the well known biblical injunction to turn your swords into ploughshares and turned it on its head. But again there is no evidence of Ned possessing more than a rudimentary understanding of the Bible.

There is nothing in the Irish tradition that could have led Ned to adopt protective armour as either an offensive or defensive strategy, unless one turns to the notion of an inherited Irish memory of the medieval period, chivalrous knights, staged combat, castles and the like. Literary and historical accounts of Greek and Roman warriors played a formative role in shaping Irish republican attitudes and of course they were well known to the classically-educated English. There is a possibility then that Ned may have taken the idea for the Kelly armour from the breastplates worn by Greek and Roman soldiers or other ancient world warriors, but the suggestion is a long shot.

Local models are more likely. In the six months before the Stringybark Creek police murders, Ned and his mates took over an abandoned miner's hut on the Bullock Creek near Mansfield which they fortified against attack. The hut was composed of interlaced thick logs with several loopholes and a cut-up ship's metal ballast tank covering the door which had a metal loophole similar in design and conceptual detail to that of the headpiece of the Kelly armour. The hideout was intended to withstand the strongest assault from the outside and was a possible inspiration and model for the Kelly armour.

A second and much more likely contender for Ned's idea to use armour has a Beechworth connection. Joe Byrne and Aaron Sherritt spent much of their wayward youth in and around the camp of the Woolshed's Chinese community. Joe could speak Mandarin and through his contact with Chinese goldminers he became addicted to smoking opium. During the mid 1870s a travelling exhibition of oriental artefacts was brought to Beechworth and one of the central exhibits which caused a considerable amount of local interest was a complete suit of traditional Japanese Samurai armour. Joe, Aaron and possibly even Ned himself, who spent a significant amount of time in the Beechworth area stock thieving, would have been aware of the popular exhibition and may have attended a viewing. Ned may have remembered the armour and applied the principle of its offensive/defensive use to his own Glenrowan needs.

Ned's plan called for the four members of his gang to be in the open, exposed but protected by their armour. No practical need for leg protection was required, as the tactical purpose of the armour was to shoot down train wreck survivors from atop a steep railway embankment. Its battlefield purpose was offensive rather than defensive and the armour was never meant to be used in the defensive fashion it was. Joe, Steve and Dan were from the outset against Ned's daft idea of encasing themselves in armour which restricted vision and turned its wearers into slow moving, lumbering targets. When Ned and Joe were both wounded in the first volley of police shots fired at Glenrowan. Joe angrily turned to Ned and said *It's your fault, I told you this bloody armour was no damn good and would bring us to grief.* The gang, thinking practically, did not share the grandiosity of their leader who would make himself invincible.

* * * * *

If the police were to be drawn in large numbers to the north-east some spectacular outrage must be committed. The gang decided to murder Aaron Sherritt who was a friend to Joe Byrne but whom they suspected of supplying information to the police. Four policemen were stationed in his house to protect him and to keep night-time watch for the outlaws. A debate still rages around whether Sherritt was a police spy or a double agent for the outlaws. Joe Byrne had a more personal grudge against his boyhood friend who it was rumoured had insulted Joe's mother Margaret when she accused Aaron of betraying her son. Sherritt had supposedly said to her: *I'll shoot Joe and I'll fuck him before his body gets cold!*

In the early evening hours of Saturday 26 June 1880, Joe and Dan were to perform the deed. Ned and Steve Hart were awaiting them at Glenrowan where the train was to be wrecked. Joe and Dan forced Anton Wick, a German neighbour of Sherritt's, to entice Aaron to the door of the hut pretending he had lost his way in the dark and needed direction to find his way home. Aaron opened the door and stood there framed by the dim light of candles coming from inside. Without a challenge or a warning of any kind, Joe Byrne stepped from out of the shadows and fired a double shotgun blast directly into his childhood friend's neck and chest saying: *the Bastard will never put me away again!*

Dan Kelly smiled and laughed as he heard Aaron's young wife of only six months scream hysterically as Sherritt staggered and fell backwards, dashing his head against a table or some other piece of furniture as his body hit the ground. He died instantly without recognising his murderer or knowing the reason why he had been shot.

Following this brutal death a bizarre two hour 'bushranger' performance of bullying, intimidation, feigned negotiation and constant name-calling began. The policemen hiding in the bedroom could hear several voices outside Sherritt's hut and they wrongly believed that all four members of the Kelly Gang were waiting outside to murder them. Joe and Dan did nothing to disabuse them of this notion; in fact they actively encouraged the belief that Ned and Steve were present in order to raise the anxiety level of those inside the hut.

The four policemen have been unfairly portrayed as cowards hiding behind two women and afraid to confront the outlaws. They were at a huge disadvantage. Within a minute or so of the shooting of Sherritt, Dan, loudly cursing and calling on the police to come out, fired a shotgun blast through the bark partition wall of the bedroom where the policemen were hiding. The policemen were armed but trapped inside a windowless bedroom with no way out except past the outlaws who had a clear view of the bedroom door even from outside the hut. Constable Armstrong, the man in charge of the police, who even Ned's defenders acknowledge was a courageous policeman, proposed to his colleagues that they rush out together but he got no takers.

After two hours of bloodcurdling threats and occasional gunfire, Joe and Dan unsuccessfully tried to set fire to the outside wall of the sawn-timber hut, taunting with a fiery death those who were inside. Their attackers kept up the pretence that the Kelly Gang and several of their friends were watching every move and waiting to shoot down anyone who emerged from the hut. With the timber hut smouldering but failing to burn, Joe and Dan silently rode away from the scene sometime around 8:30 pm in the evening without those cowering inside suspecting they had departed. Paddy Byrne, Joe's brother, spent the rest of the night and the early morning hours trampling around the bush and calling out bloodcurdling threats to maintain the charade of a Kelly Gang presence.

Around 6:30 am Constable Armstrong ventured outside to find someone to carry the news of Sherritt's murder to Beechworth. When the messengers all returned saying they were afraid of the Kelly sympathisers, Armstrong decided to make the journey himself fearful at every moment that he would be noticed by the gang's relatives and friends. He 'requisitioned' a horse from a traveller and galloped towards Beechworth without interference.

He arrived at 1 pm on Sunday afternoon some 19 hours after Sherritt's Saturday evening murder. The news was telegraphed to Benalla and Melbourne immediately. After a staggering nine hours further delay a police special train finally left Melbourne at 10 pm to respond to the Kelly Gang's provocation.

The outlaws had expected the police train to pass through Glenrowan sometime around dawn on the Sunday morning. Ned's plan went terribly wrong, he tells us, because *the police did not do as I expected*. Ned had grossly overestimated the police's ability to react immediately to his Beechworth challenge. But his followers had made the delay much longer by keeping the police cooped up in Sherritt's hut. Harassing cowering police was simply too much fun.

* * * * *

The railway station at Glenrowan was a mile (1.5 kilometres) from the town. Here was the stationmaster's house and two pubs, Paddy McDonnell's Railway Tavern close to the station and over the railway lines and on rising ground Ann Jones's Glenrowan Inn. Ned and the Greta Mob larrikins were regular patrons at McDonnell's. Although a licensed pub it was viewed by Glenrowan's respectable residents, selectors and townspeople alike, as only marginally better than the rough bush shanties that usually catered for the district's criminal and larrikin toughs. Ann Jones catered for a better class of clientele, although the Kellys and their rowdy friends would occasionally drink there as well. The Glenrowan Inn was locally regarded as a police pub and was generally avoided by the district's criminals. Ann provided meals and accommodation to the police and stabled their horses.

Ned correctly suspected Ann Jones of assisting the police in their campaign against him.

McDonnell's pub was the chosen headquarters of Operation Police Massacre. Ned and Steve arrived there at 10 pm on Saturday night. They left a small group of friends and relatives behind and set off to accomplish their first task, the lifting of the railway tracks half a mile (800 metres) to the north of the station. The location *was chosen with diabolical fitness for bringing about the total destruction of the special train. The line takes a sudden turn down an incline, and is then carried over a gully on an embankment. There is a little creek in this gully, and to carry it under the line, a substantial culvert had been built. This culvert is situated just at the end of the sharpest part of the curve, and at the foot of the incline. It was just at this point that the rails were torn up. Had the special train continued its journey without any warning having been given, it would have been impossible for the engine driver to see the breach in the line until too late, and the inevitable result would have been that the train, with its living freight, would have rushed over the embankment into the gully beneath. If it had gone on the left side it would have had a fall of about twenty feet, and if on the right a fall of about thirty feet.*

Ned and Steve brought their own tools to lift the line. After an hour and a half they had made no progress. They returned to the station, stuck up the stationmaster's residence and enlisted the help of two railway plate-layers, James Reardon and Dennis Sullivan, and several quarry workers who were camped nearby. It was now after midnight. As Ned barged into the tent of the quarry foreman Alphonse Piazzi, who had a woman in bed beside him, the feisty Italian challenged the intruder and pointed his revolver at him. Instantly Ned's temper exploded: *You bastard, you lift a gun to me!* and he fired his rifle point blank at the quarry worker. Fortunately Piazzi escaped injury by pushing Ned's rifle aside at the crucial moment just as he pulled the trigger. George Metcalf, a labourer in Piazzi's quarry gang, was later accidentally shot in the eye by Ned, while the outlaw was recklessly playing around with Piazzi's confiscated revolver. Or as another story has it, while Ned was skylarking about with his Spencer repeating rifle.

By around 2 or 2:30 am on Sunday morning a 7 metre section of the railway track had been removed and the scene was now set for mayhem and carnage. Ned and Steve marched their railway captives back to the house of John Stanistreet the Glenrowan stationmaster, where the Stanistreet family, the Reardons and Ann Jones the proprietor of the Glenrowan Inn and her family had been held hostage for the past two hours. The Jones family had been roused and taken into captivity by Ned following the Piazzi confrontation. Ned feared his rifle shot may have been heard and he took the family to the Stanistreet's house just in case.

The massacre plan orchestrated from McDonnell's pub was meant to be completed by the early hours of Sunday morning, with possibly only a handful of key Kelly sympathisers directly assisting. From inside the pub the bushrangers would watch the police train steam through Glenrowan station and after its destruction, they would ride out in their armour to confront the survivors and finish the job. Ned may have toyed with the idea of stopping the train before it reached the point of no return; he quizzed the stationmaster concerning railway protocols while telling him emphatically not to warn the train. Disingenuously, he said later he had sent a man to warn the train because he wanted him to have the reward and spoke of taking the police hostage to force the release of his mother from gaol. Ned did nothing to put such a life-saving plan into effect, though he later adopted it as a condemned man's reprieve tactic to influence the Governor in the weeks before his execution.

Since the train was failing to appear, Ned was forced to change his plan. Already the stationmaster's house had become a holding place for hostages. As day began, anyone who came near the railway station had to be taken and held. Ned decided to move the majority of the gang's growing band of hostages (the captive men only at this stage) to Jones's pub where many more hostages would be added as the day wore on. The women and children remained at the stationmaster's residence. At the peak of the hostage taking sixty-two hostages were detained inside Jones's pub and the Stanistreet house.

Why Ned at this early stage decided on separating the men from the women and children is not known. It may have been done for easier hostage control to keep the married men submissive or perhaps a more sinister purpose was intended which was never realised. Maybe the women and children held inside the stationmaster's house were to be used as a bargaining chip to force the police to surrender if things went wrong. The fact that until late on Sunday afternoon the women and children remained in the Stanistreet residence guarded by one or other of the outlaws gives weight to the idea. Then they too were moved to Jones's pub.

As Sunday morning became afternoon and evening and the police train still failed to arrive, Ned became increasingly bad tempered. There were arguments with the rest of the gang. Dan had lost faith in Ned's plan and wanted to abandon it all together. Ned would not agree: *I'm tired of running. We'll stand and fight.*

At 10 pm on Sunday night Ned decided to go into the town and capture the local cop Constable Hugh Bracken, who was still unaware that the Kellys had taken charge at the railway station and the two pubs. Why Ned would have allowed Bracken to remain free for as long as he did is curious indeed. Possibly the police barracks and Bracken were watched throughout Saturday night and most of Sunday by Ned's sympathisers. To have taken Bracken hostage earlier would have alerted the town proper to the gang's presence. Bracken knew Ned from his days as a warder at Beechworth prison in the early 1870s when Ned was incarcerated there. Later he visited the Kelly shanty as a serving police officer and met Ned again before the Kelly outbreak. Bracken was captured without incident. He opened the door and Ned said *throw up your arms or you are a dead man!*

The police barracks were part of a large building owned by Hillmorton John Reynolds who lived at the other end of it. Ned called on him, they had a long discussion but he did not take him prisoner. This has led some writers to assume he was a sympathiser. A less likely sympathiser would be hard to find. He was a licensed store owner, the local postmaster, a dealer in livestock and a property speculator owning a selection and many Glenrowan township blocks. He was not a man to mix with livestock thieves and criminals and he eschewed their company whenever he could. When Ned returned to the pub Ann Jones asked him why Reynolds was not taken as a pub hostage; Ned smugly said *he is as right as if he was locked up* tapping his pocket where he kept his Colt revolver — meaning that Reynolds feared the midnight match and far worse retaliation, if he did or said anything against the outlaws. A rich man with a lot to lose, whose young son was already a prisoner, did not need to be locked up.

For 15 hours the Kelly Gang and its growing band of hostages had remained sequestered together in and around Jones's pub. They drank Ann Jones's alcohol freely 'without limit' as Ned had commanded of his hostess at the outset. Throughout the day and well into the night of that Sunday the captives engaged in sporting contests, danced and sang together. Ann's son John encouraged by his mother and the outlaws sang the Wild Colonial Boy. The pub atmosphere was boozy, garrulous and on the surface laid-back and relaxed.

Behind this facade was a growing misgiving among the hostages about the carnage they knew lay at the centre of Ned's Glenrowan plan. The bushrangers made no secret of their intention to wreck the police train but kept their armour concealed for some time. When hessian bags containing the armour were carried through the bar and lodged in Ann Jones's bedroom, speculation among the hostages reached fever pitch. One well-known Kelly sympathiser when asked what he thought was in the hessian bags cryptically replied: *I know and if things go as planned, you'll all soon know!*

Glenrowan schoolmaster Thomas Curnow, his wife Jean, baby daughter Muriel, his sister Catherine and his brother-in-law David Mortimer, aged 19, were taken hostage around 11 am on Sunday morning. David Mortimer played concertina for the singing and dancing. Thomas Curnow was appalled by the ruthlessness of Ned's plan and he decided soon after his capture to take the necessary steps to foil *the outrage which the outlaws had planned* by convincing Ned he was a Kelly sympathiser. He took Ned aside and informed him that John Stanistreet the stationmaster had a revolver in his office and was waiting for an opportunity to use it. Ned angrily confronted Stanistreet and threatened to shoot him; Curnow intervened and calmed the situation down achieving his twofold purpose of protecting Stanistreet from harm and fooling Ned into believing he was a Kelly loyalist.

When Steve Hart complained of *sore and swollen feet* Curnow arranged for a basin of hot water to soothe Steve's discomfort. He advised Ned to take into custody Constable Bracken at the police barracks and bring him to Jones's pub. Earlier Curnow had tried to convince Ned to accompany him home *to get his dancing shoes* knowing that they would pass by the police barracks where Bracken might be expected to see them and raise the alarm. Ned refused the request and Curnow made the best of dancing Irish jigs and reels in his hobnail boots. Curnow assured Ned he had no cause to fear him, *as I was with him heart and soul.* Ned replied *I can see it.*

When Kelly set off to arrest Constable Bracken, Curnow asked to go with him and then go home. Ned agreed to Thomas, the two Curnow women and baby Muriel leaving with him, with the admonition *to go quickly to bed and don't dream too loud*. Curnow did not go to bed; he went to the railway line with a candle and a red scarf to stop the train.

At 1:30 am on Monday morning after an interrupted journey of three and a half hours the police train arrived at Benalla where it was met by Superintendent Francis Hare and a contingent of Benalla policemen, some railway employees and a civilian volunteer. The police and railway officials were aware of a rumour and possibly of more solid information that the Kelly Gang had interfered with the railway line. The scuttlebutt floating about the platform was that the railway line between Benalla and Wangaratta had been torn up. As a precautionary measure a pilot engine was placed at a distance of two hundred metres in front of the police train, which was now carrying twenty-four people and seventeen horses as it cautiously made its way towards Glenrowan and Wangaratta.

With the pilot engine in front of the passenger train, the Kelly Gang's Glenrowan plan to murder a large number of policemen was effectively brought to an end. Even if the pilot engine was derailed without sounding a warning whistle, there was no way the police steam engine would share its fate.

Curnow's improvised stop light worked. The pilot engine stopped and the train behind ground to a halt. *What's the matter*, yelled the guard. *The Kellys are here!* replied Curnow. The trains went on slowly to the Glenrowan station.

Inside the pub Ned was addressing the captives about the evils of the police (at 2:30 am in the morning!). He broke off his speech cursing *that bloody Curnow, he has betrayed us!* Ned and Joe were already wearing their armour minus the heavy helmets; they waited impatiently, while Dan and Steve kitted themselves out for the coming fight. David Mortimer later wrote: *this was the first time I had seen the men in their full dress and the thought inwardly struck me that the police would stand a very poor show indeed when opposed to these desperate men clad as they were in what seemed complete armour.*

Ned ordered the lights and the parlour fire extinguished as he left the pub, mounted his horse and rode towards the railway tracks. He witnessed the police train and the pilot engine coupled together with six armed policemen riding shotgun watching both sides of the tracks as the train slowly made its way to Glenrowan station. Realising there was now little chance the train would continue on to the spot where the railway line was torn up, Ned hurriedly rode back to the Jones's pub to convey the news to his mates.

Inside the pub the hostages were huddled together on the floor, intimidated by the outlaws and fearful about what was to come. Even the Kelly sympathisers among them had lost their previously cocky sense of 'bring on the fight'. Ned and his bushranging mates were discussing what they should do. Ned wanted to stay and fight and the others pleaded with him to escape into the bush.

Constable Bracken had earlier taken the pub's front door key from the mantelpiece where Joe Byrne had carelessly placed it. He seized an unguarded moment to escape and ran towards the station where the police were hurriedly unloading their horses. To cover his escape Bracken locked the door on his way out, which prevented other hostages from escaping this way when the shooting commenced. As Bracken reached the station he breathlessly informed Superintendent Hare the Kelly Gang was at Jones's pub and that he should go there immediately before the outlaws escaped. Hare called out to several policemen who were nearest to him and strode towards the Glenrowan Inn unsure of exactly who was inside the pub.

Almost immediately Bracken's disappearance from the pub was noticed. Brandishing his revolver menacingly in the air, Dan Kelly *proclaimed that the first man who left the house would be shot*. Dan's words immobilised the hostages long enough for the police to form a cordon around the hotel making escape dangerous and difficult.

As Superintendent Hare led his small band of policeman through the railway reserve gate with the verandah of Jones's pub completely immersed in shadow, Ned Kelly stepped from out of the darkness into the clear moonlight and fired the Spencer repeating rifle he had taken from Constable Scanlan at Stringybark Creek. He taunted the police: *Come on you bloody cocktails! You can't hurt me, I'm in iron*. Constable Gascoigne standing next to Hare called out: *That is Ned Kelly's voice* not comprehending what was being said. All the eyewitnesses agree that Ned fired the first shot and then calmly stepped back into the shadow of the verandah as the battle commenced. Hare was seriously wounded with his left wrist badly shattered by Ned's bullet. He exclaimed: *Good gracious, I am hit the very first shot!* and fired his Webley revolver in the direction of Jones's pub. *See Appendix III Superintendent Hare's Wound. A few seconds later a volley of three shots was fired from the verandah and Hare's police party returned fire shooting at the muzzle flashes they saw in the darkness.

In a brief exchange lasting only a few minutes in which upwards of 100 shots were fired, the battle scene became so heavily clouded by a thick gun smoke haze that neither side could see the other to continue the skirmish. Ned was severely wounded in the first volley of police shots with a bullet travelling the length of his right foot damaging several bones and the ball of his right thumb was shot through. His left arm was badly injured with a bullet entry and exit wound in the forearm and elbow area. He was bleeding profusely, his mobility was very much restricted by his armour and his ability to fire a weapon was greatly impaired. Thus with only a few shots fired both of the opposing leaders were badly wounded.

Ned's wounds were serious but not life-threatening. Joe Byrne had also been shot. *I think my leg is broke* he complained to Ned as he hobbled around cursing the *bloody armour* as well as the *bloody police*. Joe was to become, as one hostage later said, *perfectly reckless of his life* which was partially caused by Ned's disregarding of his advice. Again all three of Ned's mates said they must discard the armour and escape into the bush. Ned again refused. He was not thinking of survival.

The scene inside Jones's pub when the bullets began to fly was chaotic and unpredictable: *The firing commenced and we dropped to the floor. The bullets whizzed through the weatherboards in all directions. Our feelings at the time were indescribable. The poor women and children were screaming with terror and every man in the house was saying his prayers. We could do nothing and the bullets continued to whistle through the building.* The police were firing through the wooden building from all sides, with police bullets fired from the front going over the heads of the policemen firing from the back, which they took to be the outlaws shooting at them and increased their rate of firing.

John Jones son of the publican was shot. A police bullet entered at the young boy's left hip and exited his body under his right armpit. He bled profusely and calling out for his mother he soon lost consciousness. When *poor little Johnny Jones was shot, I put my fingers in my ears so as not to hear his screams of agony and the lamentations of his mother and Mrs Reardon who had a baby in her arms* In a rarely acknowledged act of bravery, Piazzi quarryman Neil 'Jock' McHugh carried the unconscious young boy through the police lines on his back to obtain medical attention. He died in the Wangaratta Hospital without ever regaining consciousness on the day following the siege.

Most at risk from being directly fired upon by the police were those few hostages who made an attempt to escape from Jones's pub in the pre-dawn darkness. Sergeant Steele, hyped up and single minded, shot at and narrowly missed Margaret Reardon, a distraught woman escaping with a baby in her arms. Baby Bridget was slightly grazed by Steele's bullet, which passed through her mother's shawl, but luckily mother and baby suffered no more serious injury. Immediately Steele was challenged by Constable Arthur who threatened to shoot him: *if you fire at that woman again, I'm damned if I don't shoot you!* It was a rash and reckless act for which Steele was later rightly criticised by the public and his fellow police officers.

Beyond a few hurried words spoken to a fleeing female hostage by Dan that she should tell the police *to wait till daylight and allow all these people to go out and we shall fight for ourselves*, the gang did nothing to protect its more than 40 pub hostages or to arrange with the police for their release even after the daylight hours came. They were accustomed to taking captives while they robbed banks. Now they were keeping terrified captives in the line of police fire. By this time the outlaws, desperate to protect themselves, had completely lost interest in the fate of the hostages. They said they were free to go, but added that if they did *the police would surely shoot them*.

For many hours the police laboured under the false impression that those trapped inside the Glenrowan Inn were all diehard Kelly sympathisers intent on fighting with the gang against the police. Heedless of the screams and pleas coming from the hostages that could be heard over the gunfire, they continued to believe this even after some of the escaping hostages informed them of the true situation inside Jones's pub. To be fair to the police the information they received from the fleeing hostages was mixed and confused. Neil McHugh who escaped from the pub carrying on his back the seriously wounded John Jones told Constable Gascoigne: *There are 30 of them and they have armour on, for God's sake don't go near the hotel for they intend to shoot you all in the morning.* Gascoigne was later to say: *I thought from what he said the whole lot had armour.* After failing to catch the Kellys for two years and suffering regular humiliations, the police had no thought other than that the bushrangers were at last cornered and in this battle they would either surrender or die. The simple truth of the matter is that the police and the Kelly Gang showed little concern for anything other than the fight itself.

During the night at around 3 am in the morning, Ned Kelly left the pub and was absent for about two hours. How far he went and with what purpose has been a matter of great dispute which will be examined in the next chapter. Sometime after 5 am before police reinforcements had arrived from Benalla and Wangaratta, Ned was again back inside Jones's pub having successfully breached the still flimsy police cordon. Within minutes of Ned's arrival, Joe Byrne celebrating his return was raising a glass to toast the gang, when a police bullet severed his femoral artery and without uttering a single word he quickly bled to death. What Ned and the two remaining outlaws did next is difficult to comprehend. They could have escaped and left the scene of their failed Glenrowan venture. But Ned alone left the pub for a second time, while Dan and Steve, whom he had supposedly returned to rescue, remained behind dispirited and leaderless. McIntyre was later to write: *Dan Kelly and Hart were much depressed after the death of Byrne and the disappearance of Ned for whom they had been singing out all night.*

After Joe's death, Ned lost confidence in his companions' will to fight. He said as much to Superintendent Sadleir after his capture. *The heart's gone out of them. They won't come out fighting like men, they're only boys; they'll stay in there until they're finished.* Dan was 19 and Steve was two years older. Constable Dwyer confirms Ned's presence inside Jones's pub when Joe Byrne was shot and notes his disgruntled view of his comrades, who Ned said *are too cowardly and would not surrender. When he saw his best friend dead he had no more faith in them; he left the house.*

Some writers allege that Ned left the pub for the second time promising to return for the boys, telling them that together they would take on the police and win the day. Other accounts describe Ned as leaving the pub believing Dan and Steve were following him only to discover he alone had successfully escaped for a second time. The real reason the boys had failed to follow Ned was they no longer had any confidence in his leadership. Ned had told them they were cowards and his only plan was to confront the police. Dan and Steve were disheartened and feared for their lives; it is significant that later in the siege they took their own lives rather than openly face police bullets or surrender. With Ned now gone and Joe dead, Dan and Steve retreated inside the pub where one hostage would later describe them as looking *for all the world like two condemned criminals waiting for the bolt to be drawn.*

Ned strode off angrily into the bush to sulk and consider what he should do next. It was an hour and a half later around 7 am as the winter sun was rising, that he appeared from behind police lines in the early morning mist, striking his armour with the butt of the Webley revolver he had taken from Constable Lonigan's dead body at Stringybark Creek and calling out to the police: *You bloody dogs, you can't shoot me!*

Ned had reached the fateful decision that the situation he was in was hopeless. He may have revived himself with alcohol during this time: Doctor John Nicholson said Ned *smelt strongly of brandy* when he was captured but he was clearly not drunk. Ned could do no better than to die game with a gun in his hand. He was not a coward and he would never surrender or so he thought as he prepared himself to attack the police. But he had the secret weapon of his armour. He was planning something more than suicide by cop; it was to be death defying spectacle by cop — to be followed when death was imminent by mercy plea to cop.

Ned's attack from behind the police cordon surrounding Jones's pub took everybody completely by surprise. Thomas Carrington whose famous illustrations drawn at the scene appeared in the *Australasian Sketcher* said *it was the most extraordinary sight I ever saw or read of in my life and I felt spellbound with wonder, I could not stir or speak*. Carrington later described what he said seemed to be a headless apparition: *in the dim light of morning with the steam rising from the ground, it looked for all the world like the ghost of Hamlet's father with no head.*

Constable Arthur *thought at first it was some madman in the horrors who had put a nail can on his head.* Sergeant Steele cried out *it's a blackfellow!* believing it to be Tommy Reid a local Aboriginal man with a drinking problem. As the police struggled to come to grips with the extraordinary situation confronting them, Ned called out to Dan and Steve: *Come out boys and we'll whip the beggars!* Some revolver firing came from the back of Jones's pub where Dan and Steve briefly appeared in armour, but they failed to join Ned in his quarter-hour fight against the police and hurriedly retreated inside as the police nearest to them fired back. From inside the pub they would fire more shots in Ned's defence and Dan would briefly appear outside again when Ned was finally captured.

Benalla railway guard Jesse Dowsett described police bullets as striking and bouncing off Ned's armour *like parched peas*. Ned experienced much difficulty in firing and reloading the three revolvers he had carried into battle. As an injured man, Lonigan's Webley revolver was the only weapon he could easily reload. Constable George Devine's Colt Navy revolver taken during the Jerilderie bank robbery and the underpowered Colt pocket revolver Ned used to wound Constable Fitzpatrick both caused Ned problems in loading and firing and he was forced to abandon them once their chambers were empty.

Constable Arthur said Ned's movements were unsteady and his firing aim was inaccurate. *He could not raise his arm properly, he seemed to be crippled.* To others *he seemed to be drunk, like someone in a trance from the way he was staggering about.* Ned was greatly handicapped by his injuries but he was determined to fight on regardless, until as he was brought down by Sergeant Steele's well placed shotgun blast to his legs causing him to say *that's enough, I have got my gruel.*

The police recovered their composure after their initial surprise and began to form a semicircle around the injured bushranger, who no longer cared whether he lived or died. Ned later said, when *I was at last surrounded by the police and only had a revolver* [from] *which I fired four shots, I had half a mind to shoot myself.* Ned suffered many bruises and abrasions as police bullets struck but failed to penetrate his ploughshare armour. Both of his eyes were severely blackened, portions of his nose and cheeks were rubbed raw, discoloured and swollen. By the end of the encounter his unprotected legs and other parts of his body were found to have sustained in excess of two dozen gunshot wounds.

Sergeant Arthur Steele the most important eyewitness participant in Ned's capture gave a detailed account of the encounter from its beginning. *He was not far from us when he began firing a revolver at several of the police who were closer to him. They ran for shelter and fired a number of shots at him and I could plainly hear the bullets strike his armour. All this time he kept gradually approaching the hotel, moving to the side from time to time to fire at a constable sheltering behind a tree. He discharged three revolvers and was thus engaged for about fifteen or twenty minutes.* During this time Ned fired at anybody he could see through the narrow slit of his helmet visor. *Come on you bastards, Come on you dogs! You can't hurt me!* he shouted as he fired his revolver at Jesse Dowsett who quickly fired back making Ned's armour plate ring like a bell. *How do you like that old man?* Dowsett hollered. Immediately Ned sent a bullet whizzing past Dowsett's right ear quipping: *How do you like this?*

All the while Ned fired his revolver awkwardly and inaccurately due to his many wounds and the restricted vision of his helmet, which undoubtedly saved the lives of several policemen. As Ned engaged various policemen he continued to bellow out an endless round of insults. *Come on you bastards, I don't care for you!* he shouted as he went after Constable James Dwyer and was about to fire point blank at him. When a voice from behind the policeman cried out: *Look out Dwyer, he has you covered!* Dwyer stepped to the side and narrowly missed a bullet that was meant to shatter his skull.

Sergeant Steele's narrative continues. *Kelly then sat down between three trees and I could see he was reloading his revolvers. Some police were quite close to him and I called out to rush him as his revolvers were empty but no one made the attempt. I then thought of doing it myself, immediately I showed my head two shots were fired* [from the hotel] *but I had determined to take the risk and rushed at Kelly. He stood up at once and resting his revolver on a tree fired two shots at me. At the same time a bullet fired from the hotel struck the ground at my feet.* Steele hurriedly threw himself to the ground getting sand in his eyes as he did so, which caused him momentary pain; he rubbed his eyes and struggled to see his adversary. *Just at this time a number of civilians ran from near the hotel to the railway station. Kelly levelled his revolver* and fired at the running figures and seeing his attention thus diverted, I stood up and rushed him.

As Steele closed in on Ned, *by some peculiarity of fate his mare* [Music] *trotted between us before I had reached him,* and then galloped away as she was fired upon and wounded by the police. Ned said that earlier in the siege: *I got away into the bush, found my mare and could have rushed away but wanted to see the thing out.* The mare's presence distracted Ned long enough for Steele to detect the strategic chink in his armour, his unprotected legs. *As he was levelling his revolver at me I fired at his leg which I saw was not protected by armour and he staggered back. As he staggered he spread his legs apart to save himself from falling and while he did so he exposed an opening in the armour on his hip and I fired a second shot at that spot. He then sank down his helmet falling off and partly supporting his head. I'm done! I'm done!* Ned cried out as he crashed to earth accompanied by the resounding metallic thud of his armour.

Ned was lying on the ground, bleeding heavily, finally beaten and thoroughly exhausted. A reporter gained from him this account: *He fell from loss of blood, was unable to stand from weakness, the helmet he wore was choking him and the rifle bullets completely stunned him.* Ned was down but the fight was not yet over. Steele said *I rushed to seize him and as I stooped he raised his arm and pointed his revolver backwards at me. The shot was discharged into the air as I grabbed his wrist. The bullet cut the rim of my hat and my face was slightly blackened from the smoke. I at once wrenched the revolver from his hand.*

Jesse Dowsett, who souvenired Ned's Navy Colt revolver and several other Kelly items, claims he wrested the weapon from the outlaw's up-raised hand. Nearly all of the eyewitnesses to the event say it was Steele and not Dowsett who disarmed the bushranger. Dowsett held onto one of Ned's arms, while Steele wrestled with the outlaw and took his weapon away. As Steele roughly wrenched the revolver from Ned's iron grip the outlaw said s*teady, do not break my fingers!* Enraged by Ned's close range attempt to shoot him, Steele angrily cried out. *You bloody wretch I swore I would be in at your death and I am!* Ned called out to Constable Hugh Bracken. *Save me, I saved you!* Bracken intervened saying *I'll shoot any bloody man that dares touch him!* Steele quickly regained his composure and lowered his Webley revolver which had been pointing directly at Ned's frightened face.

For saving Ned's life Bracken endured the lingering resentment of many of his police colleagues, who believed that Ned deserved to be shot dead in the same callous manner he had shot Kennedy, Lonigan and Scanlan at Stringybark Creek. Bracken was devastated by this rejection and he suffered a nervous breakdown. He was declared medically unfit and discharged from the police force on 9 May 1883.

Steele's narrative continues. *A number of men soon rushed to where I was holding Kelly. One of the men said to me 'Take your hand away and I'll shoot him through the head' and the outlaw said 'Don't let them kill me Steele, I never hurt any of you fellows'.* Constable James Dwyer said *Kelly was trembling with fear and said: 'Do not kill me, let me live as long as I can. I never injured one of you'.* In his narcissist way, Kelly judged people solely on whether they helped or hindered him. If they interfered with him, they were enemies. He thought the police surrounding him should be the same: because he had not harmed them why should they harm him? They had abundant reason: a loyalty to their dead comrades beyond Kelly's understanding. It was he who had just deserted Steve and Dan so that he could go out in a blaze of glory. They were now in his eyes cowards. Dwyer said: *when he said he never injured any of us, I said 'You damn wretch you shot my comrade* [Lonigan] *and Mr Hare and when poor Kennedy was begging* [for] *his life as you are begging yours of us, you shot him like a dog'.* Dwyer rushed in and *made a kick at the outlaw but missed and struck an end of his iron apron making him limp away with a painful injury on his shin.* Dwyer later said he had kicked Ned *to show my contempt* for his cowardice in surrendering when he always said he would never be taken alive. Ned's only response was to repeat his earlier plea for clemency. *'For God's sake'*, he said to Dwyer *'let me live as long as I can'.*

As Ned's armour was being removed several shots were fired from Jones's pub. Doctor John Nicholson, the same Benalla doctor who had tended to Constable Fitzpatrick's wrist wound more than two years earlier, quickly assessed Ned's many wounds. Nicholson described Ned as *shivering with cold and ghastly white; a wild beast brought to bay and evidently expecting to be roughly used.* It seemed to Nicholson that Ned was in danger of dying and he needed to be promptly removed to a quiet place where his wounds could properly be attended to.

When asked if he would get Dan and Steve to surrender Ned replied *the heart's gone out of them* and said they would not listen to him. He had completely lost interest in his mates. The police had to deal with them. At 10 o'clock in the morning they allowed the remaining hostages to come out of the pub. They emerged with their hands raised and their heads bowed. They had undergone eight hours of terror. A newspaper reporter wrote: *the faces of the poor fellows were blanched with fear and some of them looked as if they were out of their minds.* After being interviewed by the police, most of the hostages hurriedly departed the scene to escape the absolute nightmare of their encounter with the Kelly Gang.

The police thought of rushing the pub or pulling it down with ropes. Someone even suggested that a cannon be sent for to blow the pub apart. At 3 pm the police set it alight. At some point early in the afternoon, Dan and Steve decided on suicide as the only solution to their predicament. Each of the bushrangers carried a small satchel of poison. They either took this or fired a revolver into their hearts.

Dean Matthew Gibney, a Catholic priest, who happened to be passing through Glenrowan, bravely entered the burning pub as the fire raged to give the lads the last rites. He found them already dead and was sure they had committed suicide. *When I came into their presence they were very composed looking both lying at full stretch side by side and bags rolled up under the heads the armour on one side of them. I took hold of the hand of the one that was near me to see whether or not they had recently killed themselves-whether there was life in them and I found* [the body] *quite lifeless. Then I looked at his eyes and found unmistakable signs that he was dead for some time. I satisfied myself that life was completely extinct in both of them before I left.* The bodies were then burnt in the fire beyond recognition.

Throughout the day reporters were telegraphing regular reports of the state of the siege to Melbourne. There was huge public interest with people crowding outside the newspaper buildings to read the latest bulletin — as they did during cricket test matches and to follow the outcome of elections. Ned's last stand was already a national event of equal importance.

Ned survived the horror of Glenrowan; his three mates, having failed to persuade him to lead them to safety, perished. The illustrated papers carried drawings of Ned's last stand in his armour, Joe's dead body and a depiction of the burning bodies of Dan and Steve.

The police had ample reason for hating Kelly. He had not only killed three of their number; he had proclaimed them fools and cowards and he kept making them appear as fools and cowards. But just by a whisker the police upheld the principle to which they were sworn that the law should prevail. So Kelly was nursed back to health, tried and hanged. This gave him one last chance to leave his mark; he talked back to the judge as sentence of death was being passed and said if he had examined the witnesses he could have shown that his killing of police was not murder. That delusion never left him.

9

A Bank Robbers' Republic

In every paper I am called the blackest and coldest blooded murderer ever on record. But if I hear any more of it I will not exactly show them what cold blooded murder is but wholesale and retail slaughter, something different to shooting three troopers in self defence and robbing a bank.

Ned Kelly The Jerilderie Letter (1879)

The Kelly myth has kept growing. Since the 1960s the myth-makers assert that after Kelly had massacred the police at Glenrowan he was planning to proclaim the Republic of North East Victoria. Not immediately. Kelly and his sympathisers would progress to Benalla; the gang protected by their armour and equipped with gunpowder and dynamite, would blast open the safes of the banks and then a republic, headed by the bank robbers and with an ample treasury, would be inaugurated.

Certainly Kelly sympathisers were present at Glenrowan. When the police and the gang began their gun battle at the pub, two rockets went up into the sky, fired from McDonnell's pub. Presumably they were to have been used to signal that the police train had been wrecked. It is not clear what they were now signalling. Were more sympathisers being summoned or was the message for a small contingent of Kelly loyalists waiting in the shadow of Mount Morgan to assist the gang after the train had been wrecked? In either case the number would have been small, restricted to Ned's most trusted sympathisers.

The siege of the pub went on for hours and attracted many onlookers and no doubt more sympathisers. But not every civilian carrying a gun was a Kelly sympathiser nor every Glenrowan rubbernecker a Kelly Gang spy. Estimates of a sympathiser army of 150 is much too high and however many sympathisers there were, they never looked like an army. It is notable that the four gang members remained the police's only attackers; in the wide zone of the conflict no move was made by the sympathisers against the police either directly or indirectly. Not a single shot was fired by a sympathiser. But perhaps Kelly had told them he no longer wanted their assistance?

For two hours from 3 am and until 5 am Ned was absent from the besieged pub. Sometime after 5 am he again left the pub and was next seen behind the police lines at 7 am. There is much debate about what he was doing. On his own evidence, Ned tells us he spent much of this time lying in a semi-conscious state in the bush close to where he made his escape. He would later speak of overhearing policemen discussing the siege as he lay bleeding and occasionally fainting from blood loss within 100 yards of Jones's pub. Upon regaining his senses and moving on, Ned left behind him the Spencer repeating rifle and his helmet's skull-cap now completely soaked in blood from trying to staunch his wounds.

Ned was slowly and cautiously moving about the bush outside the police cordon. But in his bleeding and wounded condition exacerbated by too much alcohol, he was clearly experiencing difficulty in maintaining consciousness. Since he was physically weakened and psychologically disoriented, the suggestion that he held a prolonged council of war with his friends and relatives seems unlikely. He may have briefly spoken to Tom Lloyd junior in the bush close to the pub. He may even have reached McDonnell's pub where, revived by brandy, he spoke with other sympathisers concerning the increasingly desperate plight of the gang before heading off again to rejoin his mates in the besieged Glenrowan Inn.

On the flimsiest of oral history evidence the myth-makers claim that the badly wounded Ned rode off into the hills and turned back the Kelly sympathisers converging on Glenrowan; with Ned telling them: *this is our fight* and *I am prepared to die*. Brandishing his revolver in the air, he then rode back to rejoin the pub fight and save his trapped mates. None of this is referred to in contemporary records and only became part of the myth in the 1960s, when the sympathisers were cast as the force which would have robbed more banks and created a republic if the destruction of the police train had been accomplished. After his capture Ned said: *I could have got away last night, for I got into the bush with my grey mare and lay there all night. But I wanted to see the thing end.* That is a more plausible account of what Kelly was doing during those missing hours.

None of the early works on Ned Kelly, not even the many penny dreadfuls published before the First World War, mentioned a Kelly republic or discussed the Kelly outbreak in terms other than bushranging that enjoyed popular support. Ned was portrayed as a lawbreaker, courageous and bold, but always within the bushranging tradition and having no wider purpose. In 1948 author Max Brown declared, without revealing any evidence, that *in the first hour of his capture, the police took from Kelly's pocket a declaration for a Republic of North Eastern Victoria*. Every myth-making author since Brown has simply taken for granted the Kelly Gang's revolutionary intentions. Each author presents the same paucity of credible information and takes the Kelly story no further than the romanticised imaginings of their predecessors, confirming the republic by dint of numbers and repetition.

An even more questionable source is the former Melbourne journalist Leonard Radic. During a visit to the Public Records Office in London in 1962, Radic claims to have seen a printed copy of the long missing Declaration of the Republic of North East Victoria. Why a 'printed' copy is not explained except by a later source who from hearsay alone talks of handbills. No one has managed to find the document Radic claimed to have seen and the Public Records Office denies ever having such a document in its possession. Another printed copy is said by Kelly enthusiasts to exist in private hands, kept with a few romantic letters and the famous handkerchief Ned wore around his neck the day before his execution. If Radic did see the document why didn't he copy and publish it? A document that can't be viewed is no evidence at all.

Tom Lloyd junior the unofficial fifth member of the Kelly Gang failed to speak of the declaration or of the Kelly republic even in J.J. Kenneally's book *The Inner History of the Kelly Gang* (1929) for which he was the major oral history source. His son, Thomas Patrick Lloyd, only began to talk about both topics when he entered the public arena as the official spokesman for the Lloyd family in the 1960s and it is largely on his word alone that the declaration and the republic are today accepted by many as established historical fact.

Tom allegedly told Kelly researchers over a period of more than forty years captivating tales of secret meetings and seditious discussions between Ned and his leading sympathisers. The researchers said he spoke of exercise books containing the minutes of secret meetings where a Kelly republic was discussed. The pièce de résistance of Tom's tales was the mention of a handwritten copy of the Declaration of the Republic of North East Victoria. All of what

Tom said was anecdotal without confirmation or acknowledgement from within the Kelly family or those of its principal sympathisers.

I visited Tom many times when researching my own work on the Kelly outbreak. Tom was a likeable, knowledgeable source on most things Kelly. But never once did he raise the topic of secret meetings and exercise minute books in our discussions on the Kelly republic, despite on several occasions bringing out Lloyd family treasures for me to see. He did say, however, that he once *overheard* his father Tom junior say something about a notebook which he *assumed* contained the names of those associated with the Glenrowan debacle. In whispers Tom junior had said: *those books should have been destroyed, because they incriminated too many people and were dangerous.* Beyond that old Tom commented no further on the incriminating notebook, except to say that in the Kelly books he was quoted *out of context* and he was not at all pleased about it.

Tom occasionally talked of the Declaration of the Republic of North East Victoria, but only in general nonspecific terms, never mentioning a handwritten copy or who he thought might have written it. In his opinion if such a dangerous document had existed it would have been destroyed immediately after the Kelly Gang's demise for, if discovered, it would have put his father's and others lives at risk. Tom an ex-policeman who had suffered a paralysing injury from a fall from a police horse possessed an impish, roguish nature and a wry sense of humour. He told me he disliked many of the writers and researchers on both sides of the Kelly debate who had interviewed him over the years; *because they listened to my story, asked their questions, then went away and wrote what they wanted regardless of what was said.*

On more than one occasion, Tom indicated to me that he had told many of these writers and researchers what it was they wanted to hear and he further hinted that he had sometimes embellished what he was saying *to get a rise out* of them. Tom's stories changed over the years and their veracity increasingly depended on whether he liked or disliked his audience. Tom's tall tales are now a permanent feature of the Kelly canon.

As far as I can ascertain, the first documented public reference to a Kelly republic appeared in the radical and republican *Bulletin* magazine on 9 June 1900. *The Bulletin* was no longer so firmly republican as in its wild youth in the 1880s, but in 1900, against the mass of Australian opinion, it was opposing the British empire for its war against the Boers in South Africa and colonial governments for supporting it and sending troops there to fight. It was the only mass circulation journal prepared to make a bit of mischief with a Kelly republic. Its report was no more than a paragraph appearing in the section Aboriginalities, which published odd-ball and quirky bits of news and information. It was unsigned and the police reports it referred to have not been found by anyone else.

If certain statements contained in reports in the Victorian Police Department regarding the Kelly Gang, are to be believed, that crowd narrowly escaped making a political landmark in Australian history. These reports indicated the existence of such a widespread state of disaffection in North East Victoria, owing to what was called the 'remanding' as applied to persons 'guilty' of being Kelly sympathisers that the Kellys had determined to take advantage of it for their own purposes. They had resolved it was said, after having upset the special train containing the police from Melbourne, to make a cut across country from Glenrowan to Benalla, destroying bridges and telegraph lines en route, and there to have proclaimed North East Victoria a republic with Benalla as capital. This move was stopped by the failure of the effort to destroy the train. But for this hitch, it is asserted, nothing could have averted the railway catastrophe as a prelude to the Presidency of Edward Kelly, Esq, supported by nine men out of every ten in the disaffected district.

The Bulletin was partially correct on the effect of the remanding of the Kelly sympathisers. It did cause widespread disquiet. In January 1879 the police arrested around thirty men, brought no charge against them in court, but had them remanded until the next court sitting, a process which continued week by week. They remained locked up for three and a half months and so were unable to assist the gang. The disquiet did not indicate support for the Kelly Gang and their activities. Still less for a republic with them in charge. Rather, respectable people were disturbed at the flouting of the hallowed British principle of *Habeas Corpus*, which required that a person under arrest be brought promptly to court to face his or her accuser and that the case against them be produced.

The Bulletin's claim that nine out of ten people would have supported a republic is absurd. Supposing a wide level of disaffection on various grounds has been the basis for all the more recent republican stories. But as we have seen, the suggestion that all selectors were a disaffected group is completely misleading. Generally they were doing well on the land and they were part of the great mass of respectable people, who saw themselves as British and were loyal to Queen and empire.

There was no disquiet at the Victorian government's policy of denying new landholdings under the Selection Act to suspected and known Kelly sympathisers during and after the Kelly outbreak. Recommendations against an application for land were made by the police on the basis of the applicant's kinship, criminality and association with the Kelly Gang. With a few exceptions land denials were fairly administered and proved to be effective in disrupting and eventually smashing the livestock stealing network, which had produced and sustained the bushrangers. Contrary to what is said in the Kelly literature, land denial of this kind had the strong support of the majority of north-east residents, squatters and selectors, anyone indeed who wanted to hold on to their livestock and not have thieves and criminals living next door.

Because Ned was Irish he is thought of as a natural republican. Though he was a native-born Australian, his Irish heritage certainly enraged and emboldened him. He felt Ireland's woes keenly. *They were all Catholics before the Saxons and Cranmore yoke held sway. Since then they were persecuted, massacred, thrown into martyrdom and tortured beyond the ideas of the present generation.* And Ireland still awaited the moment when it could be free. There is no evidence that Ned was a Fenian or a Fenian sympathiser, the armed movement that in his times was trying to free Ireland. He had a pub-talk confidence that the Irish filled important posts throughout England and the Empire — they had command of *her armies, forts and batteries even her life guards and beef tasters* [beefeaters] *are Irish*. If England went to war, say with America, these Irishmen would turn around and fight England with her own arms: *for the sake of the colour they dare not wear for years and to reinstate it and rise old Erin's isle once more, from the pressure and tyrannism of the English yoke.* Bold strokes would free Ireland — and free Kelly himself from the local tyrants. It was easy for Ned to imagine that, by violently opposing one, he was just as much opposing the other. He was particularly good at mixing his political and cultural metaphors; the colonial authorities and the police were imaginatively transformed into the traditional racial and political enemy. So Irishmen joining the Victorian police was a complete betrayal of Ireland: these were men *who for a lazy loafing, cowardly billet, left the ash corner, deserted the Shamrock the emblem of true wit and beauty, to serve under a flag and nation that has destroyed, massacred and murdered their forefathers by the greatest of torture.*

Kelly had no sense that he lived in a self-governing, democratic colony. Victoria in his eyes was ruled by a tyrannical English government supported by the British army (whose small Australian contingents had fully departed in 1870). Actually Victoria had the most forceful liberal and democratic movement in Australia. The liberals had fought the squatters to get access to the land and when the first attempts failed they persisted and acquired finally an effective land law. The land board sitting at Benalla was the local sign of this. When Kelly took to the bush, the liberals under firebrand leader Graham Berry had recently returned to power. They passed a land tax to break up large free-hold estates and were then locked in battle with the conservative upper house over the rest of their reformist programme. In 1877, Berry had visited Beechworth as the crisis with the upper house loomed and he had been given a tumultuous welcome. He swore he would never give in to those *thirty tyrants* and become the abject slave of the Melbourne Club. His language and threats were quite Kellyesque. None of this touched Kelly. *You are all damned fools,* he said at Glenrowan, *to bother your heads about parliament for this is our country.* When asked his opinion of Berry, he replied *no bloody good, as he gave the police a lot of money to secure the capture of the gang.*

In Kelly's 'English' colony, Irish politicians had held high office. John O'Shannassy the grand old man of Melbourne's Irish Catholics was an early premier, a radical in his early years who became more conservative with age and growing wealth. His Minister of Lands was the Irish rebel Charles Gavan Duffy who had been imprisoned for his part in the Young Ireland rebellion of 1848. He was the author of one of the earliest Selection Acts that took his name, the Duffy Land Act of 1862, and in the 1870s he was briefly premier. Duffy called the colonial form of parliamentary self-government that Ned hated so much: *The most perfect system of liberty that exists in the world.*

Kelly's Australia was simply the scene of English cruelty. *More was transported to Van Diemens Land to pine their young lives away in starvation and misery among tyrants worse than the promised Hell itself. All of true blood, bone and beauty, that was not murdered on their own soil, or had fled to America or other countries to bloom again another day were doomed to Port MacQuarie, Toongabbie, Norfolk Island and Emu Plains, and in those places of tyranny and condemnation, many a blooming Irishman, rather then subdue to the Saxon yoke, were flogged to death and bravely died in servile chains, but true to the shamrock and a credit to Paddy's Land.* He learnt this Australian history not at the national school but from his father John (Red) Kelly, who had been a convict in Tasmania, and his relatives, the older generation of Quinns and Lloyds. In these circles, the convict ballad Moreton Bay must have been regularly sung for Kelly to remember from its lyrics the place names of the penal settlements and the phrase *places of condemnation* to which he added from another line *tyranny*. In loyal British Victoria there was still this subculture from another age.

But Ned's form of Irish allegiance isolated him from most of the Irish in the district. On purely tribal occasions all Irishmen remembered rebellions and the tyranny of the English, but for most their Irish patriotism was accommodating itself to the immigrants' shared sense of Britishness. They did not talk of 'breaking the English chain' by force of arms; they believed with the majority of Irishmen in Ireland and those living in England's colonies that constitutional and parliamentary means was the only practical road to achieving Ireland's independence. Their heroes were the Irishmen who had worked for Catholic Emancipation and Home Rule for Ireland, Daniel O'Connell and Charles Stewart Parnell. Irish Republicanism, the successor movement to Fenianism, only became a popular force following the 1916 Easter Rebellion. Before that time the 'men of violence and assassination', the garrulous Ned Kellys, were relatively few in number and never attracted widespread popular support.

Whitty and Byrne, Ned's declared 'squatter' enemies, were the respected leaders of the Moyhu Irish Catholic community who put their Irish patriotism effectively to work. Andrew Byrne was a supporter of the Irish Land League. At the inaugural meeting of the Wangaratta branch in October 1881: he said *when first the League came into existence, I feared they entertained some wild, foolish scheme of rebellion and that no good would come of their action; but after waiting patiently, I found the League to be a really useful organisation.*

Around the same time Jane Byrne and Kate Whitty, daughters of the patriarchs, together established the Moyhu branch of the Victorian Native Ladies' Land League, collecting donations and generally promoting the interests of the Irish National Land League. In an open letter to the Catholic Advocate newspaper, they praised Miss Parnell *for the sacrifice she is making for the poor and homeless evicted families in Ireland* and assured her *that although we never saw the 'Emerald Isle' our love for it is as strong as our parents*. In Whitty and Byrne's hands, Catholicism and Irish patriotism were inseparable and lay at the core of their colonial identity. Their children were equally culturally Irish Catholic and enthusiastic about Ireland's cause, outspoken and practical and never just rhetorical in their colonial Irish patriotism.

Ned, his relatives and his leading sympathisers, contributed nothing in a practical sense to the colonial work for Irish independence and charitable relief. They may have made an occasional small donation to Irish and Catholic fund-raising causes. There is no evidence of this or that they did anything other than engage in wild pub talk and violent threats. Theirs was a rhetorical Irish Catholicism, very different from the plodding organisational work of Catholic charitable relief and Irish political activity.

The support for a Kelly republic, had it been attempted, would have been minimal. Contrary to the myth-making, Ned was not a man in touch with the people of his district. He lived too much in an archaic Ireland of his mind. But he might still have attempted to found a republic. It is true that in the Jerilderie Letter Kelly is envisaging a new order of things in his part of the world. Whether it should be called a republic is debatable.

Kelly had almost no sense of the state, the public good or of an institution. The only allegiance he understood and respected was that to kin and his mates – and to his abstraction of Ireland. After killing three policemen, robbing banks and intimidating a whole district, he could not understand why ordinary civilians had assisted the police to hunt him down. What had he ever done to them? The only institution he knew in any detail was the police, over which he had puzzled much. Beyond the specific failings of individuals, to Kelly the police force in very essence was corrupt beyond repair. Only cowards joined it, men who wanted to throw their weight around and were too scared to do it on their own account (as Kelly did). Policemen were themselves rogues for it is well known that *it takes a rogue to catch a rogue*. In joining the force recruits took an unnatural oath because, in Ned's view, they swore to arrest *brother sister father or mother* if required. That seems to rule the police out as a body necessary to a state. Kelly's policy on the police was not to call for its reform, but to tell any policeman under his power to leave the force and to threaten violence to anyone who considered joining or assisting it.

Ian Jones, the most widely-read of Kelly's biographers, accepts the plan for a republic and a document proclaiming it and sees its principles foreshadowed in the closing passage of the Jerilderie Letter. This reads:

I wish those men who joined the Stock Protection Society to withdraw their money and give it and as much more to the widows, and orphans and poor of Greta district, where I spent and will again spend many a happy day, fearless, free and bold, as it only aids the Police to procure false witnesses and go whacks with men to steal horses and lag innocent men. It would suit them far better to subscribe a sum and give it to the poor of their district, and there is no fear of anyone stealing their property, for no man could steal their horses without the knowledge of the poor.

I give fair warning to all those who has reason to fear me to sell out, and give £10 out of every hundred towards the widow and orphan fund and do not attempt to reside in Victoria but as short a time as possible after reading this notice, neglect this and abide by the consequences, which shall be worse than the rust in the wheat in Victoria or the druth of a dry season to the grasshoppers in New South Wales.

I do not wish to give the order full force without giving timely warning, but I am a widow's son outlawed, and my orders <u>must</u> be obeyed.

Kelly's politics are highly personal. The good times will come when his enemies disappear or give up. The members of the Stock Protection Society will cease their subscriptions. His other enemies are to sell up and leave Victoria. Then he will be able to live again *fearless, free and bold.* The social justice element of the message is the age-old one that the rich should care for the poor, the widows and orphans, but the appeal is to self-interest: the poor will ensure that the rich don't have their horses stolen. No policy or law is to ensure this result. Whether the horses of the rich would be safe, given the excitement and profits of horse stealing, is to be doubted. In a nearby passage Kelly boasts again of having stolen *horses and cattle innumerable.*

Preceding this passage Kelly imagines that he is in control of affairs, issuing edicts. Any of his enemies he cannot catch himself, he will offer *a payable reward for.* Presumably Kelly felt that officialdom did not always pay out on the rewards it offered; his would be guaranteed. The punishment awaiting his enemies is fearful: *pegged on an ant-bed with their bellies opened, their fat taken out, rendered, and poured down their throats boiling hot will be cool to what pleasure I will give some of them.* And here is the Kelly state in operation: *Any person aiding or harbouring or assisting the Police in any way whatever, or employing any person whom they know to be a detective or cad, or those who would be so depraved as to take blood money will be outlawed and declared unfit to be allowed human burial. Their property either consumed or confiscated and them, theirs and all belonging to them exterminated off the face of the earth.*

You can call this a republic if you like; a better description would be a holocaust of revenge, the fantasy of a criminal megalomaniac.

Conclusion

A Lawless Life

Is my mother, her infant baby and my poor little brothers and sisters not to be pitied who has no alternative only to put up with the brutal and unmanly conduct of the Police.
Ned Kelly, The Cameron Letter (1878).

Ned Kelly was a man of many parts. He lived the life of a larrikin horse and cattle thief, used the rhetoric of a poor man's hero, publicly spoke of his respect for people's lives and yet never hesitated to threaten the lives of those who got in his way. Of his chief enemies the police, he killed three and planned to massacre a whole contingent. He was physically tough, a good bushman, handy with a rifle and an accomplished horseman. He was charismatic in his relationships with other people, a natural-born leader whose judgement was often impaired by impulsive and reckless behaviour. He provided vicarious thrill for a public hungry for sensation and entertainment.

He was egomaniacal in behaviour and attitude, a wild man who would brook no opposition from friend or enemy insisting his *orders must be obeyed*. He was subject to huge mood swings from sentimentality to towering rage that bordered on paranoia. He was a narcissist, with little regard for other people's feelings and a grandiose self-confidence in his own abilities; he was excessively opinionated with a glib, garrulous charm, setting unrealistic goals for himself while remaining vulnerable to the slightest criticism. If challenged or threatened, Ned reacted with violent threats and wild boasting. His rage at those he called his enemies led to plans and fantasies of terrible revenge.

Ned told the world he was unfairly harassed by the police both before and after he became an outlaw. Valiantly defending his family from oppressive police behaviour, he took to the bush following the trumped-up Fitzpatrick Affair. Nothing was his fault; Fitzpatrick lied, Flood seduced and outraged his sister Annie, Constable Lonigan had him by the balls when he resisted being handcuffed and the Mansfield police came into the bush to shoot rather than arrest him. Ned self-righteously told his captive listeners he had no choice but to fight back and fight back with every means at his disposal.

Whether he consciously lied or genuinely believed he was the innocent party, his propensity for making self-serving excuses formed a major part of his make-up from his earliest days. The lies and exaggerations he peddled varied little over time; he was in every instance a peaceful man, wronged and provoked by others into taking precipitous action he would rather have avoided: It was the police, it was his Moyhu enemies Whitty and Byrne, it was those who crossed him or opposed his will at any time who were to blame. Anybody but Ned and his reckless behaviour, which brought catastrophe down on his own head and the heads of others.

Ned came to believe in his increasingly paranoid assessment of events and the concocted excuses he offered to explain them. He saw himself as *an honest man* and the aggrieved victim rather than the natural aggressor. *Am I not an honest man?* Ned light-heartedly asked Constable Bracken at Glenrowan. *I'm damned if you are!* Bracken tetchily replied. There was humour here, but also insight into Ned's competing good and bad sides which governed his personality and shaped the predominant metaphor of the Kelly myth.

The labels we apply to people and the moral judgements we pronounce explain nothing, but make us feel comfortable that we know who and what they are. Ned the arch criminal with perhaps a semblance of conscience or Ned the poor man's hero fighting against oppression and tyranny reveal no more than the outside shell of a complicated human being, acting and reacting often in convoluted fashion to the challenges of his personal and communal life.

A week after the Euroa bank robbery, the *Ovens and Murray Advertiser* carried an editorial that presents a different side to Ned's larrikin character. *There is not the slightest shadow of doubt that the 'enforced outlaw' as he is pleased to call himself some three or four years ago made a bold attempt at reformation. A storekeeper at Greta assures us that Kelly was very industrious while living there. He was by no means quarrelsome and vindictive* [and] *frequently quelled unseemly rows at the public house. He bitterly complained of not being allowed to get an honest living. To use his own expression he was 'hounded down'. If anyone lost a bullock the police would visit his mother's place at Greta and rouse its inmates in the middle of the night without assigning any reason for their action.*

Although overstated, there is no reason to believe that Ned was not, for a period of time at least, living on both sides of the fence. His involvement in stealing Henry Lydeker's mare and foal when he was supposedly trying to put his larrikin past behind him attests to the complexity of his position. For Ned there was nothing incongruous in this, it was simply how things were. At times he was sober and quiet and probably *quelled unseemly rows in the public house*. There were of course other times, when the exact opposite was true and larrikin rowdiness and crime was at the centre of his activities. Horse and cattle stealing was never far away from Ned's honest and dishonest dealings. It was a matter of opportunity and profit not right or wrong. Ned's constant attention from the police was his own doing; if he and his family were not constantly engaged in lawbreaking, the police would have left them alone as they did the majority of Greta's selectors.

Ned grew up in a family atmosphere of lawless violence, larrikin bravado and horse and cattle theft. His Quinn, Lloyd and Kelly relatives intentionally placed themselves on the wrong side of the law and they brought up their children in the same vein. From an early age Ned watched as his ex-convict, alcoholic father and his wild uncontrollable uncles served time in gaol for horse and cattle stealing, other types of property crime, drunkenness and brawling. When released, he watched as they continued to pursue their chosen lives of crime with abandon. He learnt from them the criminal code of fleecing the 'mugs' and outsmarting the 'traps'. But he also learnt from his long suffering Quinn grandfather who was sadly disappointed by his children's lawlessness, a more respectable way of life that he never quite forgot and at times even aspired to. Going straight however was never a real option for Ned; the lure of easy money, the ease of livestock theft and his own inclination for the wild life encouraged and supported by his family and friends, inexorably drew him in the direction of crime and the shanty lifestyle.

Ned derived a boyhood criminal reputation from his bushranging apprenticeship with Harry Power; a reputation he revelled in and placed at the forefront of his perception of himself as a flash bush larrikin, a professional livestock thief and later a proclaimed outlaw. He was also intensely proud of a green silk sash, which was awarded to him as a boy for rescuing a drowning child at Avenel. When captured at Glenrowan, Ned was wearing the green silk sash under his armour as a symbol of his earlier bravery. The two central motifs of Ned's boyhood which shaped his later life, one respectable the other antisocial, offer a rare insight into Ned's paradoxical perception of himself as both a wild bush larrikin and a conventional hero.

As he grew older and became proficient in lawbreaking and larrikin behaviour, Ned used his charisma, his physical toughness and his flash highwayman reputation to take over the leadership of the Greta Mob. Among his friends and larrikin followers, Ned was feared as much as he was admired. He intimidated those around him, had an evil temper and a fearsome reputation for settling disputes with his fists or a revolver. Ned was aware of the disquieting and exhilarating power of control he exerted over others to get them to engage in crime or simply see him as an extraordinary individual.

The Kellys were sub-cultural fringe dwellers existing in a predatory shanty world of crime and debauchery, content to live in the moment without much thought for the future; residing on their underdeveloped selection as a shanty base from which to carry on sly-grog selling and horse and cattle stealing. Shanty culture thieves and wild bush larrikins, such as Ned and his livestock stealing friends, eschewed traditional values and middle/working class notions of decency as the restricting convention of 'mugs' and wealthy squatters. Their view of themselves was based on shanty flashness and larrikin mischief making. Once he became an outlaw, Ned paraded himself before the public as a 'gentleman' bushranger with a bushranger's feigned respect for traditional values and customary concern for the plight of the poor man. In reality, the social and cultural gap existing between shanty culture fringe dwellers and the respectable selector community remained wide and unbridgeable.

What is constantly overlooked when discussing Ned's role as a selector champion is that Ned never spoke directly about selectors' rights and squatter iniquity. At Glenrowan, Ned told his captive pub audience: They were *all damned fools to bother their heads about parliament for this is our country.* Which has been interpreted to mean not belonging to politicians, squatters and the wealthy. Arguably, this is as close as Ned came to identifying himself with the political struggle of selectors. When Ned had the unique opportunity to hold forth in Jones's pub about what had brought him to Glenrowan, he said nothing at all. His lengthy speech was more of the same old Kelly blather; emotive and self-justificatory, with little substance and devoid of any rousing political content. Its chief theme as always was the iniquity of the police.

Despite apocryphal stories of the Kelly Gang's Robin Hood largesse toward selectors, only selectors associated with the Kelly sympathiser network of bush larrikins and livestock thieves shared in the bank robbers' booty. Ned rewarded those who actively supported him to ensure their continued support and he simply ignored everybody else. Ned's poor man's rhetoric never matched his bushranging deeds. He did nothing to improve the lot of selectors nor did he protect them from the predatory crimes of his associates, who continued to steal selectors' livestock and intimidate anyone they suspected of acting against the Kelly Gang. Fear and not passive selector support was the prevalent mood in and around Greta before, during and after the Kelly outbreak.

Following his capture, Ned's narcissistic image of himself as an avenging champion and righter of wrongs grew stronger as he embraced his fate and sought to ensure his legacy. In his famous courtroom dialogue with Judge Sir Redmond Barry, Ned reveals the proud and manly image of himself he wished to pass on to posterity. *My mind,* he said, *was as easy as the mind of any man. I am the last man in the world that would take a man's life. Two years ago even if my own life was at stake and I was confident a man was going to shoot me, I would give him a chance of keeping his life and would rather part with my own.*

Another more egotistical side to Ned's character emerged from the bushranger's back and forth courtroom jousting with Redmond Barry. *I wish I had insisted on examining the witnesses myself, if I had examined the witnesses I would have thrown a different light on the case. I thought that if I did so it would look like bravado and flashness.* Barry having experienced such bombastic conceit from others sarcastically remarked. *I will give you the credit for all the skill you desire to assume.* Unwilling to relinquish ground to his opponent, Ned said. *No, I don't wish to assume anything. There is no flashness or bravado about me. I would have been capable of clearing myself of the charge and I could have saved my life in spite of all against me.*

Several times following his capture at Glenrowan, Ned declared *the last of* [my] *name has not been heard. Avengers,* he said, *would arise after his death and another gang would be formed* [whose] *deeds would astonish and affright the country.* Confident in the efficacy of the Kelly myth and full of larrikin flashness and bravado to the end, Ned said *he would come back to help them.* Another gang was not formed; Ned did not come back from the grave and the north-east district did not erupt in political turmoil. With the Kelly Gang destroyed and the Greta Mob's larrikinism and horse and cattle stealing brought under control, the rebellious spirit and intimidating behaviour of the Kelly sympathisers was broken and the Kelly country settled into a peaceful and less dramatic phase of its history.

Ned Kelly was a man of many extraordinary capacities, among them self-justification and self-publicity. For reasons that can't be pursued here, Australians have made him their national hero. The mistake of the historians and biographers has been to believe what Ned said about himself.

If we avoid that trap, a different picture emerges. Ned chose from boyhood to live the life of a flash bush larrikin and shanty culture criminal and accepted murder as a consequence of his choice. Ned is not and never was a victim of squatter oppression and police persecution. It suited his bushranger purpose to portray himself as such; the evidence however suggests otherwise. Peter Fitzsimons says at the end of his recent book *Mate, we remember you* and so we shall. We should remember that along with the daring deeds and the suit of armour was an ugly history of professional crime and murder, a man who sought to bully and intimidate society *while God gives me strength to pull a trigger.*

Railway line ripped up at Glenrowan, June 1880 (Illustrated Australian News)

Appendix I

The James Murdock Connection

One of the enigmas of the Kelly story concerns Constable Hall's police informer James Murdock. In the Jerilderie Letter, Ned blames Murdock and Hall for giving evidence that sent him to gaol for three years for receiving a horse 'borrowed' by Wild Wright. Hall *got James Murdock who was recently hung in Wagga Wagga to give false evidence against me. On Hall and Murdock's evidence I was found guilty of receiving and got three years.* Murdock is a mystery man and the Kelly literature has nothing to say about him beyond Ned's brief words.

James Murdock, or Murdoch, the former being a Northern Ireland derivative of the surname, was born in Tumut, New South Wales, in 1839. It is clear from Murdoch's prison record sheet that his name was spelt Murdoch and not as Ned spelt it in the Jerilderie Letter, Murdock. His Scots/Irish parents were James and Mary and his siblings were John, Catherine and most importantly for what is to come Peter Murdoch, who was hanged in Wagga Wagga Gaol on 18 December 1877.

James senior arrived in Australia in 1830 or thereabouts, having been a Chelsea Pensioner receiving a small government allowance following an eye infection contracted during his military service. He married Mary Kelly an Irish convict maid in 1836. In 1850 James Murdoch senior took up the pastoral lease to the Jeremiah squatting run near Tumut and for the next five years he busied himself with horses, cattle and sheep farming. He did so in much the same slap-dash way that Ned's grandfather James Quinn was to later run his remote King Valley Glenmore run. Whether Murdoch's squatting run was the resort of livestock thieves and other criminals is not known, although the King Valley and Tumut were both 'cross' destinations used by livestock thieves travelling the clandestine stock routes from New South Wales across the Victorian border and back again.

John Murdoch his eldest son was clearly a livestock thief and a shanty culture criminal. On 3 August 1870, he was arrested for cattle stealing, tried at Wagga and sentenced to 12 months gaol. Two and a half years later in 1873, he was again arrested *for stealing eighteen sheep* and sent to Darlinghurst Gaol to serve a sentence of eighteen months. John it would seem, like Ned, managed to evade arrest and punishment for many of his crimes. His younger brother James's life of petty crime and shanty dissipation at Greta seems amateurish by comparison.

James Murdoch married Ann Maree Kershaw at Tumut on 1 March 1868. According to another source they were married at Greta on 19 October 1872, which if true reveals that the Murdochs did not marry until after the birth of their second child, William Henry.

The Murdochs do not seem to have selected or purchased land but probably rented or stayed on their employer's property, following an itinerant lifestyle moving about to find employment. James' occupation as a splitter and labourer provided a perfect cover for his role as a police informer. At some stage, he broke his left arm and crippled his shoulder limiting his ability to work.

The young married couple moved to Oxley in Victoria. Soon after, with their newly born eldest child Lucy Ann, they relocated and settled at Greta early in 1869 and became associated with the Kellys. They visited Ellen's grog shanty as paying customers and perhaps stayed on for a while as guests. They soon became active shanty culture participants in the Greta-Glenrowan criminal underworld and were prosecuted by the Greta police for their involvement in petty crime.

In addition to serving time in Beechworth Gaol together in 1871, Ned and Murdoch served overlapping prison sentences in Pentridge between 1873 and 1874, Murdoch serving time for a horse theft committed at Wangaratta in December 1872.

While her husband was in gaol, and Ann Maree was living with her brother at Winton she conceived a third child, Martha Jane. Of course, James could not have been the father, but she was engaged in a torrid shanty romance with local hawker Charles Petterson who may have fathered the child. With her new love she took the Murdoch children and went to live in New South Wales. The pair seem to have bigamously married in 1876.

James was released from Pentridge Gaol in May 1875 and remained in the Greta area. In 1884, he was arrested at Benalla for housebreaking and gaoled for 10 months. What happened to him after that remains a mystery. He may have lived with his daughter Lucy Ann who had returned from New South Wales and married into the McAuliffe clan, a prominent Kelly sympathiser family. Lucy Ann and her husband Patrick went to New Zealand in the 1890s. James may have gone with them. This would account for the lack of a documented record of his later life or death in either Victoria or New South Wales.

In February 1877, Peter Murdoch, James's younger brother, brutally murdered Henry Ford staving in Ford's skull with an axe and disposing of his body in the Murrumbidgee River. He then went on a drunken shanty spree with the stolen pay cheque and was arrested at the Barmedman Station. Murdoch was also suspected of involvement in another brutal murder, as many of the details mirrored the bashing death of Henry Ford. There was a stronger suspicion he was responsible for the disappearance several years before of a *half caste woman* with whom *he was on intimate terms* at Barmedman. She disappeared in suspicious circumstances and her body was never found.

On 3 October 1877, Peter Murdoch was convicted of murdering Henry Ford and sentenced to death. He had pleaded not guilty and said little throughout the trial. While awaiting execution, Murdoch tried to escape by lifting his cell door off its hinges and hiding in the prison kitchen. When told that he was not to be granted a reprieve, *he completely gave way falling to the floor of his cell and writhing most frightfully*. He refused to eat for the remaining days of his incarceration *brooding in silence over his impending doom.*

On 18 December 1877 at a few minutes past nine, Peter Murdoch *placed himself beneath the beam. He refused to make any statement. As the hangman withdrew to pull the bolt, he trembled violently on the drop. With a heavy fall the drop gave way and Murdock seems to have made a clutch at the rope, but it passed through his hands and he dropped about eight feet with the usual telling thud, the body giving two spasmodic jumps and not relaxing into silent death until 15 minutes after. After the body had been hanging for 20 minutes, it was cut down, placed in its coffin and conveyed almost immediately to the cemetery.*

Did Ned intentionally name the wrong Murdoch brother to make his Jerilderie Letter claim of perjury seem more believable? He may have known Peter through his Greta shanty association with James and his horse and cattle stealing activity in New South Wales. But it was James who informed on him and he was not hanged in Wagga gaol.

References

McDermott Alex, *Ned Kelly: The Jerilderie Letter* (2001), p 15.

Morris Sherry, *Wagga Wagga Thrillers* (2000), pp. 37-43.

Australian List of Executions 1870 to 1967, 18 December 1877. www.capitalpunishmentuk.org/aus1900

Murdoch family history information, Ancestry.com.au; The Monaro Pioneers Project: Pioneers and Settlers Database. wc.rootsweb.ancestry.com/cgi-bin/igm.cgi?db=monaropioneers

New South Wales Police Gazette, 3, 31 August 1870, 4 October 1871, 25 March 1874, 8 December 1875.

The Australian Town and Country Journal, 24, 31 March, 13 October, 8, 22, 29 December 1877.

The Maitland Mercury and Hunter River General Advertiser, 29 March, 27 December 1877.

The Sydney Morning Herald, 3 April, 11, 25 October, 27 December 1877.

The Wagga Wagga Advertiser, 4, 18 April, 17, 28 March 1877.

James Murdoch, Prisoner No. 10634, Central Register of Male Prisoners, volume 16, p. 486, 1872.

North Eastern Ensign, 7 January 1873.

Ovens and Murray Advertiser, 9 January 1873.

Victoria Police Gazette, 11 May 1875.

North Eastern Ensign, 2 September, 3, 7, 14 October 1884.

Appendix II

The Diseased Stock Agent

The identity of the Diseased Stock Agent is a conundrum that rarely gets mentioned in the Kelly literature. This most famous of police spies was said to be an educated and professional man, with access to local rumour and more substantial information concerning the doings of the Kelly Gang and its supporters. He was almost certainly Daniel Kennedy who at different times was the Greta schoolmaster, the manager of his sister-in-law's Greta Pub and a Glenrowan selector. He knew all the parents of his pupils, those who drank at O'Brien's pub and those who didn't and he farmed alongside many of them, the respectable as well as the disreputable. In a word he was the perfect police spy, respected and trusted by all.

Daniel Kennedy was born at Mangalore in February 1843. His impoverished Irish parents Michael and Margaret Kennedy had arrived in Australia from King's County (Offaly) as bounty migrants two years before. For a time they were employed as bonded servants on the Mangalore squatting run. Throughout the 1850s and into the early 1860s the family lived on rented land in the Seymour-Kilmore area, probably working the land as small farmers. In the mid 1860s, the Kennedy family took up land in Greta with 22 year old Daniel working on his father's selection or following some other kind of employment until he could enter the teaching profession.

In December 1867, Daniel took charge of the Greta Catholic School. Although unhappy with the unsuitable schoolroom, rented from Ned's relatives the Lloyds and located next to the family's pigsty and chicken coup, the Board of Education provided financial support because *if aid be withheld then about 30 children will be allowed to grow up in utter ignorance, for the parents belong to a very low class and cannot possibly instruct their families, nor do they set much value on education at all.*

Following the Greta school's closure in September 1870 due to poor attendance and a lack of interest from the parents, Kennedy transferred to Catholic schools at Boorhaman and later Benalla. In 1874, Kennedy and his wife Julia Conway a teaching assistant whom he had married in April 1869 left teaching to assist Julia's sister Bridget, the widow of Greta publican Laurence O'Brien. Kennedy became manager of his sister-in-law's pub and store. During the Kelly outbreak, Daniel grew tired of managing Bridget O'Brien's affairs and selected 300 acres at Glenrowan. In doing so he made an arch enemy of prominent Kelly sympathiser Henry McAuliffe, who felt himself deprived of water access by Kennedy's selection application. McAuliffe's objection was dismissed as vexatious and Kennedy's application was granted.

Daniel was a law-abiding citizen, who disapproved of the Kellys' horse and cattle stealing ways. During his time as a Greta publican, storekeeper and later Glenrowan selector, Kennedy occupied a unique position in the local community, which enabled him to pass onto the police gossip, rumours and factual information concerning the activities of the Kellys and their friends. His reputation as a teacher gave him a professional standing in both communities and he was frequently called upon to play a leading role in community affairs. Among other duties, he was the Electoral Registrar for Greta and the Deputy Returning Officer for elections. In July 1880, following

Thomas Curnow's removal to Ballarat in wake of the Kelly Gang's demise, Kennedy was appointed with a recommendation from the Police Department to take charge of the Glenrowan School. He retained possession of his Glenrowan selection and continued to farm his property in addition to carrying out his teaching duties.

While there is little doubt that Kennedy gave information to the police concerning the whereabouts of the outlaws, his identity as a police spy is difficult to establish with certainty. Police agents were given nom de plumes as a precaution against accidental discovery. In a letter to Sergeant Whelan written during the Police Commission, Acting Police Commissioner Chomley refers to Kennedy as special agent Denny. But given Kennedy's respectable position and professional standing in the Greta and Glenrowan communities, which are mentioned in connection with the Diseased Stock Agent, his real pseudonym may well have been Diseased Stock rather than Denny. There is, however, a difficulty in identifying Kennedy too closely with the famous police spy. Superintendent Sadleir mentions Sergeant Whelan as the person who first brought the future Diseased Stock Agent to the notice of the Benalla Police. Presumably, Whelan, who knew the identity of the famous agent, would have corrected Acting Commissioner Chomley's reference to Kennedy as special agent Denny, if Kennedy's police pseudonym really was that of Diseased Stock. Whelan may well have informed Chomley of his error, while he was in Melbourne attending the Police Commission or perhaps the reference was simply overlooked and the matter forgotten.

Whether or not Daniel Kennedy was the Diseased Stock Agent or simply special agent Denny, he gained his appointment to the Glenrowan School as Curnow's successor by the use of police influence. In the months following Ned's hanging and the rash of disclosures made by the Police Commission concerning the identities of those who had assisted the police, the Kelly sympathisers conducted their own vendetta to seek out and punish suspected police informers. Kennedy grew increasingly worried that the Kelly sympathisers would discover his past role as a police spy and take revenge against his family. In February 1882, although he was prospering as a selector due to his teacher's additional income, Kennedy wrote to the Education Department requesting a transfer *to some other part of the colony, for I fear bodily harm may be done to me at Glenrowan.* Some months later, his request became more urgent *in consequence of a threat being made on my life.* At the same time, Kennedy wrote to Inspector Montfort pleading with him not to divulge the particulars of his appointment to the Glenrowan School. *I was appointed in July 1880 and should it be made public that Police influence secured my present position, certain revenge would follow.*

By May, Kennedy felt his position had reached breaking point. *In consequence of a threat having been made on my life, I am suffering from severe nervous shock and was compelled to close the school yesterday at noon and seek medical advice.* Montfort valued Kennedy's past services highly. In a memo to the Police Commissioner, Montfort wrote *he deserves everything the Police can do for him.* Much to his own relief and to the regret of the local community who regarded him as *a very efficient teacher and a gentleman*, Kennedy sold his Glenrowan property and was granted a transfer to a school near Winchelsea.

Daniel Kennedy using the pseudonym *B.C. Williams* (a fictitious name associated with the Diseased Stock alias) with several recommendations from senior policemen applied for and was denied a portion of the Kelly Reward. In support of Kennedy's application Superintendent Hare wrote that he was *an honest and respectable man one of the most reliable of police agents I knew employed by the police.* Kennedy is by far the most likely candidate to be the Diseased Stock Agent and we should regard him as such.

References

Pryor Len, "The Diseased Stock Agent", *Victorian Historical Journal*, December 1990, pp. 243-269.

Correspondence between the author and Len Pryor between August 1984 and October 1988.

Glenrowan School No. 1742 Building File. PRO.

Greta School No. 921 Building File. PRO.

Inspector Geary to Education Board, 15 August 1867. PRO.

Kennedy Daniel, Glenrowan Land File 10956/19.20. PRO.

Kennedy to Brown Secretary of Lands, 17 May 1882. PRO.

Kennedy to Inspector Montfort, 22 May 1882. PRO.

Montfort to Chomley the Police Commissioner, 20 May 1882. PRO.

Appendix III

Superintendent Hare's Wound at Glenrowan

Superintendent Francis Hare has been unfairly branded a coward for leaving the Glenrowan siege after receiving a minor wrist wound. This medical assessment of Hare's wound is based on a brief telegram Superintendent Sadleir sent to Sergeant Steele in Wangaratta: *Hare just arrived* [in Benalla] *not seriously injured.* Sadleir had seen Hare conscious and talking as he was about to hurriedly depart for Glenrowan and he wrongly assumed that Hare's wound was not serious. Hare was not a coward; his wrist wound was life-threatening and if it had not been attended to quickly by a doctor he may well have died. Ned would later tell a Pentridge inmate *I wish the bullet had struck him two inches lower* causing him a fatal wound, mistaking the location but not the seriousness of Hare's wrist wound.

Superintendent Hare was shot through the left wrist by Ned immediately the fighting began. With blood pouring from his wound, he withdraw to the railway station seeking assistance to stem the flow. On regaining the safety of the station, Hare continued to issue orders, with his left arm *helpless* beside him, blood covering his left trouser leg and a makeshift bandage on his still-bleeding wound. Suddenly, he staggered and fell forward in a faint calling out loudly for someone to catch him. *I had no idea how serious my wound was,* he later said. All of his attention was focused on preventing the escape of the Kelly Gang from Jones's pub. Regaining his senses, Hare brushed aside the concern of those around him and made an adrenalin-fuelled attempt to rejoin his men who were creating a cordon around the pub. He remained with them for around fifteen minutes. *I began to feel very faint and dizzy; I was bleeding fearfully, a bullet had entered at one side of my wrist and gone out at the other and feeling that I was losing large quantities of blood, I returned to the railway platform.* He collapsed to his knees, fainted again and was carried to a railway carriage, where those present feared for his life.

On being revived Hare, who was *staggering, getting very weak and faint from loss of blood* and experiencing bouts of nausea and occasional loss of consciousness, allowed himself to be persuaded to return to Benalla for police reinforcements, extra ammunition and the urgent medical treatment he so clearly required. *For God's sake, Rawlins,* he had said to Charles Rawlins as he fainted again: *Send me back to Benalla!* Hare delegated battlefield command to Sub Inspector O'Connor and Constable Kelly before dazed, bewildered and *with the blood still flowing* from his arm, he reluctantly boarded the steam engine that would take him and the sensational news of the Glenrowan encounter with the Kelly Gang back to Benalla.

Upon his arrival in Benalla, Hare went straight to the telegraph office and sent for the doctor to meet him there. *When I got to the Telegraph office I was much exhausted. I sent messages to all surrounding* [police] *stations and just as I had finished the Doctor came in. He took the handkerchief off my arm and said I was bleeding from an artery. I asked him to attend to it at once as I wished to return to Glenrowan. I said I was determined to go back. I remember their pulling a mattress on to the floor of the telegraph office and my lying on* [it] *and then I fainted away and continued unconscious for some time. When I recovered consciousness I felt terribly weak and could scarcely stand. I was assisted to my hotel and went to bed.*

Hare's path back to health was a drawn-out and perilous affair.

His wound required constant medical attention; it remained extremely painful, and was slow to heal. He recuperated at the Rupertswood farming property of his wife's relatives, the Clarkes, and was under the medical care of his cousin Dr Charles Ryan, a former military surgeon and gunshot specialist who had treated Ned's wounds at Glenrowan and was still attending him at the Melbourne Gaol. Whilst there, he became gravely ill and almost died as a consequence of contracting Erysipelas, a severe bacterial infection which ulcerated his still unhealed wound and was accompanied by fever, chills, headaches and vomiting.

A long period of convalescence followed; Hare eventually recovered his health, although his severely injured wrist was to bother him for the rest of his life. He subsequently received a government annuity as compensation for the serious wound he had sustained at Glenrowan and he left the police force soon after.

References

Clarke Michael, *Clarke of Rupertswood* (1995), pp. 59-60, 297.

Hare Francis, *The Last of the Bushrangers* (1892), pp. 271-273.

Shaw Ian, *Glenrowan* (2012), p. 160.

Royal Commission on the Police Force of Victoria (1881), Q 1503-1515, pp. 86-89.

Appendix IV

The Makers of the Modern Kelly Myth

Peter Carey, *True History of the Kelly Gang*, University of Queensland Press, 2000.

Peter Fitzsimons, *Ned Kelly: The Story Of Australia's Most Notorious Legend*, William Heinemann, 2013.

Ian Jones, *Ned Kelly: a short life*, Lothian Books, 2003.

John McQuilton, *The Kelly Outbreak 1878-1880: The Geographical Dimension Of Social Banditry*, Melbourne University Press, 1979.

John Molony, *I am Ned Kelly*, Allen Lane, 1980.

Ian Jones is the best-known of the myth-makers and, despite his lack of academic credentials, is regarded in some quarters as *the best bloody historian there ever was*. For his biography of Ned, Jones randomly mined the 1881 Police Commission evidence and depicted Ned as a selector champion and proto-revolutionary hero, planning to establish a Republic of North East Victoria. He gave readers the dramatic excitement of Ned's Glenrowan rebellion; thrilling them with mysterious skyrockets and over-stated tales of armed men *not the police* riding through the hills surrounding the besieged township.

With no examination of the community in which they lived, Jones accepts the Kelly Gang as typical north-east selectors. He uncritically accepts Ned's Jerilderie Letter assessment of the Whitty and Byrne land empires, their impounding of selectors' livestock and their 'squatter' domination of land in and around Moyhu and Greta. As selectors, Ned's impoverished family is hemmed in by the district's squatters leaving Ned no choice but to rebel. In such repressive circumstances, horse and cattle theft and other agrarian crimes were an 'on the ground' reflection of a bitter land war and selector fight back against tyranny and police oppression. The community presented by Jones is completely polarised without relationship or behavioural nuance and on the verge of tearing itself apart.

Ned's misdeeds are exonerated and forgiven by Jones; Ned is a criminal in name only, harassed by the police persecution of his family into taking up a gun and defending himself. It was they and not he who were to blame for everything wrong in Ned's life; he had no choice but to resist and *seek revenge for the name and character which has been given me and my relations, while God give me strength to pull a trigger.* Jones excuses as legitimate selector rebellion Ned's professional horse and cattle stealing, a dishonest profession, which had little to do with class conflict and was bragged about by Ned in the Jerilderie Letter where he berated the police for not catching him.

Jones was following in the footsteps of previous popular Kelly authors J.J. Kenneally, Max Brown and Frank Clune, who presented a highly romanticised view of the bushranger's life. Jones's interpretation went further turning Ned into a powerful political force for radical change, transcending his previous role as a bushranger and making him into something he clearly was not, a revolutionary hero fighting for the usurped rights of impoverished selectors. Jones's work has influenced a new generation of Kelly-philes, who unabashedly glorify Ned's memory and give a false legitimacy to the Kelly myth.

In the late 1970s, historian John McQuilton embraced Jones's work adding a more complex dimension of land war and social banditry to explain the Kelly outbreak. According to McQuilton, Ned was not a political revolutionary per se; he was a social bandit, a surrogate leader of the selector class. McQuilton paints a highly contentious picture of the north-east as wracked with community division and political dissent, experiencing a *rural malaise* and a *culture of poverty* in which selectors felt themselves dispossessed and powerless. Ned steps in as a Clayton's leader, the leader you have when there is no other leader available. The malaise and poverty arguments fall apart when assessed in light of the high farming success rate in Greta and Moyhu, 79% and 84% respectively; these were the selectors who stayed the course of the selection process to gain freehold title to their selections. There were tough times to be sure, but nothing resembling widespread selector poverty or rural melancholy was present as McQuilton would have us believe.

McQuilton interprets the Kelly source material according to the dictates of Eric Hobsbawm's social bandit thesis, which was an academic fashion of its time but now seems rather antiquated. Bushrangers and criminals are generally not the harbingers of social and political justice to impoverished peasants and selectors, unless of course there is something tangible in it for them. Usually it is about seeking to avoid police bullets and the gallows for their criminal misdeeds. Hobsbawm's thesis was too optimistic in its reading of rural revolts and McQuilton's acceptance of the same distorts the Kelly outbreak and misrepresents Ned's motivation and behaviour as a reckless bush larrikin engaged in criminal activity which led to bushranging and several murders. Outlaws adopt the mantle of working class and peasant hero, rarely is it thrust upon them by those they rob and terrorise, no matter how neatly packaged the academic theory may be.

McQuilton's analysis of the land war is no more convincing, for he fails to take into consideration that Whitty and Byrne were 'boss cocky' selectors (who acquired land by purchase before the Selection Acts and by selection when the acts became law) and were not squatters as he suggests. They engaged in a family cluster style of land settlement, which McQuilton mistakes for a squatter monopoly unfairly squeezing everybody else out. Whitty held the pastoral license of the Myrrhee run for a brief period of time only before its cancellation, when the run was no more than a mere rump version of itself. He was also in a two year business partnership with the Byrne family, leasing by tender forfeited Union Bank land. What did Whitty do during his brief tenure as a last-gasp pastoralist and entrepreneur lessee of bank land? He leased out grazing rights to other selectors, who were just as protective of their rented grass as Whitty himself. There was no squatter conspiracy, as McQuilton suggests, to dominate the land at Moyhu or Greta. There was no attempt by either the Whitty or Byrne families to deliberately disrupt the land selection process by keeping selectors from selecting. Ned criticises Whitty and Byrne because of the extent of their family landholdings and for their use of the usual impounding practice. Ned more likely disliked them, because he was jealous of their success as farmers and in their position he and his family would have acted in precisely the same manner.

McQuilton denigrates and mocks the police, presenting them as squatters' men intent only on protecting the property and interests of the squatter class. Every policeman from Fitzpatrick to Flood, Hall and Steele, he castigates as Kelly enemies seeking an opportunity to fit up Ned and his family. He says nothing about Fitzpatrick's friendly larrikin relationship with Ned, except to describe Fitzpatrick as *a liar and a larrikin*. Flood is the seducer of Ned's sister Annie, while Hall is Ned's Greta nemesis. Steele is criticised as a reckless policeman, who at Glenrowan shot at Mrs Reardon and her infant baby and brought Ned down with a shotgun blast to his legs.

McQuilton's social bandit assessment of the Kelly outbreak, and his misinterpretation of the land war, are the shonky foundations upon which successive Kelly writers have built their edifices ever since.

John Molony, writing in 1980, blended poetic imagination with historical fact and wrote about Ned in heroic terms emphasising his Irish heritage and native-born larrikinism. In Molony's creative hands Ned emerges, yet again, as an impoverished selector's son harassed by the police and never given a fair go by anybody else. Molony's book was history but history written with romantic admiration based on the formulas of Jones and McQuilton. It put a more humanly recognisable face to Ned, was mesmerising and exciting to read, but ended up mired in the same old imaginings of the Kelly Myth.

As a novelist Peter Carey made no pretence at historical objectivity, although subtly and not so subtly his work on Ned pretends to offer a true history of the Kelly Gang, clearly associating itself with J.J. Kenneally's earlier fiercely partisan *Inner History of the Kelly Gang*. Both works loosely play with historical fact shrouding the past in myth and imaginative reconstruction, making it difficult to tell where imagination begins and fact ends. Carey's novel is all the more insidious, for it appears to be based on documentary evidence which in fact is bogus. The novel is presented as being closer to the truth than the truth itself, but it is in truth no more than a novel.

The latest Kelly biographer is journalist Peter Fitzsimons, whose *Ned Kelly: The Story Of Australia's Most Notorious Legend* appears to be a weighty tome extensively researched. In fact Fitzsimons has written yet another Kelly book that is pure fantasy, misleading his readers at every point of Ned's dramatic story. His novelistic style of writing enables him to distort Ned's behaviour, while pretending *to get inside* an event and plumb the depths of psychological meaning and emotional trauma present. His Ned Kelly story not only reads like a novel; it is a novel with distorted historical fact and copious footnotes added to give verisimilitude.

Fitzsimons makes no apology for presenting Ned as the acclaimed bushranging hero and would-be saviour of the downtrodden selector farmer. He makes this the predominant metaphor of the Kelly outbreak and the principal reason why selectors supported Ned's bushranging rebellion. He makes no distinction between the small band of active Kelly sympathisers and the majority of selectors who prudently kept out of the way of the Kelly Gang and the police. The Kelly family emerge from Fitzsimons lengthy book as the quintessential, hard-pressed, poverty-ridden selector family of popular myth. As in the works of Jones and McQuilton, they engage in horse and cattle theft and other agrarian crime as a rebellious response to squatter oppression and police harassment. They were as Ned so often claimed in his public pronouncements, and echoed by Fitzsimons throughout his book, driven to a life of crime through no fault of their own. The police Fitzsimons calls *the bastard police*, who thoroughly deserve the occasional thrashing they receive at Ned's avenging hands.

While this makes for exciting reading and gives the reader a vicarious thrill at Ned's noble fight for freedom, none of it stands up to critical analysis any more than the previous works. The land war has again been grossly exaggerated and made a convenient excuse for Ned's criminal excesses, which far from being sympathised with by the majority of selectors was something they abhorred. Fitzsimons fails to make this crucial distinction and rolls selector grievances, which were not nearly as divisive as he accepts, into one neatly-packaged bundle of Kelly Gang grievances.

The Kellys were not typical selectors; they were notorious horse and cattle thieves belonging to an extensive criminal network, using their selections and in some cases 'bent' squatting runs for livestock stealing purposes. Fitzsimons tarnishes all of the region's selectors with the wide brush of criminality and livestock theft. He simply ignores the respectability of most selectors, preferring to see them as Kelly associates and criminals in their own right. Even a cursory examination of the Greta community reveals the basic decency and honesty of the majority of selectors, who feared rather than sympathised with Ned and his predatory Greta Mob of larrikin livestock thieves. They simply had no truck with the local toughs who stole their farm animals and terrorised the neighbourhood.

In all Ned's confrontations, Fitzsimons unreservedly takes Ned's side. His account of the McCormick Affair, where Ned wilfully rode his horse over a Greta hawker in a bitter dispute over the illegal use of a cart horse, misrepresents what happened. Fitzsimons portrays Ned as a brave teenager, heroically defending himself against the unwarranted aggression of an adult intent on giving him a beating. The truth however is far less flattering to Ned, who was the instigator of the incident sending McCormick's wife an indecent note and challenging her husband to fight when he took offence. He does the same with every other major and minor Kelly Gang event from the Stringybark Creek police murders, where he blames the police rather than the Kelly Gang for what happened, to the Glenrowan pub siege where Ned's murderous plan to derail a police train and massacre its passengers is excused as legitimate warfare rather than the terrorist act it was.

At Stringybark, Fitzsimons accepts Ned's insistence that the police were heavily armed and came into the bush to shoot him down. He tells us: *for there, inside the* [police] *tent, is stored a rifle, a shotgun with thirty-*

six shells, breach loading shotguns and so much ammunition it is dizzying. This is nonsense; the police carried their regular service revolvers with some extra ammunition and two borrowed rifles, one an old fowling piece and the other a Spencer repeating rifle that none of them knew how to use properly. There was no over-the-top arsenal of weapons or a *dizzying* amount of ammunition. Any more than there was a sinister police intention to shoot rather than arrest the fugitive Kelly brothers. Whatever amount of ammunition there was at Stringybark Creek was stolen by the Kellys and used against Scanlan and Kennedy in place of their home-made bullets.

According to Fitzsimons, the new house Ned built for his mother with the proceeds of livestock theft was something of a bush marvel. *The outside walls of the new house are carefully crafted slabs of bark that fit neatly together, with bark on the interior to give insulation. A veranda provides somewhere shady to sit, while the interior is divided into one large room for the kitchen and living room, boasting an expertly built enormous fireplace, and three bedrooms. Most impressive is that the hut has real interior walls. No more hessian or partitions.* Constable Fitzpatrick, who visited the new house, describes at least one of Ned's bullets lodging *in a bark partition. I know that* [because] *the first shot fired at me grazed the bark behind my back and lodged in it.* He said that when he returned to the Kelly house sometime later to find the piece of partition bark it had been replaced. It is evident from Fitzpatrick's remark that the Kellys new house was not the grand affair described by Fitzsimons and was still divided by partitions. Fitzsimons, who gives sources for the information in his book, gives no reference for his description of the new house so it seems to be the work of his imagination.

There are many other occasions when Fitzsimons allows his imagination to run away with him. He writes of George Devine, the policeman held prisoner by the Kelly Gang during the Jerilderie raid and who did not pursue them afterwards: *George Devine had an even better idea. He decides to go to bed instead, where at his wife's insistence he remains for several days.* The implication is one of police cowardice, when in reality Devine was suffering from a severe rupture injury sustained before the Kelly Gang raid. Fitzsimons should have been aware of this as he follows Ian Jones's work closely where it is clearly mentioned.

Fitzsimons book adds nothing new to Ned Kelly studies. A reader expecting to gain some insight into the Kelly outbreak and the emotional and psychological life of the participants will be sadly disappointed. Fitzsimons offers up the same old clichés and metaphors as Jones and McQuilton. While the story they tell is dramatic, exciting and the stuff of national myth, it not truthful history and should not be portrayed as such. Fitzsimons is a better journalist than he is a skilled historian and like many Kelly authors seeking to identify themselves with Ned's criminal celebrity, he would have found himself culturally and socially no match for the cunning of the bush larrikin and bushranger he writes about so admiringly. Ned knew how to manipulate the journalists he encountered; Fitzsimons has proven himself to be equally susceptible.

Appendix V

The Jerilderie Letter Annotated

The Jerilderie Letter is an expanded version of the earlier Cameron Letter sent to Donald Cameron MP at the time of the Euroa bank robbery. Ned wanted to have it printed and distributed as a pamphlet during the Jerilderie bank raid but failed to capture Samuel Gill the newspaper proprietor. Although it was written 16 months before his capture at Glenrowan, the letter today is regarded as the principal source of Ned's defence of his life as a horse thief and bushranger. It covers 56 pages containing around 8,000 words in one continuous rambling monologue with poor grammar, numerous spelling mistakes and almost no punctuation. Only parts of 'Ned Kelly's Letter' as it was called were published during Ned's lifetime. It was published in full as 'Kelly's Manifesto' in a 1930 newspaper serialisation 'The Kellys Are Out!' and as 'The Jerilderie Letter' in Max Brown's 1948 Kelly biography *Australian Son*. The original manuscript is in the State Library of Victoria. Two copies were made and can be found in the Victorian Public Records Office and the National Museum of Australia. This version is a precise rendering of the original Jerilderie Letter.

* * * * *

Annotations

1 Ned's brother Jim was working for Gould and his employer resented the McCormick's intrusion into his hawking territory. J.J. Kenneally's account gathered from Ned's cousin Tom Lloyd states Ned found McCormick's horse and used it to pull Gould's wagon out of the mud. In all likelihood, Ned or one of his family took the horse for just this task and later returned it minus its blanket. Ned took pleasure in taunting McCormick, saying he knew where the blanket was. Ned wrote the indecent note and gave it and a parcel of calf testicles to his cousin Tom to deliver. The note suggested that McCormick use the contents *to better shag* his wife the next time. Gould was at the centre of this incident and may have been the brains behind it.

2 Ben Gould was an ex-convict from Tasmania, ready as his convict record states *to join in riot and disorder*. He was sent to Port Arthur and Norfolk Island as punishment for his bad behaviour. During the Kelly outbreak, Gould was arrested suspected of assisting the Kelly Gang during the Euroa bank robbery. He said of the Stringybark police murders: *it served the bastards right, there will be more of them shot before Kelly is caught*. In May 1881, Gould was found guilty of arson and received a 12 months gaol sentence. That Gould should befriend the Kellys and set up his hawker's camp near their shanty, employing young Jim Kelly as his assistant, is entirely consistent with his criminal background and shady activities.

3 It is accepted by most scholars that Ned was born in December 1854. That would mean he was 15 years and 10 months old at this time.

Dear Sir

I wish to acquaint you with some of the occurrences of the present past and future, In or about the spring of 1870 the ground was very soft a hawker named Mr Gould got his waggon bogged between Greta and my mother's house on the eleven mile creek, the ground was that rotten it would bog a duck in places so Mr. Gould had abandon his waggon for fear of loosing his horses in the spewy ground. he was stopping at my Mother's awaiting finer or dryer weather Mr McCormack and his wife. hawkers also, were camped in Greta the mosquitoes were very bad which they generally are in a wet spring and to help them Mr John had a horse called Ruita Cruta, although a gelding was as clever as old Wombat or any other Stallion at running horses away and taking them on his beat which was from Greta swamp to the seven mile creek consequently he enticed McCormack's horse away from Greta. Mr Gould was up early feeding his horses heard a bell and seen McCormack horse for he knew the horse well he sent his boy to take him back to Greta. When McCormack's got the horse they came straight out to Goold and accused him of working the horse; this was false and Goold was amazed at the idea I could not help laughing to hear Mrs McCormack accusing him of using the horse after him being so kind as to send his boy to take him from the Ruta Cruta and take him back to them. I pleaded Goulds innocence and Mrs McCormack turned on me and accused me of bringing the horse from Greta to Goolds waggon to pull him out of the bog I did not say much to the woman as my mother was present but that same day me and my uncle was cutting calves Gould wrapped up a note and a pair of the calves testicles and gave them to me to give them to Mrs McCormack.[1] I did not see her and I gave the parcel to a boy to give to her when she would come instead of giving it to her he gave it to her husband consequently McCormack said he would summons me I told him neither me or Gould[2] used their horse. he said I was a liar & he could welt me or any of my breed I was about 14 years of age[3] but

4   Ned's uncle John Lloyd gives the lie to his nephew's 'fist in the face' statement, when he testified he saw *Kelly try to ride over McCormick*. Ned had arrived at the McCormick's camp as the sun was setting intent on provoking them. He was aggressive and shouting insults and was clearly spoiling for a fight. He rode past the McCormicks saying: *I will ride my horse over you and kill the bloody lot of you, you bloody wretches!* At one point in the confrontation, Ned was wielding a stirrup-iron and called out to McCormick: *Come on you old bastard and fight me!*

5   It is Ned who is telling the lies. At the violent height of the argument, Kelly menacingly said to Catherine McCormick: *I have got your horse covered*, meaning the horse would be maliciously attacked or stolen. In consequence of Ned's threat her frightened husband told the court: *I had to sit up at night watching the horse with a loaded pistol.*

6   Both Jeremiah and Catherine McCormick were convicts. Jeremiah had served as a convict policeman in Tasmania before arriving in Victoria in the early 1850s. Catherine had been married before to another convict policeman in Tasmania. The pair were married (possibly a bigamous relationship) in Beechworth in 1856. There is no evidence that Jeremiah was responsible for Catherine's release, nor that he sought her out as a wife while she was still a convict. On the mainland, neither Jeremiah nor Catherine offended again. The McCormicks travelled Victoria and southern New South Wales as hawkers for many years before their confrontation with Ned and continued to do the same beyond the Kelly outbreak. Hatred of convict policemen ran deep with the Kellys and their rowdy ex-convict friend Ben Gould. Catherine McCormick never got over Ned's malicious behaviour and she gave information to the police on several occasions during the hunt for the Kelly Gang.

7   Ned reports here that he rode his own horse and took the Mansfield mare to Wangaratta, where he spent four days enjoying a larrikin's 'holiday'. Larrikins often rode stolen or borrowed horses about before disposing of them. By the time he returned to Greta to be confronted by Constable Hall, Ned was riding the Mansfield horse. He knew the horse was dishonestly acquired and he was thumbing his nose at Hall as he had earlier done to the Wangaratta police.

accepted the challenge and dismounting when Mrs McCormack struck my horse in the flank with a bullock's skin it jumped forward and my fist came in collision with McCormack's nose and caused him to loose his equillibrium and fall postrate[4] I tied up my horse to finish the battle but McCormack got up and ran to the Police camp, Constable Hall asked me what the row was about, I told him they accused me and Gould of using their horse and I hit him and I would do the same to him if he challenged me McCormack pulled me and swore their lies[5] against me. I was sentenced to three months for hitting him and three months for the parcel and bound to keep the peace for 12 months. Mrs McCormack gave good substantial evidence as she is well acquainted with that place called Tasmania better known as the Dervon or Vandiemans land. and McCormack being a Police man over the convicts and women being scarce released her from that land of bondage and tyranny, and they came to Victoria and are at present residents of Greta[6] and on the 29th of March I was released from prison and came home Wild Wright came to the Eleven Mile to see Mr Gunn stopped all night and lost his mare both him and me looked all day for her and could not get her Wright who was a stranger to me was in a hurry to get back to Mansfield and I gave him another mare and he told me if I found his mare to keep her until he brought mine back I was going to Wangaratta and seen the mare and I caught her and took her with me all the Police and Detective Berrill seen her as Martains girls used to ride her about the town during several days that I stopped at Petre Martains Star Hotel in Wangaratta,[7] She was a chestnut mare white face docked tail very remarkable branded (M) as plain as the hands on a town clock. The property of a Telegraph Master in Mansfield he lost her on the 6th gazetted her on the 12th of

8 The Mansfield mare was listed in the Police Gazette as a stolen animal on 25 April, more than a month later than Ned states. The fact that Ned was in Beechworth Gaol when Wild Wright took the horse is true; but that does not absolve Ned of guilt in receiving a stolen horse.

9 Hall had been trying to apprehend Ned for some time, but Ned would pretend not to see the policeman and gallop away. Hall's ruse to arrest Ned was necessary because the policeman knew Ned's reputation for using his fists and resisting arrest. He planned successfully to intercept Ned on the Greta Bridge and have him come to the police barracks to sign some papers. Ned was suspicious and difficult to persuade and when they reached the barracks wanted to sign the paperwork on horseback. When Hall insisted he go inside, Ned said *I will see you damned!* turning his horse away. Hall said to Kelly: *You are my prisoner for horse stealing and made a jump and caught him by the neck, but* [his] *coat, waistcoat and shirt all gave way*. Hall then caught him by the shoulder and pulled him off the horse.

10 Hall says that Ned sprang away and ran for the scrub across the road. Hall called on Kelly to stand and when he did not he fired at him three times. The gun did not work. Hall said he *presented the revolver straight at* [Ned's] *face and pulled the trigger* but gives no indication of the distance involved. Ned said he stood still when he *heard* the misfires and waited for Hall to close the gap between them. Unless Ned was running away backwards, he was not facing the policeman when the revolver was fired. If it happened as Hall reported, Ned would surely have said so to make the *shaking with fear* policeman look an even greater coward.

11 Ned was on a 12 months good behaviour bond as part of the McCormick conviction. As he assaulted Hall while resisting arrest, his sureties would have forfeited their bond money of £60.

March and I was a prisoner in Beechworth Gaol until the 29 of March therefore I could not have Stole the mare.[8] I was riding the mare through Greta Constable Hall came to me and said he wanted me to sign some papers that I did not sign at Beechworth concerning my bail bonds I thought it was the truth he said the papers was at the Barracks and I had no idea he wanted to arrest me or I would have quietly rode away instead of going to the Barracks. I was getting off when Hall caught hold of me[9] and thought to throw me but made a mistake and came on the broad of his back himself in the dust the mare galloped away. and instead of me putting my foot on Halls neck and taking his revolver and putting him in the lock up. I tried to catch the mare Hall got up and snapped three or four caps at me and would have shot me but the Colts patent refused.[10] This is well known in Greta Hall never told me he wanted to arrest me until after he tried to shoot me when I heard the caps snapping I stood until Hall came close he had me covered and was shaking with fear and I knew he would pull the trigger before he would be game to put his hand on me so I duped and jumped at him caught the revolver with one hand and Hall by the collar with the other. I dare not strike him or my sureties would loose the bond money[11] I used to trip him and let him take a mouthful of dust now and again as he was as helpless as a big guano after leaving a dead bullock or a horse. I kept throwing him in the dust until I got him across the street the very spot where Mrs O.Briens Hotel stands now the cellar was just dug then there was some brush fencing where the post and rail was taking down and on this I threw big cowardly Hall on his belly I straddled him and rooted both spurs onto his thighs he roared like a big calf attacked by dogs and shifted several yards of the fence I got his hands at the back of his neck and

12 Hall said when he heard the misfires, Ned rushed at him and tried to take his revolver. Ned took hold of the barrel but Hall kept hold of the stock and managed to wrench it off him. Hall then struck Kelly with the gun four or five times over the head trying to stun him. This seemed to have little effect except for the bloody wounds to Ned's head. The fight over the gun resumed with Kelly trying to turn the gun on Hall and Hall trying to turn it towards Kelly. Both were kick boxing and Ned bit Hall. Eventually they fell over a brush fence both still holding the gun. There was no humiliating spur raking, as Ned relates, just a head over heels tussle with Hall delivering a powerful box to Kelly's ear which stunned him. Two blacksmiths came up and, with the assistance of some passersby, Hall got Kelly to the lockup. Neither Hall's police superiors nor any of the onlookers complained about the severity of the beating and the misfiring pistol episode. Commissioner Standish simply remarked: *I think it is a very fortunate circumstance that Senior Constable Hall's pistol misfired.* Hall was not reprimanded for his actions, rather he was awarded £5 for arresting and gaining a conviction against Ned a rising young star in the Greta criminal community.

13 As Ned was 16 years old at this time, it is inconceivable that he could have defeated seven men. In the Cameron Letter, Ned exaggerates the number of men subduing him. He says: *at the time I was taken by Hall and his 14 assistants.*

14 Dr James Hester (not Hastings) of Wangaratta attended to both Ned and Hall's wounds. A fortnight later, on 1 May 1871, he died suddenly following a short illness.

15 Hall was alone at Greta and knowing the Greta Mob's lawlessness, he sent for reinforcements and a doctor from Wangaratta. Kelly's friends and relatives came around shouting, using wild language and threatening to take Ned out of the police camp. Darkness fell and Hall had a fire lit, so he could see the lockup door and the stable where the stolen horse was sheltered. Hall was on guard in the shadows for several hours waiting for reinforcements, which luckily arrived before a sufficiently strong mob could form. Extra police came from Benalla and Wangaratta.

tried to make him let the revolver go but he stuck to it like grim death to a dead volunteer[12] he called for assistance to a man named Cohen and Barnett, Lewis, Thompson, Jewitt two blacksmiths who was looking on I dare not strike any of them as I was bound to keep the peace or I could have spread those curs like dung in a paddock.[13] They got ropes tied my hands and feet and Hall beat me over the head with his six chambered colts revolver nine stitches were put in some of the cuts by Dr Hastings[14] And when Wild Wright and my mother came they could trace us across the street by the blood in the dust and which spoiled the lustre of the paint on the gate post of the Barracks Hall sent for more Police and Doctor Hastings[15] Next morning I was handcuffed a rope tied from them to my legs and to the seat of the cart and taken to Wangaratta. Hall was frightened I would throw him

16   It is doubtful that Constable Arthur laughed at Hall and it is understandable that Ned was tied in place, as Hall was taking no chance of Ned being rescued by his Greta Mob friends on the journey to Wangaratta. The stolen mare was also taken to Wangaratta and extraordinary measures were taken to make sure this evidence did not disappear.

17   The claim that Doctor Hester could prove Hall a perjurer is puzzling. Did Ned mean the doctor had overheard something about the ownership of the mare, or did he think that Hester could contribute evidence about the severity of injuries sustained in the fight with Hall?

18   Hall twice got into trouble for stretching the truth before a Police Magistrate. In January 1870 in the Eldorado district, he was overzealous in arresting a drunk who was mouthing off and resisting being taken into custody. The arrested man an ex-policeman later apologised saying: *he was drunk* [and] *very much regretted having offered such violent resistance to Constable Hall*. Hall had a bad relationship with Police Magistrate Wills and was censured from the bench for downplaying the amount of force he employed in the encounter. Wills described Hall *as too hot tempered* and unfairly recommended he be transferred to another district. A short time later, Hall was again in trouble; prompting Superintendent Wilson to write in Hall's police service record: *An intelligent and active Senior Constable well fitted for police duties, but in my opinion too confident in his own construction of the Victorian Statutes*. Hall was an effective policeman, who responded forcefully to offenders when carrying out arrests and he defended the same in court. Ned's 'tried for perjury' claim against the policeman was not serious nor was it regarded so by Hall's superiors. In May 1870 with Hall now in Greta, Superintendent Wilson commented: *I have a very high opinion of this man's activity and ability*. Hall had a successful policing career and, in 1889, he was promoted to the rank of Sub Inspector.

19   Ned was not innocent and neither were the other offenders Hall arrested.

20   There is no evidence that Hall was indebted to Greta Publican O'Brien and the subscription O'Brien collected, which amounted to 20 gold sovereigns, came from Greta's farmers as recognition of Hall's policing achievements. In comparative terms, this represents more than a year's rent (£16) for a selector farming 160 acres, half of the 320 acres permitted under the 1869 Land Act.

out of the cart so he tied me whilst Constable Arthur laughed at his cowardice for it was he who escorted me and Hall to Wangaratta.[16] I was tried and committed as Hall swore I claimed the mare the Doctor died or he would have proved Hall a perjurer[17] Hall has been tried several times for perjury[18] but got clear. as this is no crime in the Police force it is a credit to a Policeman to convict an innocent man[19] but any muff can pot a guilty one Halls character is well known about El Dorado and Snowy Creek and Hall was considerably in debt to Mr L. O.Brien and he was going to leave Greta Mr O.Brien seen no other chance of getting his money so there was a subscription collected for Hall[20] and with the aid of this money he got James Murdock who was recently hung in Wagga Wagga[21] to give false evidence against me but I was acquitted on the charge of horsestealing[22] and on Hall and Mur-

21 James Murdoch(k) was not hanged in Wagga Gaol.

22 Ned was originally arrested for horse stealing but never charged, tried or acquitted for it. The charge for which he was convicted was receiving.

23 Murdoch was Hall's informant and he told the court Ned had tried to recruit him to steal some horses. Ned said to Murdoch that the Mansfield horse he was riding would also be sold; in larrikin parlance he said *take up*, which meant sold on as a stolen animal. When Murdoch asked where the horse had come from Ned said she was *brought up from the Plenty* near Whittlesea and was as *right as old cheese;* that is stolen and not yet gazetted.

24 Ned did not steal or borrow the Mansfield horse but there is good reason to believe he knew the horse was 'lifted' from the moment the mare came into his possession. Ned had in all probability exchanged a horse of his own or bought the mare outright from Wild Wright. The story of Wright's stolen mare wandering in the bush, and Ned giving him a horse to return to Mansfield, was most likely concocted by Ned and his friends to hide the truth.

25 In September 1877, Dan and his cousin's Tom and John Lloyd faced court over a ruckus they caused at Davis Goodman's Winton store. Tom was also charged for manhandling Goodman's wife. Dan, Tom and John were fined and each given three months hard labour for damaging property. Tom was charged with assault with intent to rape and given an additional four months for common assault. Ned's Cameron Letter claim, *Goodman got four years for perjury concerning the same property,* tells us the Winton storekeeper went to gaol for lying about the cost of the goods and property damaged. This is untrue. Goodman was a recent bankrupt and Morris Unger a Melbourne creditor removed over £200 of goods from the Winton store several days before the Kelly/Lloyd fracas. Unger was convicted of defrauding Goodman's creditors and went to gaol for 18 months. Goodman's only role was acting under duress to assist Unger to remove the goods. Goodman may have been guilty of exaggerating the cost of the goods damaged in the fracas, but if he did no legal action was taken against him in the matter.

26 The Quinns Lloyds and Kellys went to the police on numerous occasions to settle their disputes. The fact that Ned did not take this opportunity to report the crime and take revenge on Flood for the childbirth death of his sister Annie points to the conclusion that the horses were 'lifted' to begin with or his relatives and friends were responsible for taking the animals or the whole story is a fabrication.

docks[23] evidence I was found guilty of receiving and got 3 years experience in Beechworth Pentridge's dungeons.[24] this is the only charge ever proved against me Therefore I can say I never was convicted of horse or cattle stealing My Brother Dan was never charged with assaulting a woman but he was sentenced to three months without the option of a fine and one month and two pounds fine for damaging property by Mr. Butler P.M.[25] a sentence that there is no law to uphold therefore the minister of Justice neglected his duty in that case, but there never was such a thing as justice in the English laws but any amount of injustice to be had. Out of over thirty head of the very best horses the land could produce I could only find one when I got my liberty. Constable Flood stole and sold the most of them[26] to the navvies on the Railway line one bay cob he stole and sold four different times the line was completed and the men all gone when I came out and Flood was shifted to Oxley. he carried on the same game there all the stray horses that was any time without an owner and not in the Police Gazette Flood used to claim He was doing a good trade

27 Ned's characterisation of Constable Flood, as equivalent only to himself in horse stealing, has no basis in fact. His version of Squatter Brown having Flood removed from Oxley for horse stealing is wrong. Flood became embroiled in an agistment argument between a fellow ex-policeman and Squatter Brown and he helped his former colleague remove his horse from Brown's paddock. Brown a Justice of the Peace and a vindictive and argumentative man with influence, took offence. He went after Flood, who was removed from the district to appease Brown, and he left Oxley without a blemish on his character.

28 George King was Ned's stepfather and with Ned established a fast track method of Greta Mob horse and cattle stealing in the mid 1870s. The pair bragged about their thieving and blamed the police for hounding them when they stole other people's horses. In February 1874, George married Ellen Kelly in the same month that Ned was released from gaol for receiving the Mansfield mare. They joined forces and terrorised the north-east district as professional stock thieves. In 1877 George disappeared from Greta at the time of the Baumgarten arrests, riding away it is said from his wife and young children as the police began to close in. Whatever happened to him, George King suddenly vanished; he was not heard from again and the Kellys never commented on his disappearance.

29 Is this a case of Ned's guilty conscience or sense of indignation coming to the fore? What horse and saddle he is referring to is not clear, but obviously the accusation still rankled him many years later.

30 Ned was in goal in February 1873 and was not released until 2 February 1874.

31 The 'wild bull' story could have been correct and James Whitty's bull was not involved. Ned is lying when he said he went straight for a few years. In 1876, Henry Lydeker brought a charge of stealing a mare and a foal against Ned, who only beat the rap because his livestock stealing uncle John Quinn had shady business dealings with Lydeker and criminal loyalties soon asserted themselves. There is no doubt that Ned and his cousin Tom Lloyd stole the animals.

32 Ned is being disingenuous here in blaming Whitty, Farrell and Byrne for his return to horse and cattle stealing. He needed no excuse to return to the trade for in truth, as the Lydeker theft proves, he never actually left it.

at Oxley until Mr Brown of the Laceby Station got him shifted as he was always running his horses about.[27] Flood is different to Sergeant Steel, Strachan, Hall and the most of Police as they have got to hire cads and if they fail the Police are quite helpless. But Flood can make a cheque single-handed. he is the greatest horsestealer with the exception of myself and George King[28] I know of. I never worked on a farm a horse and saddle was never traced to me[29] after leaving employment since February 1873[30] I worked as a faller at Mr J. Saunders and R Rules sawmills then for Heach and Dockendorf I never worked for less than two pound ten a week since I left Pentridge and in 1875 or 1876 I was overseer for Saunders and Rule. Bourkes water-holes sawmills in Victoria since then I was on the King river, during my stay there I ran in a wild bull which I gave to Lydicher a farmer he sold him to Carr a Publican and Butcher who killed him for beef. Sometime afterwards I was blamed for stealing this bull from James Whitty Boggy Creek I asked Whitty Oxley racecourse why he blamed me for stealing his bull he said he had found his bull and never blamed me, but his son-in-law Farrell told him he heard I sold the bull to Carr, not long afterwards I heard again I was blamed for stealing a mob of calves from Whitty and Farrell which I knew nothing about.[31] I began to think they wanted me to give them something to talk about. Therefore I started wholesale and retail horse and cattle dealing.[32] Whitty and Burns not being satisfied with all the picked land on the Boggy

33 Ned is, in a confused way, referring to Duffy certificates issued under the 1862 Land Act to compensate landowners, who had earlier paid more than £1 per acre at public auction for their properties. Duffy Certificates were valued at four shillings for every acre of land subsequently purchased. Certificates were traded enabling selectors and squatters alike to take up crown land beyond the maximum number of acres permitted by the Land Act. Ned is complaining about Whitty and Byrne using certificate land to graze their livestock 'free'. He may, however, simply mean Commons land which has nothing to do with land acquired by Duffy certificates and was land used by everybody to pasture their livestock. It is not clear precisely what Ned means here.

34 Heavy rent refers to the Moyhu land Whitty and Byrne temporarily leased from the Union Bank in 1877 and again in 1879. The land was forfeited by Hugh Glass to the bank as mortgagee. Glass was a Melbourne-based entrepreneur who purchased huge tracts of land, employing dummies and using borrowed money. In 1878, the bank tried to sell a portion of the Glass property which covered some of the land parish of Moyhu. When they failed to sell it all, they leased the remainder as grazing land for a year at a time. Whitty and Byrne used the land they leased together to run their own livestock and to lease out grazing rights to other selectors. To provide for his growing family's grazing needs, Whitty separately took up the pastoral licence to a small part of the Myrrhee run from 1877 to 1881 just before the licence was cancelled.

35 Like everybody else, poor farmers running stock on this land were trespassing. But they were entitled to pasture their animals on Commons land and were not hemmed in or unable to keep livestock as Ned implies.

36 Whitty and Byrne impounded wandering livestock, though it is doubtful they did so in the exaggerated numbers claimed by Ned. Impoundings rarely went into double figures and when they did selectors were as guilty as squatters in driving wandering animals to the pound. Ned's emotive image of dirt poor farmers, leaving their work with little money to redeem impounded animals, was just as applicable to livestock impounded by his own relatives and friends, as it was to Whitty and Byrne.

Creek and King River and the run of their stock on the certificate³³ ground free and no one inter fering with them. paid heavy rent³⁴ to the banks for all the open ground so as a poor man could keep no stock,³⁵ and impounded every beast they could get, even off Government roads. If a poor man happened to leave his horse or bit of a poddy calf outside his paddock they would be impounded. I have known over 60 head of horses impounded in one day by Whitty and Burns all belonging to poor farmers they would have to leave their ploughing or harvest or other employment to go to Oxley. when they would get there perhaps not have money enough to release them and have to give a bill of sale or borrow the money which is no easy matter.³⁶ And along with this sort of work, Farrell the Policeman stole a

37 There is no proof of this statement and, if true, Michael Farrell the policeman, the brother of Whitty's son-in-law John Farrell, must have been a pretty dumb horse thief to hide a stolen horse on his relatives' Moyhu property in plain sight of Ned and his livestock stealing friends.

38 Eleven horses were stolen, not just from Whitty and Farrell but from Moyhu selector Jeffrey. Two months later, Ned and his mates stole several horses from Greta selectors Smith and McDonald.

39 In 1877, the Baumgarten horse stealing case lifted the lid on Ned and George King's Greta Mob livestock stealing operation. The Baumgarten brothers, and the others named, were receivers and their selections safe havens in the Greta Mob's intercolonial network of horse and cattle thieves. The police and the public glimpsed, for the first time, the highly organised nature of professional livestock theft in the region. Ned is trying his best here to shield his associates, as he did at Stringybark Creek, by taking the blame with his now disappeared stepfather George King for the Moyhu and Greta stock thefts. It was the arrest warrant for this crime that set Ned on the downward spiral to murder and bushranging.

40 Ned is mockingly portraying himself as the saviour of the police during the Berry government's 1878 Black Wednesday public service cutbacks. Priding himself on providing his old enemy with *double pay* and *good employment* after he was declared an outlaw.

41 Ned's colonial stratagem became his grisly plan to massacre a train-load of police and civilians.

horse from George King and had him in Whitty and Farrells Paddocks until he left the force[37] and all this was the cause of me and my step-father George King taking their horses[38] and selling them to Baumgarten and Kennedy. the pick of them was taken to a good market and the culls were kept in Petersons paddock and their brands altered by me two was sold to Kennedy and the rest to Baumgarten[39] who were strangers to me and I believe honest men. They paid me full value for the horses and could not have known they were stolen. no person had anything to do with the stealing and selling of the horses but me and George King. William Cooke who was convicted for Whittys horses was innocent he was not in my company at Petersons. But it is not the place of the Police to convict guilty men as it is by them they get their living had the right parties been convicted it would have been a bad job for the Police as Berry would have sacked a great many of them only I came to their aid and kept them in their bilits and good employment and got them double pay[40] and yet the ungrateful articles convicted my mother and an infant my brother-in-law and another man who was innocent and still annoy my brothers and sisters and the ignorant unicorns even threaten to shoot myself But as soon as I am dead they will be heels up in the muroo. There will be no more police required they will be sacked and supplanted by soldiers on low pay in the towns and special constables made of some of the farmers to make up for this double pay and expence. It will pay Government to give those people who are suffering innocence, justice and liberty. if not I will be compelled to show some colonial stratagem[41] which will open the eyes of not only the Victorian Police and inhabitants but also the whole British army and now doubt they will acknowledge their hounds were barking at the wrong stump. and that Fitzpatrick will be the cause of greater slaughter to the Union Jack than Saint Patrick was to the snakes and toads in Ireland. The

42 A warrant was out for Ned for stealing Whitty's horses and those belonging to other selectors; a short time later a similar warrant was issued for Dan's arrest.

43 Fitzpatrick says, while he was speaking to Williamson, two riders entered through the sliprail into the Kellys' homestead paddock. He identified one as Skillion whom he spoke to and the other as Dan who had entered the shanty. No horse dealer was present. Skillion was one of the accused and his defence was that he was not present. Ned wants to discredit Fitzpatrick and support the defence argument.

44 There may have been other witnesses to the shanty wounding whom Fitzpatrick did not see; however as the defence failed to call these witnesses it is doubtful that they existed.

45 Fitzpatrick was sent to Greta to relieve Strahan not Steele.

46 None of those present claim the policeman drew his revolver and threatened to shoot Ned's mother Ellen. The allegation was not raised at the trial and only surfaced when Ned raised it here.

Queen of England was as guilty as Baumgarten and Kennedy Williamson and Skillion of what they were convicted for When the horses were found on the Murray River I wrote a letter to Mr Swanhill of Lake Rowan to acquaint the Auctioneer and to advertize my horses for sale I brought some of them to that place but did not sell I sold some of them in Benalla Melbourne and other places and left the colony and became a rambling gambler soon after I left there was a warrant for me and the Police searched the place and watched night and day for two or three weeks and when they could not snare me they got a warrant against my brother Dan[42] And on the 15 of April Fitzpatrick came to the Eleven Mile Creek to arrest him he had some conversation with a horse dealer whom he swore was William Skillion this man was not called in Beechworth,[43] besides several other Witnesses,[44] who alone could have proved Fitzpatricks falsehood after leaving this man he went to the house asked was Dan in Dan came out. I hear previous to this Fitzpatrick had some conversation with Williamson on the hill. he asked Dan to come to Greta with him as he had a warrant for him for stealing Whitty's horses Dan said all right they both went inside Dan was having something to eat his mother asked Fitzpatrick what he wanted Dan for. the trooper said he had a warrant for him Dan then asked him to produce it he said it was only a telegram sent from Chiltren but Sergeant Whelan ordered him to releive Steel[45] at Greta and call and arrest Dan and take him into Wangaratta next morning and get him remanded Dans mother said Dan need not go without a warrant unless he liked and that the trooper had no business on her premises without some authority besides his own word. The trooper pulled out his revolver[46] and said he would blow her brains out if she interfered. in the arrest she told him it was a good job for him Ned was not there or he would ram the revolver down his throat Dan looked out and said Ned is coming now. the

47   There are several different accounts of what took place at the Kelly shanty when Fitzpatrick visited. As a template for what occurred, Ned's Jerilderie Letter account is totally unreliable.

48   It is unlikely that Fitzpatrick would have warned Dan to clear out as he was there to arrest him. The key, which gives the lie to this claim, is that Fitzpatrick knew Strahan was away in New South Wales collecting evidence concerning the Moyhu horse stealing case. Therefore, Strahan would not have been able to call the next day.

49   The German community living at Barnawartha and *over the Murray* included the Baumgarten brothers, who Ned had earlier in the letter sought to protect. Now he was intimidating and denigrating the community as 'grasses' to stop anyone anyone who would name Dan as one of the horse stealers. When fleeing from the Stringybark Creek murders, the gang unsuccessfully tried to cross the flooded Murray River not far from the Baumgarten's selection. They sought shelter from Mrs Baumgarten, who out of pique at her husband's arrest, refused to help the fugitives. The Kellys spent the night within sight of the Baumgarten selection and watched next day as Mrs Baumgarten pointed out to a party of police the direction in which she saw the bushrangers depart.

50   The police do not choose the jury. The defence can prevent a juror's inclusion and would have done so if they thought a discharged sergeant would not be impartial.

51   After his capture, Ned admitted to being present and wounding Fitzpatrick.

trooper being off his guard looked out and when Dan got his attention drawn he dropped the knife and fork which showed he had no murderous intent and slapped Heenans hug on him took his revolver and kept him there until Skillion and Ryan came with horses which Dan sold that night. The trooper left and invented some scheme to say that he got shot which any man can see is false,[47] he told Dan to clear out that Sergeant Steel and Detective Brown and Strachan would be there before morning[48] Strachan had been over the Murray trying to get up a case against him and they would convict him if they caught him as the stock society offered an enticement for witnesses to swear anything and the germans over the Murray would swear to the wrong man as well as the right,[49] Next day Williamson and my mother was arrested and Skillion the day after who was not there at all at the time of the row which can be proved by 8 or 9 witnesses and the Police got great credit and praise in the papers for arresting the mother of 12 children one an infant on her breast and those two quiet hard working innocent men who would not know the difference a revolver and a saucepan handle and kept them six months awaiting trial and then convicted them on the evidence of the meanest article that ever the sun shone on. it seems that the jury was well chosen by the Police[50] as there was a discharged Sergeant amongst them which is contrary to law they thought it impossible for a Policeman to swear a lie but I can assure them it is by that means and hiring cads they get promoted I have heard from a trooper that he never knew Fitzpatrick to be one night sober and that he sold his sister to a chinaman but he looks a young strapping rather genteel more fit to be a starcher to a laundress than a policeman. For to a keen observer he has the wrong appearance or a manly heart the deceit and cowardice is too plain to be seen in the puny cabbage hearted looking face. I heard nothing of this transaction until very close on the trial[51] I being then over 400 miles

52 Ned's claim that he was 400 miles from Greta and a *rambling gambler* in New South Wales, at the time of the Fitzpatrick Affair, is disproven by his cousin Joe Ryan and what Ned told his Faithfull's Creek captives. He was not outlawed at this time, although there were warrants out for his arrest for wounding Constable Fitzpatrick and stealing the Moyhu horses.

53 This was a one-off remark made as an argument clincher by Constable Strahan during a heated altercation with Ned's police informer uncle Pat Quinn. Strahan had spoken in the heat of the moment.

54 We only have Ned's unsubstantiated word that the police acted in this unruly manner. Outrageous police behaviour, against defenceless women and children, would not have gone unnoticed in a close-knit community like Greta. Yet following the attack on their colleague Fitzpatrick, the police may not have been too nice in their methods. The Kellys had plenty of relatives with whom the children could have stayed if the behaviour of the police became too intimidating. Their married sister Maggie was caring for them.

55 Ned is referring to the Stringybark police murders, which were widely reported and condemned in the press.

from Greta when I heard I was outlawed and a hundred pound reward for me for shooting at a trooper in Victoria and a hundred pound for any man that could prove a conviction of horse-stealing against[52] me so I came back to Victoria knew I would get no justice if I gave myself up I enquired after my brother Dan and found him digging on Bullock Creek heard how the Police used to be blowing that they would not ask me to stand they would shoot me first and then cry surrender[53] and how they used to rush into the house upset all the milk dishes break tins of eggs empty the flour out of the bags on to the ground and even the meat out of the cask and destroy all the provisions and shove the girls in front of them into the rooms like dogs so as if anyone was there they would shoot the girls first-but they knew well I was not there or I would have scattered their blood and brains like rain I would manure the Eleven Mile with their bloated carcasses and yet remember there is not one drop of murderous blood in my Veins Superintendent Smith used to say to my sisters, see all the men I have out today I will have as many more tomorrow and we will blow him into pieces as small as paper that is in our guns Detective Ward and Constable Hayes took out their revolvers and threatened to shoot the girls and children in Mrs Skillions absence the greatest ruffians and murderers no matter how deprived would not be guilty of such a cowardly action, and this sort of cruelty and disgraceful and cowardly conduct to my brothers and sisters who had no protection[54] coupled with the conviction of my mother and those men certainly made my blood boil as I dont think there is a man born could have the patience to suffer it as long as I did or ever allow his blood to get cold while such insults as these were unavenged and yet in every paper that is printed I am called the blackest and coldest blooded murderer ever on record[55] But if I hear any more of it I will not exactly show them what cold blooded murder is but wholesale

56 Here Ned is foreshadowing what he intended to do at Glenrowan. In the earlier Cameron Letter (1878), he signed off with the implied threat: *Remember your railroads*.

57 Ned and Dan were keeping a low profile, hiding out from the police in the Wombat Ranges. There were warrants out for them for stealing Whitty's and the other Moyhu horses and for attempting to murder Fitzpatrick.

58 The police camped near a derelict goldminer's hut known locally as the shingle hut.

59 Ned objected to the police carrying long firearms (rifles). The police had two rifles, an old borrowed fowling piece and a modern Spencer repeating rifle which none of them knew how to use. Ned's gang had four rifles and therefore they outgunned the police. The police also carried revolvers which Ned did not object to in the Jerilderie Letter, but were a handicap to them as they were enclosed in a button-down holster and could not be accessed quickly. Kennedy had only his Webley revolver to fight off the gang and was at a grave disadvantage as the bushrangers had their rifles and captured police weapons. While waiting for Kennedy and Scanlan to return from their patrol McIntyre said: *Kelly inquired if Kennedy and Scanlan had any long firearms, on my hesitating to reply to this question I was threatened in the usual manner, and had to admit that they had a rifle with them. Upon hearing this he became very enraged and said 'Well that looks like you had come out to shoot me, you had no right to carry anything but revolvers'*. Ned's obsession with the police carrying rifles does not translate into a plan to murder him. His insistence they carry revolvers only has an irony to it, given that Ned and his mates were themselves armed with rifles.

60 While awaiting execution, Ned wrote a letter to the Governor where he said that in addition to Kennedy's Mansfield patrol, he expected two other police search parties making a total of *thirteen police to meet at Stringybark Creek to search for me*. Ned's plan was to make a pre-emptive strike against the Mansfield police before (as he wrongly believed) the other police patrols arrived. There were in fact just two search parties, one from Mansfield and another from Greta. The Hedi police station, situated near the Glenmore run and not Stringybark Creek, was the agreed meeting point for the Mansfield and Greta search parties. From there, they would scour the bush for Ned and his brother Dan.

and retail slaughter,⁵⁶ something different to shooting three troopers in self defence and robbing a bank. I would have been rather hot-blooded to throw down my rifle and let them shoot me and my innocent brother, they were not satisfied with frightening my sisters night and day and destroying their provisions and lagging my mother and an infant and those innocent men but should follow me and my brother into the wilds where he had been quietly digging neither molesting or interfering with anyone he was making good wages as the creek is very rich⁵⁷ within half a mile from where I shot Kennedy. I was not there long and on the 25 of October I came on Police tracks between Table top and the bogs. I crossed them and returning in the evening I came on a different lot of tracks making for the shingle hut I went to our camp and told my brother and his two mates me and my brother went and found their camp at the shingle hut⁵⁸ about a mile from my brothers house, saw they carried long firearms⁵⁹ and we knew our doom was sealed if we could not beat those before the others would come as I knew the other party of Police would soon join them⁶⁰ and if they came on us at our camp they would shoot us down

61   There is no evidence, apart from Ned's vivid imagination and the overblown Strahan story, that either police search party contemplated doing such a thing. Whether Inspector Brooke Smith said to Ned's sisters that the police would blow their brother Ned *into pieces as small as* [the] *paper that is in our guns* is debatable, and is probably no more than the usual anti-police rhetoric.

62   According to McIntyre the gang had four rifles and at least one revolver.

63   McIntyre rounded up the horses before breakfast and may have had the fowling piece with him. Around lunchtime, Lonigan strapped on his Webley revolver after hearing a strange noise in the bush. Later McIntyre took the rifle down the creek and shot at some parrots. Both the rifle and McIntyre's revolver were at the tent 24 yards to his right, when he was cooking the evening meal and the Kelly Gang appeared.

64   Ned tells us the Kelly Gang only had two guns and these were the guns they brought to Stringybark Creek. In describing the moments immediately following Lonigan's death, McIntyre states: *After shooting Lonigan the four men rushed over to me, Ned Kelly with a revolver in his right hand and carrying his rifle in the other. Dan Kelly whisked round and presenting his gun at the tent called out 'Come out here you bloody bastards!'* If Ned had the two guns, how could Dan keep McIntyre covered? Clearly, the bushrangers had more than two guns when they bailed up the police camp and added to their weapons soon after they shot Lonigan.

65   McIntyre was unarmed when Ned shouted for him to Bail Up! The fowling piece was at the tent and not as Ned states resting against a stump, when he closed in on McIntyre and Lonigan.

66   Constable McIntyre, who was standing facing Ned, tells us: *Ned Kelly shifted the muzzle of his gun to the right and without taking it from his shoulder shot at Lonigan who had started to run, putting his hand down as if to get his revolver, he had no time to open the case and must have been looking over his right shoulder when he was shot in the right eye by Ned Kelly. The whole affair occurred so quickly that Lonigan did not run more than four or five paces before he was shot.* Ned's story of Lonigan coming up from behind a log and his firing only in self-defence is contradicted by McIntyre's account, which describes Lonigan's death as the cold-blooded murder it was. Ned was the aggressor from the start with his rifle closely following Lonigan's every move. Thirty-five years later Superintendent Sadleir, 80 years old and retired, wrote in his memoirs that two days after the police murders, McIntyre related to him a version of Lonigan's death similar to Ned's. Only on this one

like dogs at our work⁶¹ as we had only two guns.⁶² we thought it best to try and bail those up take their fire arms and ammunition and horses and we could stand a chance with the rest we approached the spring as close as we could get to the camp as the intervening space being clear ground and no battery we saw two men at the logs they got up and one took a double barreled fowling-piece and fetched a horse down and hobbled him at the tent⁶³ we thought there were more men in the tent asleep those being on sentry we could have shot those two men without speaking but not wishing to take their lives we waited. McIntyre laid the gun against a stump and Lonigan sat on the log I advanced, my brother Dan keepin McIntyre covered⁶⁴ which he took to be Constable Flood and had he not obeyed my orders, or attempted to reach for the gun or draw his revolver⁶⁵ he would have been shot dead. but when I called on them to throw up their hands McIntyre obeyed and Lonigan ran some six or seven yards to a battery of logs insted of dropping behind the one he was sitting on, he had just got to the logs and put his head up to take aim when I shot him that instant or he would have shot me⁶⁶ as I took him to be Strachan the man who said he would not ask me to stand he would shoot occasion did McIntyre's many accounts of Lonigan's death differ from what he said above. It seems probable that Sadleir got it wrong and attributed to McIntyre what Ned had said in the Jerilderie Letter.

67 Even if it had been Strahan, would this have excused cold-blooded murder?

68 Ned is referring to a fight at a Benalla boot maker's shop, where he refused to be handcuffed and fought the police who attempted to subdue him. Lonigan grabbed Ned *by the privates* as Ned lashed out at all those around him. Ned submitted, when Justice of the Peace William Maginness (McInnis) defused the tense situation, and he allowed himself to be handcuffed by him. Ned's assertion that Lonigan said: *he was the man would shoot him* is spurious and was probably never uttered. This threat may have been invented to justify the taking of Lonigan's life. In other words, he was not the hated Strahan but would do just as well as he had also threatened to kill Kelly.

69 Ned and Fitzpatrick were good friends; they drank together before the Benalla boot maker's shop fight and, a week or so later, Ned arranged for his brother Dan and his Lloyd cousins to give themselves up after the Goodman store ruckus, but only to Fitzpatrick.

70 Ned's falling-out with Fitzpatrick only came about during the policeman's April 1878 visit to the Kelly shanty. Before that time, as Kate Kelly said in a newspaper interview on the day of the Jerilderie bank robbery, *Fitzpatrick was on very intimate terms with the family.*

71 Ned's claim would seem entirely credible, if there were not several other incidents where he was careless with the use of firearms. The most famous was the accidental shooting of labourer George Metcalf at Glenrowan. Metcalf, a destitute quarry worker, told a desperate lie to the authorities of being shot by the police inside Jones's pub in order to receive medical treatment at government expense. The police quickly determined the truth of the matter and without recrimination at Metcalf's pitiable deception, arranged accommodation and medical treatment for Metcalf, whose eyesight was badly affected by the bullet wound he had received from Ned's careless hands. Metcalf later died from medical complications related to his injury.

me first like a dog.⁶⁷ But it happened to be Lonigan the man who in company with Sergeant Whelan Fitzpatrick and King the Bootmaker and Constable O.Day that tried to put a pair of hand-cuffs on me in Benalla but could not, and had to allow McInnis the miller to put them on, previous to Fitzpatrick swearing he was shot, I was fined two pounds for hitting Fitzpatrick and two pounds for not allowing five curs like Sergeant Whelan O.Day Fitzpatrick King and Lonigan who caught me by the privates and would have sent me to Kingdom come only I was not ready and he is the man that blowed before he left Violet Town. if Ned Kelly was to be shot he was the man would shoot him⁶⁸ and no doubt he would shoot me, even if I threw up my arms and laid down as he knew four of them could not arrest me single-handed not to talk of the rest of my mates, also either me or him would have to die, this he knew well therefore, he had a right to keep out of my road, Fitzpatrick is the only one I hit out of the five in Benalla, this shows my feeling towards him as he said we were good friends⁶⁹ & even swore it but he was the biggest enemy I had in the country⁷⁰ with the exception of Lonigan and he can be thankful I was not there when he took a revolver and threatened to shoot my mother in her own house it is not fire three shots and miss him at a yard and a half I don't think I would use a revolver to shoot a man like him when I was within a yard and a half of him. or attempt to fire into a house where my mother brothers and sisters was.⁷¹ and according to Fitzpatricks statement all around him a man that is such a bad shot as to miss a man three times at a yard and a half would never attempt to fire into a house among a house full of women and children while I had a pair of arms and bunch of fives on the end of them that never failed to peg out anything they came in contact with and Fitzpatrick knew the weight of one of them only too well, as it run against him once in Benalla. and cost me two pound odd as he is very subject to

72   Ned wanted to humiliate Fitzpatrick and no doubt he thought fainting was effeminate. Fitzpatrick had fainted at the Kelly shanty, after being shot by Ned, and he fainted again at Lindsay's Winton Pub. Ned's taunt about fainting ignores Fitzpatrick's wounding ordeal at Ned's hands and unfairly tars Fitzpatrick with cowardice in the Benalla fight. There is no evidence that Fitzpatrick fainted on this occasion and his bouts of fainting during the Fitzpatrick Affair are directly attributable to Ned shooting him.

73   The Kellys brought home-made ammunition with them. Ned reloaded the police fowling piece with bullets instead of pellets. Why would he do this, unless it was to take the policemen's lives? When fired from a distance shotgun pellets were less likely to kill, while solid bullets would prove deadly if they hit a vital part of the body. Here is definite proof that Ned wanted to take life rather than preserve it.

74   McIntyre, expediently, said to Ned: *You cannot blame us for what Fitzpatrick has done to you.* He said this to placate his captor in a life-threatening situation rather than passing judgement on Fitzpatrick's guilt or innocence.

75   McIntyre agreed to leave the police force because he knew if he angered Ned it was likely he would be shot.

76   Kennedy and Scanlan were looking for any sign of the Kellys but had no idea they were camped nearby.

77   McIntyre did not tell Kelly that other police were heading for Stringybark Creek. Ned tells us he was aware other police were searching for him before the Stringybark encounter. There was no plan for police search parties to meet at Stringybark Creek and McIntyre knew this.

78   Sergeant Thomas Wallings was a New South Wales police officer shot in September 1878, while pursuing a party of bushrangers. There was a suspicion that, while he was on the run because of the Fitzpatrick Affair, Ned had shot the policeman. Ned encouraged McIntyre to believe this false rumour, pretending the New South Wales police had shot the wrong man for Walling's murder.

fainting.⁷² As soon as I shot Lonigan he jumped up and staggered some distance from the logs with his hands raised and then fell he surrendered but too late I asked McIntyre who was in the tent he replied no one. I advanced and took possession of their two revolvers and fowling-piece which I loaded with bullets instead of shot.⁷³ I asked McIntyre where his mates was he said they had gone down the creek, and he did not expect them that night he asked me was I going to shoot him and his mates. I told him no. I would shoot no man if he gave up his arms and leave the force he said the police all knew Fitzpatrick had wronged us.⁷⁴ and he intended to leave the force,⁷⁵ as he had bad health, and his life was insured, he told me he intended going home and that Kennedy and Scanlan were out looking for our camp⁷⁶ and also about the other Police⁷⁷ he told me the N.S.W. Police had shot a man for shooting Sergeant Walling I told him if they did, they had shot the wrong man⁷⁸ and I expect your gang came to do the same with me he said no they did not come to shoot me they came to apprehend me I asked him what they carried spenceir rifles and breech loading fowling pieces and so much ammunition for as the Police was

79 Ned makes much anti-police capital out of the weapons and ammunition carried by the police to prove his point that they had come into the bush, not just to shoot him but to riddle his body with bullets. Every Victorian policeman was supplied with a Colt or Webley revolver and they carried their guns on bush patrol. When considered from the police point of view, the weapons and ammunition they brought with them to Stringybark Creek proved to be inadequate for an encounter with fugitives armed with rifles. In addition to their service revolvers, the four policemen had an old fowling rifle and a modern Spencer repeating rifle. The ammunition they carried was not excessive; given the fact they shot game for food and expected to be camping out for several weeks in wild and inaccessible bushland. There was nothing excessive or untoward, either in the weapons the police carried or the extra ammunition they brought with them. Constable McIntyre said Kennedy's party mistakenly believed the Kellys: *would defend themselves; but not that they would attack us.* The police understood that when an encounter came, they would have to defend themselves.

80 Ned's mates Joe Byrne and Steve Hart were present from the beginning of the encounter and stayed until the end. Ned is shielding them from responsibility for their actions, by claiming they arrived later and left the scene shortly thereafter.

81 McIntyre says Byrne and Dan hid in the rushes, where all four bushrangers had been when the ambush began. Hart took up a position inside the police tent and Ned crouched behind a log with McIntyre standing to one side.

82 McIntyre states: *I was deceived by Kelly who notwithstanding his promise to spare the men's lives if I could induce them to surrender, neither gave me an opportunity to explain nor them to learn the position they were in. He incurred no more danger in shooting Lonigan and Scanlan than he would have done in shooting two kangaroos; he simply gave the men no chance to injure him, and might have shot them down without challenging them, as they scarcely had time to realise their danger until they were shot.* The same was true of Kennedy's encounter with the bushrangers; he was fired on by Ned with his hand resting playfully on his revolver case as McIntyre attempted to blurt out words of surrender.

only supposed to carry one revolver and six cartridges in the revolver but they had eighteen rounds of revolver cartridges each three dozen for the fowling pieces and twenty one spenceir-rifle cartridges and God knows how many they had away with the rifle this looked as if they meant not only to shoot me only to riddle me[79] but I dont know either Kennedy Scanlan or him and had nothing against them, he said he would get them to give up their arms if I would not shoot them as I could not blame them, they had to do their duty I said I did not blame them for doing honest duty but I could not suffer them blowing me to pieces in my own native land and they knew Fitzpatrick wronged us and why not make it public and convict him but no they would rather riddle poor unfortunate creoles. but they will rue the day ever Fitzpatrick got among them, Our two mates came over when they heard the shot fired but went back again for fear the Police might come to our camp[80] while we were all away and manure bullock flat with us on our arrival I stopped at the logs and Dan went back to the spring for fear the troopers would come in that way but I soon heard them coming up the creek.[81] I told McIntyre to tell them to give up their arms he spoke to Kennedy[82] who was some distance in front of

83   Scanlan was carrying the Spencer repeating rifle slung across his back. To fire the unconventional rifle in the way Ned suggests, the weapon would have to have been upside down with the barrel pointed towards the ground. This would have been a foolishly dangerous way to carry such an unfamiliar rifle. Given that Scanlan was returning from a day's bush patrol and felt safe approaching the camp, it is doubtful he would have carried his rifle in this unsafe, combat-ready fashion.

84   Constable Scanlan did not *slew his horse around to gallop away*, nor did he *as quick as thought* fire his Spencer repeating rifle and he was not on his horse when the fatal shot was fired. He was in fact on his knees on the ground and had not fired a single shot, before he was hit under the armpit by either Ned or Joe Byrne's rifle bullet. According to McIntyre's account, without firing a shot Scanlan died almost immediately: *I saw the blood spurt out from the right side as he fell. At this time a great number of shots were being fired by Kelly's party*. Scanlan died in a hail of Kelly Gang bullets and Ned's claim that he alone shot the policeman is only guesswork on his part.

85   Ned is being disingenuous. Following Ned's Glenrowan capture, McIntyre visited the badly wounded outlaw in his Benalla prison cell and discussed his escape. *Kelly threatened not less than a dozen times to shoot me and several times he pointed his rifle at me. Kelly many times afterwards said that he intended to shoot me and expressed great regret that he had not done so. He told me himself that if he had thought there was any chance of my getting away he would have shot me at once.*

86   Kennedy's body was not discovered until five days after his death and animal predation is thought to account for the loss of the ear.

87   Ned's perfunctory account of Kennedy's pursuit and death masks the fact that the tree-to-tree shooting encounter went on for some time and covered a distance of around a mile. When McIntyre asked Ned in his Benalla cell: *Did Kennedy fire many shots at you?* Ned replied, *Yes, he fired a lot*. The trees along the route of Kennedy's pursuit were marked with many bullet holes. Ned's description of how Kennedy was shot and the wounds he received differs from his later accounts. He told his Faithfull's Creek captives that he shot Kennedy in the right shoulder causing him to drop his revolver. But he also said that he mistook Kennedy's blood-stained hand raised in surrender for a revolver when he had none and he immediately fired at him. Ned

Scanlan he reached for his revolver and jumped off, on the off side of his horse and got behind a tree when I called on them to throw up their arms and Scanlan who carried the rifle slewed his horse around to gallop away but the horse would not go and as quick as thought fired at me with the rifle without unslinging it[83] and was in the act of firing again when I had to shoot him and he fell from his horse.[84] I could have shot them without speaking but their lives was no good to me. McIntyre jumped on Kennedys horse and I allowed him to go as I did not like to shoot him after he surrendered[85] or I would have shot him as he was between me and Kennedy therefore I could not shoot Kennedy without shooting him first Kennedy kept firing from behind the tree my brother Dan advanced and Kennedy ran I followed him he stopped behind another tree and fired again I shot him in the arm pit and he dropped his revolver and ran I fired again with the gun as he slewed around to surrender I did not know he had dropped his revolver the bullet passed through the right side of his chest & he could not live or I would have let him go had they been my own brothers I could not help shooting them or else let them shoot me which they would have done had their bullets been directed as they intended them. But as for hand-cuffing Kennedy to a tree or cutting his ear off[86] or brutally treating any of them, is a falsehood, if Kennedy's ear was cut off it was not done by me and none of my mates was near him after he was shot I put his cloak over him and left him as well as I could and were they my own brothers I could not have been more sorry for them this cannot be called wilful murder for I was compelled to shoot them, or lie down and let them shoot me[87] it would not be wilful murder if they packed our remains in, shattered into a mass of animated gore to Mansfield, they would have got great praise and credit as well as promotion but I am reconed a horrid brute because I had not been cowardly enough to lie down for them under glosses over Kennedy's death in a few words not mentioning the fact that the wounded policeman was subjected to two hours of interrogation, before Ned placed a shotgun against the policeman's chest as he pleaded: *let me alone to live as long as I can, for the sake of my poor wife and family* and callously pulled the trigger. A Euroa bank robbery hostage said: *Kelly told me he had spoken to Kennedy for a long time after the Sergeant had been wounded.* Ned said: *he shot him to end his misery.* Kennedy died without being offered a chance to live and be taken care of by the two police search parties, which Ned was convinced were making their way to Stringybark Creek.

88 McIntyre did not acknowledge Fitzpatrick's guilt. He suggested to Ned that he should not blame all of the police for what he imagined was Fitzpatrick's crime. The fault lay with Ned for hot-headedly taking a loaded pistol into the shanty and firing it in a crowded room. Ned twists McIntyre's words to his own advantage, implying that all policemen recognised he and his family had been wronged.

89 Ned is perhaps ridiculing McIntyre here for hiding in a wombat hole following his desperate escape. McIntyre said he was sorry he ever mentioned the wombat hole as many nasty jokes were made about it.

90 Ned had a memorable way with words and his mocking portrayal of the police should not be accepted as an accurate description of police motives or behaviour. The literary strength of Ned's caricature has been instrumental in fashioning modern-day acceptance of the Kelly myth.

91 The oath taken by a constable on joining the Victoria Police made no mention of vowing to arrest one's relatives, they swear to uphold the law without fear or favour.

92 Ned, his family, relatives and friends, frequently lied in court giving false alibis to get the accused off charges of which they were usually guilty.

such trying circumstances and insults to my people certainly their wives and children are to be pitied but they must remember those men came into the bush with the intention of scattering pieces of me and my brother all over the bush and yet they know and acknowledge I have been wronged[88] and my mother and four or five men lagged innocent and is my brothers and sisters and my mother not to be pitied also who has no alternative only to put up with the brutal and cowardly conduct of a parcel of big ugly fat-necked wombat headed[89] big bellied magpie legged narrow hipped splaw-footed sons of Irish Bailiffs or english landlords which is better known as Officers of Justice or Victorian Police who some calls honest gentlemen[90] but I would like to know what business an honest man would have in the Police as it is an old saying It takes a rogue to catch a rogue and a man that knows nothing about roguery would never enter the force an take an oath to arrest brother sister father or mother[91] if required and to have a case and conviction if possible any man knows it is possible to swear a lie[92] and if a policeman looses a conviction for the sake of swearing a lie he has broke his oath therefore he is a perjurer either ways. A Policeman is a disgrace to his country, not alone to the mother that suckled him, in the first place he is a rogue in his heart but too cowardly to follow it up without having the force to disguise it. Next he is a traitor to his country ancestors and religion as they were all catholics before the Saxons and Cranmore yoke held sway since then they were persecuted massacreed thrown into martyrdom and tortured beyond the ideas of the present generation, What would people say if they saw a strapping big lump of an Irishman shepherding sheep for fifteen bob a week or tailing turkeys in Tallarook Ranges for a smile from Julia or even begging his tucker, they would say he ought to be ashamed of himself and tar-and-feather him. But he would be a king to a policeman who for a lazy loafing cowardly bilit left the ash

93   The list of place-names comes from the convict ballad Moreton Bay. The passion for Ireland is unmistakeable, which makes more puzzling McIntyre's report that he appealed without success to Kelly as a fellow Irishman: *I thought he might be possessed of some of that patriotic-religious feeling which is such a bond of sympathy amongst the Irish people. My opinion is that he possessed none of this feeling. Like a great many young bushmen he prided himself more on his Australian birth than he did upon his extraction from any particular race.*

94   Ned is creating a caricature of the police and their confrontations with larrikins. Often larrikins, particularly in the towns and cities, outnumbered the police trying to arrest them. Rather than being victims of police violence, larrikins inflicted wounds and an occasional beating to the custodians of law and order. A puny half-starved larrikin taking on police toughs, and getting the better of them, is a flash larrikin fantasy that must have amused Ned and his mates no end.

corner deserted the shamrock, the emblem of true wit and beauty to serve under a flag and nation that has destroyed massacreed and murdered their forefathers by the greatest of torture as rolling them down hill in spiked barrels pulling their toe and finger nails and on the wheel. and every torture imaginable more was transported to Van Dieman's Land to pine their young lives away in starvation and misery among tyrants worse than the promised hell itself all of true blood bone and beauty, that was not murdered on their own soil, or had fled to America or other countries to bloom again another day, were doomed to Port McQuarie, Toweringabbie Norfolk Island and Emu plains[93] And in those places of tyrany and condemnation many a blooming Irishman rather than subdue to the Saxon yoke, Were flogged to death and bravely died in servile chains but true to the shamrock and a credit to Paddys land What would people say if I became a policeman and took an oath to arrest my brothers and sisters & relations and convict them by fair or foul means after the conviction of my mother and the persecutions and insults offered to myself and people Would they say I was a decent gentleman, and yet a policeman is still in worse and guilty of meaner actions than that The Queen must surely be proud of such herioc men as the Police and Irish soldiers as It takes eight or eleven of the biggest mud crushers in Melbourne to take one poor little half starved larrakin to a watch house. I have seen as many as eleven, big & ugly enough to lift Mount Macedon out of a crab hole more like the species of a baboon or Guerilla than a man actually come into a court house and swear they could not arrest one eight stone larrakin and them armed with battens and neddies without some civilians assistance and some of them going to the hospital from the affects of hits from the fists of the larrakin and the Magistrate would send the poor little Larrakin into a dungeon for being a better man than such a parcel of armed curs.[94] What would England do if America declared war and

95 Ned's victims did not ask to have their livestock stolen or to suffer the intimidation of the Greta Mob. The bushranger is, yet again, indulging in the delusion of portraying himself as the wronged victim of those who legitimately pursued him, police and civilians alike. He declares himself ready to unleash his anger against anybody who opposes him. Ned knew his gang's murdering of three policemen at Stringybark Creek shocked, frightened and angered the public, but he would accept no responsibility for the choices he made.

96 Ned's anger here would seem to be rhetorical, if not for the grisly fact that some 16 months later he planned and attempted to derail a train carrying police and civilian passengers.

97 Ned had an abiding hatred of Alexander Brooke Smith, who as a rooky policeman in 1852 had captured the bushranger Captain Brown. Ned's dislike of Inspector (not Superintendent as Ned writes) Smith stemmed from the Beechworth policeman's early role in failing to capture the Kelly brothers following the Fitzpatrick Affair. Brooke Smith was a quintessential Englishman, a compulsive gambler, a townsman in poor health who disliked bush patrol duty and as such was a favourite lampooning target for Ned's abuse. Smith was somewhat of a pompous gentleman with poor policing skills and was an incompetent leader of men. He was criticised by the 1881 Police Commission into the Kelly Outbreak and it was suggested he should retire. Ned clearly felt himself superior to the urbane *clipped poodle* Brooke Smith and ragged him mercilessly.

hoisted a green flag as it is all Irishmen that has got command of her armies forts and batteries even her very life guards and beef tasters are Irish would they not slew around and fight her with their own arms for the sake of the colour they dare not wear for years. and to reinstate it and rise old Erins isle once more, from the pressure and tyrannism of the English yoke. which has kept it in poverty and starvation. and caused them to wear the enemys coat. What else can England expect. Is there not big fat-necked Unicorns enough paid, to torment and drive me to do thing which I dont wish to do, without the public assisting them I have never interefered with any person unless they deserved it, and yet there are civilians who take firearms against me, for what reason I do not know, unless they want me to turn on them and exterminate them without medicine.[95] I shall be compelled to make an example of some of them if they cannot find no other employment If I had robbed and plundered ravished and murdered everything I met young and old, rich and poor. the public could not do any more than take firearms and assisting the police as they have done, but by the light that shines pegged on an ant-bed with their bellies opened their fat taken out rendered and poured down their throat boiling hot will be cool to what pleasure I will give some of them and any person aiding or harbouring or assisting the Police in any way whatever or employing any person whom they know to be a detective or cad or those who would be so deprived as to take blood money will be outlawed and declared unfit to be allowed human buriel their property either consumed or confiscated and them theirs and all belonging to them exterminated off the face of the earth,[96] the enemy I cannot catch myself I shall give a payable reward for, I would like to know who put that article that reminds me of a poodle dog half clipped in the lion fashion. called Brooke. E. Smith Superintendent of Police[97] he knows as much about commanding Police as Cap-

98 Inspector Brooke Smith appeared before the court in cases where a decision had to be made about whether children should be sent to the Industrial School. The court was reluctant to take this course of action and only did so as a last resort. Ned unfairly equates Brooke Smith's courtroom role in these community sensitive cases as oppressive and akin to child exploitation. Kelly may have been familiar with the protracted courtroom drama surrounding the orphan son of James O'Neill of Greta. On three separate occasions, the Wangaratta Police Court considered the case and sought unsuccessfully to place the child with a family in the Greta community. After exhausting every other alternative the neglected child was sent to the Melbourne Industrial School for seven years.

99 Ned's warped and contradictory larrikin values are on show in this passage. He condemns Lonigan and those who show fight as *cowards,* while declaring that he has an outlaw's right to dispatch to *Kingdom Come* those who don't immediately surrender to his challenge. He said he admired Kennedy's bravery and covered the policeman with his cloak. Yet Lonigan, whom he said he did not recognise before he shot him, he fired upon immediately the policeman failed to comply with Kelly's bail up command. Similarly, when McIntyre goes forward to warn Kennedy and Scanlan that Ned and his mates are in control of the camp, he fires at Kennedy before McIntyre had a chance to speak more than a few words. Ned wants to bask in public acclaim for his quick response to act but denies others the same right; he is the hero and they are the cowards.

tain Standish does about mustering mosquitoes and boiling them down for their fat on the back blocks of the Lachlan for he has a head like a turnip a stiff neck as big as his shoulders narrow hipped and pointed towards the feet like a vine stake And if there is any one to be called a murderer Regarding Kennedy, Scanlan and Lonigan it is that misplaced poodle he gets as much pay as a dozen good troopers, if there is any <u>good</u> in them, and what does he do for it he cannot look behind him without turning his whole frame it takes three or four police to keep sentry while he sleeps in Wangaratta, for fear of body snatchers do they think he is a superior animal to the men that has to guard him <u>if so</u> why not send the men that gets big pay and reconed superior to the common police after me and you shall soon save the country of high salaries to men that is fit for nothing else but getting better men than himself shot and sending orphan children to the industrial school to make prostitutes and cads of them[98] for the Detectives and other evil disposed persons Send the high paid and men that received big salaries for years in a gang by themselves after me, As it makes no difference to them but it will give them a chance of showing whether they are worth more pay than a common trooper or not and I think the Public will soon find they are only in the road of good men and obtaining money under false pretences, I do not call McIntyre a coward for I reckon he is as game a man as wears the jacket as he had the presence of mind to know his position, directly as he was spoken to, and only foolishness to disobey, it was cowardice that made Lonigan and the others fight it is only foolhardiness to disobey an outlaw as any Policeman or other man who do not throw up their arms directly as I call on them knows the consequence which is a speedy dispatch to Kingdom Come,[99] I wish those men who joined the stock protection society to withdraw their money and give it and

100 As Ned's own professional horse and cattle stealing career attests, fear and intimidation worked equally as well on the poor as it did on the rich. Ned's definition of who was rich and who was poor is not clearly spelled out but seems to be selectors facing the hardships of farming the land. It was never as simple as comparing the asset wealth of his enemies Whitty and Byrne with the selectors around them. Only after he had taken to the bush did Ned publicly express concern for the poor who he takes to be selectors, whose livestock he had no hesitation in stealing just a few months earlier. Ned's vision of the poor protecting a rich man's property is partially confirmed by his relatives the Lloyds, who on two occasions did precisely this concerning the property of Squatter Robert McBean who they regarded as a 'good' squatter. As for the poor rising up to a man to find the thieves, this is the usual Kelly hyperbole. Ned admits he was a horse and cattle thief. Would he expect the poor to dob him in?

101 This sounds very far from the police harassment Ned claims blighted his life. On one hand the police are branded as incompetent and he was never interfered with during his horse and cattle stealing days. While, on the other hand, they are portrayed as overbearing and harassing, hounding Ned and his 'innocent' family.

102 Ellen Kelly married Ned's stepfather and partner in livestock theft George King in February 1874. She had three King children by him before the Kelly outbreak. Ellen was therefore not a widow, nor was Ned strictly a widow's son by this time. Author J.J. Kenneally tells us that the Greta locals disliked George King, presumably for his abusive behaviour towards Ellen, and continued to refer to her as Mrs Kelly. Both Ellen and Ned fiercely regarded themselves as Kellys and, in this sense, Ned's description of himself and his mother as a widow and widow's son are emotionally correct.

as much more to the widows and orphans and poor of Greta district wher I spent and will again spend many a happy day fearless free and bold, as it only aids the police to procure false witnesses and go whacks with men to steal horses and lag innocent men it would suit them far better to subscribe a sum and give it to the poor of their district and there is no fear of anyone stealing their property for no man could steal their horses without the knowledge of the poor if any man was mean enough to steal their property the poor would rise out to a man and find them[100] if they were on the face of the earth it will always pay a rich man to be liberal with the poor and make as little enemies as he can as he shall find if the poor is on his side he shall loose nothing by it. If they depend in the police they shall be drove to destruction. As they cannot and will not protect them if duffing and bushranging were abolished the police would have to cadge for their living I speak from experience as I have sold horses and cattle innumerable and yet eight head of the culls is all ever was found I never was interfered with whilst I kept up this successful trade.[101] I give fair warning to all those who has reason to fear me to sell out and give £10 out of every hundred towards the widow and orphan fund and do not attempt to reside in Victoria, but as short a time as possible after reading this notice, neglect this and abide by the consequences, which shall be worse than the rust in the wheat in Victoria or the druth of a dry season to the grass-hoppers in New South Wales I do not wish to give the order full force without giving timely warning, but I am a widows son[102] outlawed and my orders <u>must</u> be obeyed.

INDEX

References to annotations to the Jerilderie Letter are indexed. The letter itself is not indexed.

Aboriginal trackers 118
Aborigines 137
Ainge, Henry 33
Ainge, Thomas 33
Albion Travellers Rest Hotel, Jerilderie 101
Albury, NSW 5
Archdeacon, Constable John 35
armour
    Glenrowan siege 129, 131, 133, 135–40
    inspiration 119–21
    purpose 121
    symbolism 82, 117, 162–3
    thefts of mould boards 118–19
Armstrong, Constable Robert 123–4
arson 4, 26, 106, 108, 123, 128, 192n2
Arthur, Constable James Murdoch 134, 137, 138, 200n16
Ashmead, Joseph 46
Australasian Sketcher 137
Australian Son (Brown) 114, 191
Avenel, Vic. 162

Babington, Sergeant James 11
Bank of New South Wales, Jerilderie. *See* Jerilderie bank robbery (February 1879)
Barmedman, NSW 169–70
Barnawartha, Vic. 6, 212n49
Barnett, William 24–5
Barnett family 24–5
Barry, Sir Redmond 62, 65, 143, 164–5
Baumgarten, Mrs 212n49
Baumgarten brothers 6–7, 8, 28, 52, 204n28, 208n39, 212n49
Bayview Hotel, Frankston 44
Beechworth, Vic. 59, 153
Beechworth Circuit Court 37, 53, 60
Beechworth Gaol 33, 37, 128, 169, 196n8
Beechworth goldfields 16, 19
Beechworth Hospital 96
Beechworth oriental exhibition 120–1
Beechworth police 48, 123–4
Benalla, Vic. 26, 39, 47, 53, 62, 92, 118, 145, 150, 153
Benalla boot maker's shop fight 71, 73, 220n68–9, 222n72
Benalla lockup 60, 87, 226n85, 226n87

Benalla police 124, 130, 135, 175, 178, 179, 198n15
Benalla Police Court 53, 58
Berry, Graham 153
Berry government 153, 208n40
Black Wednesday (1878) 208n40
Boer War 150
Boggy Creek, Vic. 21, 22
Boorhaman Catholic School 174
Bowman, John 60
Bracken, Constable Hugh 127–32, 141, 160–1
British empire 150, 152–4
Brown, Captain 232n97
Brown, Max 114, 147, 182, 191
Brown, squatter 204n27
The Bulletin 150–1
Bullock Creek hideout 53, 60, 62, 75–7, 81–2, 120
Byrne, Andrew 155
 see also Whitty and Byrne
Byrne, farmer 95
Byrne, Jane 155
Byrne, Joe 5
  and Chinese 105, 121
  Billy King identity 51, 53
  Cameron Letter 107
  death 92, 135–6, 143
  Euroa bank robbery 100, 107, 109
  Fitzpatrick Affair 51, 53, 55, 61, 67
  Glenrowan siege 118, 120–1, 131, 133, 135–6

Jerilderie bank robbery 101, 105
Jerilderie Letter 112
murder of Sherritt 121–4
Stringybark Creek police murders 69, 77, 80, 84, 92, 224n80–1, 226n84
Byrne, Margaret 122
Byrne, Paddy 123

Cameron, Donald 100, 107, 191
Cameron Letter (1878) 47, 73, 100, 107–8, 112–14, 117, 191, 198n13, 202n25, 216n56
Canny, Maria 33
Canny, William 33
Canowindra, NSW 99
Carey, Peter 181, 185
Carrington, Thomas 137
Catholic Advocate 155
Chinese 105, 121
Chomley, Hussey Malone 62, 175
Clarke family 180
Clune, Frank 182
Colonial Artillery Corps 70
commons land 206n33, 206n35
Conway, Bridget 174
Conway, Julia 174
Cox, Charles 110
Curnow, Catherine 129, 130
Curnow, Jean 129, 130
Curnow, Muriel 129, 130

Curnow, Thomas 129–30, 131, 175
Darlinghurst Gaol 168
Declaration of the Republic of North East Victoria 147–9, 156–7
Denny, special agent 175
Devine, Constable George 106, 138, 188–9
Devine, Mary 106, 189
Diseased Stock Agent, police spy 119, 173–7
Dowsett, Jesse 137, 139, 140
Dublin Agricultural College 70
Dudley, Henry 101–2, 104–5
Dueran station 94
Duffy, Charles Gavan 153
Duffy certificates 206n33
Duffy Land Act
    see Land Acts
Dwyer, Constable James 136, 139, 141–2

Easter Rebellion (1916) 154
Education Department 174, 176
Eldorado, Vic. 200n18
Eleven Mile Creek, Vic. 47, 48
Elliott, William 111, 113
Ellis, Robert 56
English, Michael 23–4
Euroa bank robbery (December 1878)
    a public performance 99–100
    Cameron Letter 100, 107–8, 112–13, 114, 191
    country gentlemen attire 101
    Ned's statements to captives 61, 75, 88, 91, 92, 110, 111, 214n52, 226n87
    newspaper coverage 161
    removal of bank documents 108–9
    role of sympathisers 101, 102–6, 192n2
    sham argument with Gloster 105–6
    theft of watches 109

Faithfull's Creek Station 88, 92, 100–7, 214n52, 226n87
Farrell, John 28, 204n32, 208n37
Farrell, Michael 208n37
Fenianism 152, 154
Fifteen Mile Creek, Vic. 23–4
Fitzgerald, Mrs 101
Fitzgerald, William 91
Fitzpatrick, Constable Alexander
    see also Fitzpatrick Affair
    background and character 43–5, 67–8, 210n45
    friendship with Ned 46–7, 50, 67–8, 184, 220n69, 220n70
    romance with Kate Kelly 43, 46, 58, 63–8

Fitzpatrick, Charles 44
Fitzpatrick, Jane 44
Fitzpatrick Affair 39, 69, 109, 222n74, 228n88
  see also Fitzpatrick, Constable Alexander
  Ellen's fire shovel assault 50, 55, 57, 60–1
Fitzpatrick's visits 49, 65–6, 188
Fitzpatrick's wound 51–3, 58–60, 142, 222n72
  Jerilderie Letter 43, 47, 61, 212n47
  Ned's alibi 43, 60, 61–2, 67, 212n51, 214n52
  sexual assault claim 63–4, 66–7, 111
  trial 53–4, 60–5, 210n43–6, 212n50
  warrant for Dan 47–9, 212n48
  weapon 56, 57–8, 80, 138
  Williamson's evidence 51, 54–7
Fitzsimons, Peter 166, 181, 185–9
Flood, Constable Ernest 25, 58, 74, 84, 111, 160, 184, 202n26, 204n27
Flynn, ex-constable 94
Ford, Henry 169–70
Frost, William 39

Gascoigne, Constable Patrick Charles 132, 135

Gibney, Dean Matthew 143
Gill, Samuel 101, 113, 191
Glass, Hugh 22, 206n34
Glenmore run, Vic. 4, 81, 168, 216n60
Glenrowan, Vic. 173–7
Glenrowan Inn
  see also Glenrowan siege (June 1880)
  burned 142–3
  police pub 124–5
Glenrowan police barracks 127–8, 129
Glenrowan railway station 124, 126–7, 131–2, 139–40, 178
Glenrowan School 129, 175–6
Glenrowan selectors 17–18, 20, 118–19
Glenrowan siege (June 1880) 153, 185
  armour 82, 117, 118–21, 129, 131, 133, 135–40 *passim*, 162–3
  death of Byrne 92, 135, 136
  death of John Jones 133–4, 135
  gun battle at Glenrowan Inn 132–7, 145–6
  Hare's wound 132, 178–80
  Kelly republic plan 145–7, 150
  lifting of railway tracks 125–6, 130, 166
  murder of Sherritt 121–4

national event 143
Ned abandons Dan and Steve 135–6, 137, 141–3
Ned's capture 136–42, 162, 165
Ned's disappearances 131, 135–6, 146–7
Ned's wounds 132–3, 138, 139, 140, 142, 146–7, 180
Piazzi confrontation 125–6
police burn pub 142–3
police hostages 127–8, 130
pub hostages 127, 128–9, 131, 133, 142
railway hostages 125–7
role of Constable Bracken 127–32, 141, 160–1
role of Curnow 129–31
suicide of Dan and Hart 136, 142–3
sympathisers 126–31 *passim*, 134, 145–7, 148, 149, 150–1
train wreck plan 117–18, 122, 124, 125–7, 128–9, 130, 131, 187, 208n41, 216n56, 232n96
Gloster, James 105–6
gold escort guards 78
gold fossicking 60, 76, 111
gold mining 16, 23
goldfields 16, 19, 44
Goodman, Davis 47, 202n25, 220n69

Goodman, Mrs 202n25
Gould, Ben 192n1–2, 194n6
Governor of Victoria, petitions 74–5, 118, 126, 216n60
Graham, Edith 45
Graham, Jane 32
grazing land 7, 22, 25–6, 184, 206n33–5
Greta, Vic. 46, 173–5, 182, 183, 184, 187, 208n39, 214n54, 234n98, 236n102
Greta Catholic School 174
Greta lockup 198n15, 200n16
Greta lockup brawl 34–5
Greta Mob 3, 82, 101, 115, 124, 163, 165
   see also livestock theft
Greta police 8, 72, 73, 81–2, 216n60
   see also Fitzpatrick Affair; Hall, Constable Edward
Greta police station 31, 48
Greta Primitive Methodist church 46
Greta selectors 22–3, 118–19, 164, 173, 187, 200n20, 208n38
   Kelly selection 13–14, 16–20
   selector women 20
   supportive of Constable Hall 30–1
   survival rates 16–18
Gribble, Reverend John 104, 109

Habeas Corpus 151
Hall, Ben 99, 102
Hall, Constable Edward 184
   see also Mansfield horse borrowing incident
   Greta lockup brawl 34–5, 37
   McCormick Affair 36–7
   Ned's 'tried for perjury' claim 200n17–18
   partnership with James Murdoch 31–3, 37, 38–9, 167, 202n23
   partnership with young Ned 33–6
   popular at Greta 29–31, 200n20
Hare, Superintendent Francis Augustus 5, 37, 130–2, 176
   dismisses ploughshare clue 119
   on Jerilderie Letter 113
   wound at Glenrowan 132, 178–80
Hart, Steve
   Euroa bank robbery 100, 107
   Glenrowan siege 117, 121–3, 125–6, 129, 131, 135–7, 141–3
   Jerilderie bank robbery 102, 103, 109
   Stringybark Creek police murders 69, 77, 80, 82, 84, 92, 224n80–1
   suicide 142–3
Harty, Frank 62

Hayes, Constable James Joseph 111
Hedi police station 81, 216n60
Hester, Dr James 198n14, 200n17
Hobsbawm, Eric 183
Home Rule 154
Hurdle Creek, Vic. 23

Industrial School, Melbourne 234n98
Ireland 120, 152–5
Irish 112, 230n93
   in Victoria 154–5
   Ned's Irish allegiance 152–6
   Whitty and Byrne 21, 27–8, 154–5
   Irish Land League 155
Irish National Land League 155
Irish police 28, 70–2, 152

Jamieson, Vic. 70
Jeffrey, Moyhu selector 208n38
Jeremiah run 167–8
Jerilderie, NSW 6
Jerilderie bank robbery (February 1879) 138, 188–9
   a public performance 99–102
   bank documents burned 108
   Jerilderie Letter 100, 101, 106, 107–8, 112–14, 191
   Ned reads Jerilderie Letter to Mary Devine 106

Ned's addresses 64, 75, 110–12
Ned's persona 104–6, 115
police uniform attire 101
role of sympathisers 101, 102–4
sensational coverage 114–15
theft of watches 109–10
Jerilderie Herald 101, 113, 191
Jerilderie Letter (1879) 145, 191–237
   creation 107–8
   handed to bank teller Living 101
   historical accuracy 112–13
   Kelly republic 156–7
   livestock theft 3, 191
   'Ned Kelly's Letter' 113–14, 191
   Ned's attempts to publish 100–1, 112, 191
   on Fitzpatrick Affair 43, 47, 61
   on Glenrowan seige 115
   on James Murdoch 29, 39, 167, 170
   on Stringybark Creek police murders 71, 73, 74, 76–7, 78, 90, 94
   on Whitty and Byrne 21, 27, 28, 182
   publication 191
   read to Mary Devine 106
Jerilderie lockup 106
Jerilderie police station 100–1, 106
Jerilderie post office 103–4
Jerilderie pub 75, 101, 102–5, 110–12
Jones, Ann 124–5, 126, 128–9, 133–5
   see also Glenrowan Inn
Jones, Ian 156–7, 181–3, 185, 186, 189
Jones, John 128, 133–4, 135
Jones's pub, Glenrowan
   see Glenrowan Inn

Kelly, Constable John 60, 179
Kelly, Annie 39, 74, 160, 184, 202n26
Kelly, Dan 19, 28
   armour 117, 121
   Euroa bank robbery 100, 105
   Fitzpatrick Affair 50–1, 52, 56–8, 60, 65–6, 67, 210n43
   Fitzpatrick's warrant 7, 43, 47–9, 64, 210n42, 212n48
   Glenrowan siege 127, 131, 132, 134–7, 141–3
   in hiding after Fitzpatrick Affair 53–4, 62, 76, 111, 216n57
   Jerilderie bank robbery 102, 103
   livestock theft 3, 212n49
   murder of Sherritt 122–3
   Stringybark Creek police murders 69, 72, 75, 76, 80,

Index

83–4, 85, 88, 92, 93–4, 97, 110, 111, 216n59, 218n64, 224n81
  suicide 142–3
  villainous character 115
  Winton store incident 47, 202n25, 220n69
Kelly, Dennis 18
Kelly, Ellen 4, 11, 28
  fire shovel assault on Fitzpatrick 50, 55, 57, 60–1
  Fitzpatrick Affair 46, 47, 49–50, 52–5, 57–8, 60–1, 64–7, 210n46
  impoverished selector 13–14, 18–20, 188
  imprisonment 18, 54, 64–5, 109, 126
  maintenance case 39
  marriages 13, 204n28, 236n102
  sly grog shanty 19–20, 75–6, 169
Kelly, Grace 63
Kelly, Jim 3, 19, 56, 66, 192n1–2
Kelly, John ('Red') 13, 154
Kelly, Kate 43, 46, 54, 58, 63–8, 111, 220n70
Kelly, Maggie 214n54
Kelly, Mary 167
Kelly family 3–4, 8, 19, 26, 32, 34, 39, 48–9, 154, 162, 163, 186–7, 202n26

Kelly Gang 63, 70, 77, 148
Kelly selection, Greta 68, 181–2, 186–7
  see also Fitzpatrick Affair
  huts 13–14, 19, 188
  impoverished selectors 13–14, 16–19, 163
  sly grog shanty 19–20, 65, 75–6, 163, 169
'Kelly's Manifesto' 114, 191
Kenneally, J.J. 13, 62–3, 114, 148, 182, 185, 192n1, 236n102
Kennedy, Bridget 91, 92–3, 97
Kennedy, Catherine 92
Kennedy, Daniel 119, 173–7
Kennedy, James 91, 93
Kennedy, John 92
Kennedy, Julia 174
Kennedy, Laurence 92
Kennedy, Margaret 173
Kennedy, Mary 92
Kennedy, Sergeant Michael 69, 188, 216n59, 222n76, 224n79
  autopsy 90–1
  background 70–1, 78
  body looted 92, 93, 109
  death 89–92, 141, 226n87
  funeral 97
  gunfight 85, 87–8, 224n82, 226n87
  recovery of body 74, 95–7, 226n86

return to camp with Scanlan 81, 82, 84, 85, 234n99
weapons 78–9, 80
wife and family 89, 91, 92–3, 97
Kennedy, Michael, Greta selector 173
Kennedy, Roseanna 92
Kenny, William 34–5
Kershaw, Ann Maree 32–3, 39, 168–9
Kershaw, James 32–3
Kershaw, Jane 32
Kershaw family 32
Kilmore, Vic. 23
King, Billy 51, 53
King, George 4, 13, 32, 204n28, 208n39, 236n102
King River 21, 22
King Valley, Vic. 4, 10, 82, 168
Kyneton, Vic. 10

Laceby, Vic. 17–18
Land Acts 25
    1860 and 1862 14, 153
    1869 15–16, 153, 200n20
    Duffy certificates 206n33
    dummyism 14–15, 16, 21–2, 206n34
    family cluster settlement 16, 22–3, 184
    land denials 151–2
    peacocking 16, 22, 23
    selectors' survival rates 16–18
    water access 16, 22–4, 174
    Whitty and Byrne landholdings 21–2
land tax 153
land wars 14, 27, 181–2, 183, 184, 185
Lands Department 23–4
larrikin dress 82, 101, 162–3
Lindsay, David 52–3
Lindsay, Richard 52–3
Lindsay's Winton pub 49, 52–3, 222n72
livestock brands 4, 5, 8
livestock theft 56, 204n27
    see also Mansfield horse borrowing incident
    Baumgarten case 6–7, 8, 28, 204n28, 208n39, 212n49
    bogus bills of sale 6, 61–2
    Hall's informer network 30–3, 37–9, 167
    intercolonial policing 4, 71
    Lloyd-Barnett case 24–5
    Lydeker case 7–10, 161, 204n31–2
    methods 3–6
    Murdoch connection 31–3, 37–9, 167–71
    Ned accuses Flood 74
    Ned's career 162–5 *passim*

Ned's going straight years 7, 10–11, 161–2, 204n31
Ned's McCormick threat 194n5
Ned's social justice message 99, 157, 236n100
network ended 151–2, 165
policing by Kennedy and Lonigan 71
professional intercolonial network 4–7, 75, 76, 187, 204n28, 208n39
Quinn network centre 4, 168
Steele's policing 51
theft routes 4, 5, 168
Whitty's horses 43, 208n37–8, 210n42, 214n52, 216n57
Living, Edward Richard 101, 113
Lloyd, John junior 3, 47, 48, 202n25, 220n69
Lloyd, John senior 10–11, 24–5, 36, 39, 194n4
Lloyd, Thomas Patrick 148–50
Lloyd, Tom junior 3, 24, 63, 147
and Kelly republic 148
Lydeker case 7–10, 204n31
McCormick Affair 36, 192n1
Winton store incident 47, 202n25, 220n69
Lloyd family 16–17, 19, 32, 34, 100, 154, 162, 174, 202n26
and Kelly republic 148–50
dispute with Barnetts 24–5

Lydeker case 7–10, 204n31
relations with squatter McBean 26–7, 236n100
local councils 15, 27
local land boards 15, 16, 153
Lonigan, Maria 86
Lonigan, Constable Thomas 45, 69, 141, 218n64
background and family 70, 71, 86
Benalla boot maker's shop fight 71, 73, 160, 220n68
body looted 92, 93
burial 97
death 82–3, 224n82, 234n99
Ned's version of death 73, 112, 218n65–6
recovery of body 74, 90, 91, 95–6
weapons 80, 82, 136, 138, 218n63
Lorna Doone, novel 119–20
Lurg, Vic. 16–18
Lydeker, Henry 7–10, 161, 204n31–2

Macauley, William 106, 109
MacDougall, Robert 109
Maginness (McInnis), William Justice of the Peace 220n68
Mangalore run 173
Mansfield Cemetery 91, 97

Mansfield horse borrowing incident 37–9, 74, 167, 194n7, 196n8, 202n23–4, 204n28
    Hall's arrest of Ned 37–9, 196n9–11, 198n12–15, 200n16–17, 200n19, 202n22
Mansfield police
    see Stringybark Creek police murders (October 1878)
Mansfield police memorial 97
Martin, John 74–5
Maslem, Mrs Edward 109–10
Maslem family 110
Mason, Ellen 27
Mason family 27
McAliece, Andrew 23
McAliece, Charles 23
McAliece, David 23
McAliece, Robert 23
McAliece, William 23
McAliece family 23
McAuliffe, Henry 174
McAuliffe, Lucy Ann 168, 169
McAuliffe, Patrick 169
McAuliffe family 169
McBean, Mrs Robert 26–7
McBean, Robert 26–7, 236n100
McColl's farm house, Mansfield 94–5
McCormick, Catherine 194n6
    see also McCormick Affair
McCormick, Jeremiah 194n6

    see also McCormick Affair
McCormick Affair 36–7, 187, 192n1, 194n4–6, 196n11
McDonald, Greta selector 208n38
McDonnell, Paddy 124
McDonnell's pub, Glenrowan 124–6, 145–6, 147
McHugh, Neil ('Jock') 133–4, 135
McIntyre, Constable Thomas 69, 74, 76, 81, 135, 222n75–8, 224n79, 224n81, 230n93
    background 70, 71–2
    Benalla cell interview with Ned 60, 87, 226n85
    deceived by Ned 85–7, 224n82, 234n99
    escape 85, 87, 93–5, 228n89
    health issues 96
    on Fitzpatrick 43, 222n74, 228n88
    on Kennedy 88–9, 226n87
    on Lonigan's death 82–4, 111–12, 218n64–6
    on police weaponry 78–80, 216n59, 218n62–3
    on Scanlan's death 226n84
McKay, Jessie 44
McKay family 44
McMillan, Greta selector 37
McQuilton, John 181, 182–5, 186, 189
Meadow Creek, Vic. 22
Melbourne Club 153

Melbourne Gaol 110, 180
Metcalf, George 125–6, 220n71
Molony, John 181, 185
Monk, Edward 95
Monk's Sawmill 95
Montfort, Inspector William Bradish 176
'Moreton Bay,' convict ballad 154, 230n93
Morgan, Dan 102
Mortimer, David 129, 131
Mount Morgan, Vic. 146
Moyhu, Vic. 154–5
   see also Whitty and Byrne
Moyhu selectors 17–18, 20, 30, 182–4 *passim*, 206n34, 208n37–9
Murdoch, Ann Maree
   see Kershaw, Ann Maree
Murdoch, Catherine 167
Murdoch, James 29, 31–3, 37–9, 167–71, 202n21, 202n23
Murdoch, James senior 167–8
Murdoch, John 167, 168
Murdoch, Lucy Ann 168, 169
Murdoch, Martha Jane 169
Murdoch, Mary 167, 169
Murdoch, Peter 39, 167, 169–70
Murdoch, William Henry 168
Murdock, James
   see Murdoch, James
Music (horse) 140

Myrrhee run, Vic. 22, 184, 206n34
myth-makers 145, 147–8, 181–9

National Bank, Euroa
   see Euroa bank robbery (December 1878)
National Museum of Australia 191
'Ned Kelly's Letter' 113–14, 191
Neilson, Jane 44
newspapers 27, 74, 155, 214n55
   appeal for stolen watch 109–10
   Bulletin item on Kelly republic 150–1
   Carrington illustrations 137
   Jerilderie Letter 101, 113–14, 191
   Ned's sympathiser account of Kennedy's death 89–90
   positive editorial on Ned 161
   public interest in Kelly Gang story 114, 143
Nicholson, Dr John 53, 58–9, 136–7, 142
Nicolson, Superintendent Charles Hope 11, 13–14, 48–9, 119
Nolan, Sidney 117
North Eastern Stock Protection League 30

O'Brien, Bridget 174
O'Brien, Laurence 30–1, 174, 200n20

O'Brien's pub, Greta 30–1, 173, 174, 200n20
O'Brien's stable 25
O'Connell, Daniel 154
O'Connor, Sub Inspector Stanhope Edward Dunn 179
O'Loghlen, Bryan 69–70
O'Neill, James 234n98
O'Shannassy, John 153
Oxley, Vic. 25, 168
Oxley police 8–9, 74, 204n27
Oxley Shire Council 24, 27

Parnell, Charles Stewart 154
Parnell, Miss 155
Pentridge Gaol 109, 169, 178
perjury 202n25
    see also Murdoch, James
    Hall accused by Ned 200n17–18
Perkins, Henry 89
Petterson, Charles 169
Pewtress, Sub Inspector Henry 90, 93, 95, 96
Piazzi, Alphonse 125–6, 133
police 208n40, 226n83
    see also Fitzpatrick Affair; Glenrowan siege (June 1880); Hall, Constable Edward; Hare, Superintendent Francis Augustus; Stringybark Creek police murders (October 1878)
Armstrong carries news of Sherritt murder to Beechworth 123–4
as instrument of government 97, 156
assistance to Metcalf 220n71
Benalla boot maker's shop fight 71, 73, 220n68–9, 222n72
Bracken's role at Glenrowan 127–32, 141, 160–1
budget cutbacks 79
burning of Glenrowan Inn 142–3
caution with Kellys urged 48–9
confrontations with larrikins 230n94
convict policemen 192n6
decoy of Sherritt murder 120–4
downgrading of Greta police station 31
Dwyer's actions at Glenrowan 136, 139, 141–2
Flood arrests Lloyd 25
Gascoigne's reactions at Glenrowan 132, 135
Glenrowan Inn a police pub 124–5
helmets 61
hostages fired on at Glenrowan 133–5, 184–5
ignorant of Hart and Byrne 77

intelligence on Kelly Gang dismissed 118–19
intercolonial policing 4
Irish Mansfield policemen 70–2
Jerilderie Letter caricature 228n90
Kelly Gang dressed in police uniforms at Jerilderie 101
Kelly house assessed by Nicolson 13–14
Kelly house searched by Flood 58
larrikin assault on Greta lockup 198n15, 200n16
leather body straps 72, 74
Lonigan's police record 71, 73
Mansfield memorial unveiled by Standish 97
McIntyre's policing of larrikinism 71–2
Ned covers Kennedy's body with police service cloak 89–90, 234n99
Ned entraps Quinns 33–5
Ned targeted 37
Ned threatens pill for Steele 51
Ned's antipathy to Inspector Brooke Smith 47, 218n61, 232n97, 234n98
Ned's Benalla cell interview 60, 87, 226n85
Ned's hatred of Irish police 28, 152
Ned's hostility to Flood 74, 84, 111, 160, 184, 202n26, 204n27
Ned's implies wrong man shot for Walling's murder 222n78
Ned's obsession 156, 164
Ned's policy on police 156–8
Ned's wombat hole joke 93–4, 228n89
offers of assistance to young Ned 11
police do not choose jury 212n50
police holed up in Sherritt's hut 122–3
police hostages at Glenrowan 127–32
police hostages at Jerilderie 100–1, 103–5, 106, 138, 188–9
police oath 156, 228n91
policing of livestock theft 4, 5–6, 51, 71, 75, 182
reactions to Ned in armour 137–8
recommendations on land denials 151
remanding of sympathisers 151
Richards's actions at Jerilderie 101, 103–5
Sadleir's memoirs 218n66
Standish on Cameron Letter 114

Steele's eyewitness account of Ned's capture 137–41
Strahan's threat to kill Ned 72–3, 214n53, 218n61, 220n68
stymied in Lydeker case 7–10, 204n31–2
surveillance of Quinns 4
trackers 103, 118
uniform 59–60
uniforms worn by Kelly Gang at Jerilderie 101
weaponry 72, 78–81, 84, 86, 112, 187–8, 216n59, 218n63, 218n65, 224n79, 226n83

Police Commission
   see Royal Commission on the Police Force of Victoria (1881)

Police Gazette 38, 47–9, 196n8

police harassment 3, 7, 111, 112–13, 159–62 *passim*, 166, 182, 185, 186, 204n28, 214n54, 228n88, 236n101

police informers 194n6, 214n53
   see also Hall, Constable Edward; Murdoch, James
   betrayal of Power 10–11, 33, 39
   by Kelly family 39
   criminal solidarity myth 10, 31, 39
   debate over Sherritt 122
   Diseased Stock Agent 119, 173–7

nom de plumes 175
vendettas by sympathisers 176

pounds
   impoundings by Whitty and Byrne 25–6, 182, 184, 206n36
   Lloyd-Barnett dispute 24–5
   role in lifestock thefts 5–6

Power, Harry 10–11, 33, 36, 39, 81, 162

Public Records Office, London 148

Quinn, James 4, 28, 162, 168
Quinn, Jimmy junior 33–5
Quinn, John 7–10, 204n31
Quinn, Pat 33–5, 39, 72–3, 214n53
Quinn family 4, 19, 26, 32, 34, 154, 162, 202n26
   livestock theft network 4–5
   Lydeker case 7–10, 204n31

Radic, Leonard 148

Railway Tavern, Glenrowan
   see McDonnell's pub, Glenrowan

Rankin, James 105
Rawlins, Charles 179
Reardon, Bridget 134
Reardon, James 125, 126
Reardon, Margaret 126, 133–4, 185

Register News-Pictorial 114

Reid, Tommy 137
Republic of North East Victoria 152, 181
   Bulletin item 150–1
   community response 151–2, 155
   Declaration of the Republic of North East Victoria 147–9, 156–7
   Glenrowan train wreck plan 145–7, 150
   Ned's Irish allegiance 152–6
   Ned's policy on police 156–8
   Ned's views on British Victoria 152–4
   Ned's vision 156–8
   role of sympathisers 145–7, 148, 149, 150–1
   Thomas Patrick Lloyd's stories 148–50
rewards 53, 99, 126, 157, 176
Reynolds, Hilmorton John 128
Reynolds, Dr Samuel 91
Richards, Constable Henry 101, 103–5
Richmond police depot 45
Royal Commission on the Police Force of Victoria (1881) 47–9, 54, 58, 65, 81, 175–6, 181, 232n97
Royal Mail Hotel, Jerilderie 101, 105, 110
Rupertswood 180

Ryan, Dr Charles 180
Ryan, Joe 47, 61–3, 214n52

Sadleir, Superintendent John Daniel 135–6, 175, 178, 218n66
Sandiford, Reverend Samuel 78
Savage, Annie 45
Savage, Theodore 44–5
Scanlan, Constable Michael 10, 69, 80, 141, 188, 222n76, 234n99
   background 70, 71, 78, 86
   body looted 92, 93, 132
   burial 97
   death 78, 86–7, 94, 224n82, 226n84
   recovery of body 74, 90, 91, 93, 95–6
   return to camp with Kennedy 81, 82, 84, 85, 216n59, 226n83
Scott, Mrs Robert 107
Scott, Robert 100, 107–9
Selection Acts
   see Land Acts
selectors
   impact of Land Acts 14–16, 153, 200n20, 206n33
   impoundings 25–7, 206n36
   Kelly myth-makers 181–7 *passim*

livestock theft 5, 30, 187
oppression myth 14, 21, 186
poor selectors 13–14, 18–19
selector champion myth 163–4, 236n100
survival rates 16–18, 183
water access 16, 22–4, 174
Shanks, James 23
Sherritt, Aaron 5, 120–4
Sherritt, Mrs Aaron 122
Skilling, William
   see Skillion, William
Skillion, William 39
   Fitzpatrick Affair 47, 49–53, 55, 58, 60, 62–3, 65, 67, 210n43
Smith, Inspector Alexander Brooke 47, 218n61, 232n97, 234n98
Smith, Greta selector 208n38
Smyth, Charles Alexander 44–5
social bandit thesis 14, 181, 183–5
Spencer repeating rifle 78–9, 86, 126, 132, 146, 188, 216n59, 224n79, 226n83–4
squatters 13
   see also Whitty and Byrne
   demise 15–16, 21, 153
   dummyism 14–15, 16, 21–2, 206n34
   'good' squatters 26–7, 236n100
   impoundings 25–7, 184, 206n36

land tax 153
land war myth 184–6
livestock theft 4, 6, 16, 187
oppression myth 14, 21, 27, 109, 163–4, 166, 182
Standish, Frederick Charles, Police Commissioner 13, 45, 54, 97, 114, 198n12
Stanistreet, John 126–7, 129
Stanistreet family 126
State Library of Victoria 117, 191
Steele, Sergeant Arthur Loftus Maule 51, 134, 137–41, 178, 184–5, 210n45
Stock Protection Society 30, 156–7
Strahan, Constable Anthony 72–3, 210n45, 212n48, 214n53, 218n61, 220n67–8
Strathbogie Ranges 103
Stringybark Creek police murders (October 1878) 141, 192n2, 214n55, 216n58, 222n76, 224n80–2
   death of Kennedy 88–93, 226n86–7, 234n99
   death of Lonigan 44–5, 73, 82–4, 112, 218n66, 220n68, 234n99
   death of Scanlan 84, 85–7, 226n83–4
   gunfight with Kennedy 87–8
   Jerilderie Letter 71, 73, 74, 76–7, 78, 90, 94

Kelly Gang hideout 53, 62, 75–7, 81–2, 120
Kelly Gang weaponry 76–7, 80, 111, 218n62, 218n64, 222n73
Kelly Gang's escape 212n49
leather body straps 72, 74
looting of bodies 92–3, 109
McIntyre's capture 43, 84–5, 86–7, 112, 218n65, 222n75
McIntyre's escape 87, 93–5, 96, 228n89
Ned's defences 69–75, 77–8, 83, 87–8, 111–12, 187–8, 218n61, 218n66, 220n67, 232n95
Ned's plan 75–7, 82, 216n60
Ned's sympathiser newspaper account 89–90
police backgrounds 70–2, 86
police burials and memorial 97
police plan 80–2, 97, 222n77
police weaponry 72, 78–81, 84, 86, 112, 187–8, 216n59, 218n63, 218n65, 224n79, 226n83
recovery of bodies 74, 90–1, 93, 95–7, 226n86
Sullivan, Dennis 125
sympathisers of the Kelly Gang 62, 164, 165, 186
  and Kelly republic 145–7, 148, 149, 150–1
  Curnow feint at Glenrowan 129–31
  feared 57, 123, 176
  land denials 151–2
  Ned's sympathiser newspaper account 89–90
  remanding 150–1
  role at Glenrowan 126–31 *passim*, 134, 145–7, 150–1
  role in bank robberies 101–4, 109, 115, 192n2
  sympathiser families 24, 27, 32, 169, 174, 198n13

Tanner, William 27
Tarleton, John 101, 103, 105
Teffen, Henry 108
Thompson, J. 6
Tumut, NSW 167–8

Unger, Morris 202n25
Union Bank 22, 184, 206n34

Victoria Hotel, Greta
  see O'Brien's pub, Greta
Victoria Police Museum 117
Victorian Native Ladies' Land League 155
Victorian Public Records Office 191
Violet Town, Vic. 71, 73

Wagga Wagga Gaol 29, 31, 39, 167, 170, 202n21
Wagga Wagga, NSW 5, 168
Wallan, Vic 4
Wallings, Sergeant Thomas 222n78
Wangaratta, Vic. 130, 155, 169, 194n7, 198n14–15, 200n16
Wangaratta Hospital 134
Wangaratta police 135, 178
Wangaratta Police Court 33, 35, 234n98
Ward, Detective Michael Edward 111
Webley revolvers 56, 79–80, 132, 136, 138, 141, 216n59, 218n63, 224n79
Whelan, Sergeant James 48, 53, 175
Whitlow, pound keeper 56
Whitnell, Robert 56
Whitty, Ellen 27
Whitty, James
   see also Whitty and Byrne
   background 27–8
   horses stolen 43, 208n37–8, 210n42, 214n52, 216n57
   missing prize bull 28, 204n31
   Myrrhee run 22, 184, 206n34
Whitty, Kate 155
Whitty and Byrne 112
   impoundings 25–6, 182, 184, 206n36
   Jerilderie Letter 21, 27, 28, 182, 204n32
   landholdings 21–2, 182, 184, 206n33–4, 236n100
   respected citizens 27, 30, 154–5
Wick, Anton 122
'Wild Colonial Boy,' song 128
Williams, B.C. 176
Williamson, Brickey 49–58, 60, 62, 65, 67, 210n43
Wills, Police Magistrate 200n18
Wilson, Superintendent 200n18
Winton, Vic. 19, 61–2
Winton pub 49, 52–3, 222n72
Winton store 47, 202n25, 220n69
Wombat Ranges 69, 72, 97, 216n57
Wright, Isaiah ('Wild') 10, 37–8, 72, 100, 167, 196n8

Young Ireland rebellion (1848) 153

www.ingramcontent.com/pod-product-compliance
Lightning Source LLC
Chambersburg PA
CBHW042118300426
44117CB00021B/2984